HOUSE
& GARDEN
COOKBOOK

HOUSE & GARDEN COOKBOOK

ALICE WOOLEDGE SALMON

Exeter Books

NEW YORK

TO HUGO

Editor: Marilyn Inglis
Editorial consultant: Jenni Fleetwood
Designer: John Bridges
Production controller: Shane Lask

©1987 by The Condé Nast Publications Limited
© New photographs, Octopus Books Limited

First published in USA 1987
by Exeter Books
Distributed by Bookthrift
Exeter is a trademark of Bookthrift Marketing, Inc.
Bookthrift is a registered trademark of Bookthrift Marketing, Inc
New York, New York

Printed in Hong Kong

CONTENTS

INTRODUCTION

This book is the product of my explorations of food for Great Britain's *House & Garden* magazine, within which my articles have been published every other month or so during the past five years, reflecting many of my discoveries and interests throughout this period. As I review the various chapters, I find evidence of diverse flirtations and much serious involvement, a taste for simplicity as well as the suggestion that elaboration is, at times, one of life's necessities.

Each recipe, however simple or exotic, embodies a single theme: that good food is based on the best of what's available – the freshest fish and garden produce, properly prepared meat from expert butchers, decent bread made with flour of high quality. From all this excellence comes the inspiration – to buy and prepare with flair and a taste for experiment, to create something new or to re-establish classics.

I grew up in North America, in New York City, New Mexico and California, where my mother, an imaginative and epicurean cook, gave us well-planned

casseroles, crab meat, vivid salads and delicious home-made strawberry sherbet in crystal flutes. Together we made good pastry and, occasionally, big pizzas, preparing the yeasty dough from scratch. But food, in the USA of the 1950s and '60s, was something we did not make much fuss about and, when I left for London in 1970, the most exotic ingredient at my local supermarket was 'Munster' cheese, Wisconsin-produced and plastic-wrapped.

As a student I discovered how the French eat and thought the best meal in the world must be duck *à l'orange* followed by strawberries and cream in a sugar-spun cage; lunching on this at Lasserre was, to a 20-year-old in Paris, part of the ultimate gastronomy. As were, in another sense, the chewy bread on French tables – so different from the characterless wool that has largely replaced it – and the peppery *moules* dished up by my unassuming landlady.

During the 1970s, from my base in England, I often traveled to the rest of Europe, ate and shopped with increasing curiosity, brought home recipes, read Elizabeth David, Jane Grigson, and *Mastering the Art of French Cooking*, began trying to create the dishes in these books. 'And I'll start to write about food,' I thought, 'to help pay for my travels.'

Did writing do this? Only somewhat. But it caused me to grow more attentive to both cooking and its context, French and otherwise, and by the mid-1970s I had decided to become a chef. Brief formal training, a certain audacity and a great deal of luck led me first to the kitchen of Guy Mouilleron at London's Ma Cuisine, where I made all sorts of desserts and absorbed more by watching Guy work than I ever could have done from cooking schools. I became a freelance cook, coped with temperamental employers and ovens, and eventually joined the team at the Connaught Hotel, where Michel Bourdin runs a large brigade of youthful chefs devoted to meeting the repeated onslaughts of hungry customers.

All this time I continued to write and, by the early

1980s, had made it my full-time occupation. Writing about food gives me the same degree of pleasure as buying a sparkling fresh mullet whose accompanying mayonnaise will be laced with southern garlic, or as finding that the fast froth of buttermilk is an ideal finish to a chilled soup of sweet yellow peppers.

Learning to cook is like learning how to write or to live, a lengthy process filled with speculation, in which many of the best discoveries come about unplanned. Much of this is difficult, but most of it, with luck, will be highly enjoyable; and enjoyment of cooking is increased by returning to a dish you tried years earlier and finding it easier to produce and tasting much better – or by tackling something new and deciding that you do, after all, like pumpkin or calf's brains or the business of making *gnocchi*.

In preparing these recipes, I've drawn from all aspects of my culinary travels and I've relished the experience. I hope that you too will have a long and fruitful journey.

THE BASICS

Each cook needs to acquire a repertoire of basic skills; one of the most important of these is learning to select ingredients of excellent quality, however simple their nature. The familiar parsley should always have a clean, moist, just-picked aroma, carrots the clear color of youth, lettuce a snap in the leaf, fish a bright eye and a lustrous skin. Such good, simple elements should then be put to use in a variety of imaginative ways: nuts turning up as a stylish hors-d'oeuvre or as part of a main-course salad, garlic employed as an accent or an all-pervasive flavor, fruits sliced and gleaming across the surface of a pastry or transformed into unexpected dessert terrines.

The recipes in this section help put into practice the skills of choosing and combining ingredients, and the techniques for producing specific results. There are methods for marinating meat and preparing meat and poultry for terrines, procedures for boning fish, for making aspic, for a flourless garlic soufflé, a buttery puff pastry – all adding up to a collection of favorite – and fundamental – recipes.

FOR COCKTAILS AND COOLERS

When it comes to serving drinks, I'm against run-of-the-mill accompaniments; a bit of fish paste plonked onto a cracker, or the opulent but obvious smoked salmon bound with caviar are just not interesting. As dips can be a nuisance and toast grows soggy beneath the spread, I often use vegetables as the base for various embellishments. Some of these mouthfuls are quite complex, others fast and easy while several can be partially made in advance and briefly completed to serve.

ONION RINGS

This is a recipe adapted from the late American food writer James Beard, one that he invented more than forty years ago and which, in my view, remains without peer. Buy a large brioche from a good bakery; you may have to order it specially. This recipe is not for those people who hate raw onions, though the taste of them is tempered here by quantities of parsley.

---

1 or more large brioches
mayonnaise (the best available
   commercial brand will do)
white or red onions, about 1¼ inches
   across, peeled and very finely sliced
   into rounds
salt
large bunch of very fresh parsley,
   chopped

Chill brioche well, then slice across, very thinly. With a 1½ inch circular cutter, cut slices into rounds (not including any crust). Spread each round lightly with mayonnaise. Place an onion section on half the brioche rounds (to cover each

completely), grind on salt, top with a circle of brioche, and press together gently. Have ready a dinner plate spread with mayonnaise and another of parsley. Roll the edge of each sandwich first in mayonnaise, then in the chopped parsley; the latter should make a fairly heavy wreath.

If not serving right away, store sandwiches on wide plates, cover well with plastic wrap, and refrigerate.

ZUCCHINI STUFFED WITH RATATOUILLE

The ratatouille here, unorthodox with its dashes of lemon and wine, is cut to a small scale that suits its use.

RATATOUILLE
olive oil
1 large onion, peeled and diced
½ lb baby zucchini, quartered and
   thinly sliced
1 small eggplant, diced
1 sweet red pepper, seeded and diced
1 small green pepper, seeded and diced
3 large cloves garlic, peeled and minced
¾ lb tomatoes, peeled, seeded and
   chopped
dry white wine
lemon juice
granulated sugar
salt
sprig fresh thyme
1 bay leaf
black pepper

ZUCCHINI
8 slim zucchini, about 5 inches in
   length
salt

To make ratatouille, cover base of a medium, heavy-bottomed saucepan with a film of olive oil. Add the onion and cook, covered, over low heat until softened.

Add the zucchini, eggplant, peppers, garlic and tomatoes to onions, with a dash of white wine, a dash of lemon juice and a pinch of sugar. Salt well, stir in thyme and bay leaf. Cover the ratatouille and simmer over low heat, stirring frequently, until the vegetables are cooked but neither soft nor mushy. Remove from heat, taste for seasoning, leave to cool and drain.

Take the 8 whole zucchini and boil them in salted, boiling water for 5 minutes; they should be just cooked. Drain, refresh in cold water to cool zucchini completely, dry well in paper towels. Cut ends from each zucchini and halve them lengthwise. With a small, sharp knife, cut and scoop away inner flesh, not too close to the skin or each 'boat' will be unable to bear its weight in filling (use the scooped flesh elsewhere).

Drain each half, cut-side down, on paper towels until ready to use. (If preparing zucchini well in advance, keep them whole and refrigerate, covered, until ready to use.)

When ready to serve, slice each zucchini half across into thirds and mound a little well-drained ratatouille into each. Makes 48.

Clockwise from top right: Zucchini stuffed with ratatouille, Vegetable kebabs, Cheese and apple turnovers, Mushrooms filled with scrambled eggs, Curried walnuts, Watercress tarts, Onion rings

Curried walnuts

CURRIED WALNUTS

I discovered this during my travels years ago and still love it. Easy and interesting; effortlessly doubled or tripled in quantity.

---

vegetable oil
¾ cup walnut halves
¼ teaspoon salt
¼ teaspoon mild Madras curry powder
pinch of paprika

Lightly oil a baking dish and sprinkle on a single layer of walnuts; stir. Bake in a preheated oven at 350°F, for about 10 minutes until the nuts just color. Remove to a large sheet of waxed paper, sprinkle with salt, curry powder, and a good pinch of paprika, gather ends of paper into a bag and shake walnuts to coat evenly with curry mixture. Serve warm.

These mouthfuls are likely to be eaten as fast as you can make them.

MUSHROOMS FILLED WITH SCRAMBLED EGGS

This is a sort of informal relation to the watercress tarts on page 13.

---

3 cups small, firm button mushrooms, very white
juice of 1 lemon
salt
3 eggs
black pepper
1 tablespoon butter
light cream
fresh chives, chopped

Carefully cut entire stem from each mushroom (use stems elsewhere); thoroughly wash and drain. Put into a heavy saucepan with lemon juice and a good pinch of salt, cover pan, and heat mushrooms over a fairly high heat. Stir carefully once or twice until just done. They will cook quite rapidly and give off a lot of liquid.

Put the mushrooms to drain thoroughly in a colander, then arrange them, stem side upward, across a working surface (use mushroom stock in soup).

To scramble eggs, whisk them well with salt and pepper, melt butter in a small, heavy saucepan. Add the eggs while pan is still quite cool, and over low heat, use a wooden spoon to stir eggs rhythmically, scraping them constantly from the pan's base, until soft, creamy curds are formed. Beat in a dash of cream to stop the cooking, taste for seasoning, and with a small spoon, fill center of each mushroom with a little of the mixture. Transfer the mushrooms to a serving platter, sprinkle the egg with the chives, and serve immediately.

CHEESE AND APPLE TURNOVERS

I often make small turnovers of cheese pastry, around a variety of sweet or piquant fillings.

PASTRY
3½ cups all-purpose flour
pinch of salt
1¼ cups sweet butter, chilled and diced
2½ cups shredded sharp Cheddar cheese
2 eggs

FILLING
1 large, firm eating apple, quartered, pared and cored
apple pie spice
about 14 oz Mozzarella or Cheshire cheese
2 egg yolks

To make the pastry, sift the flour with the salt and cut in the butter; rub it in and add the Cheddar cheese. Beat the eggs together and add enough to bind the pastry without making it wet. Wrap in waxed paper and a plastic bag and refrigerate for 6–8 hours.

Remove pastry from refrigerator about 30 minutes before use, roll it into

2–3 rounds about $\frac{1}{8}$ inch thick and cut into circles about $2\frac{1}{2}$ inches in diameter.

Slice the apple into short slivers, and dust lightly but uniformly with apple pie spice. Shave the Mozzarella or Cheshire cheese into thin pieces. Mound some cheese and 1 slice of apple slightly off-center of each pastry round, brush borders with a little of the egg yolks beaten in a dash of water, fold pastry over to make a compact turnover, pressing edges together with the tines of a fork. Trim borders, and brush the tops with the egg wash. Transfer to heavy baking sheets.

Re-roll the pastry trimmings and use all the dough. It softens quickly, so don't let it get too warm as you work. Refrigerate turnovers for 4–5 hours or overnight, lightly covered with foil.

Bake in a preheated oven at 375°F for about 20 minutes until the pastry has turned a rich light-golden color. Serve hot. Makes 30–40.

VEGETABLE KEBABS

No cocktail picks or traveling dips in this dish; the 'skewer' is edible and the cheese is ready-spread.

---

very fresh, straight, and fairly thick
  carrots, peeled
cucumber
radishes
Boursin cheese: garlic and herb

Slice away ends of carrots to give about 5 inch length. Cut each length neatly into slim, firm sticks, tapering in one direction.

Cut green skin from cucumber and cut skin into medallion-like shapes. Slice cucumber across into $\frac{1}{8}$ inch circles; put these together in pairs and trim edges to neaten. Slice radishes through center into thin rounds.

Use a metal skewer to pierce centers of a pair of cucumber slices; thread one of these on to the tapered end of a carrot

stick, spread Boursin onto the other slice and push it carefully along carrot to make a sandwich with the first piece. Proceed in the same way with Boursin and 2 circles of radish; clean excess cheese from the stick, pierce a hole in the center of a medallion of cucumber skin and thread this onto the carrot.

Proceed with more kebabs until you reckon you've had enough; they *are* rather fiddly to do, but a great surprise and very tasty. Cover the kebabs with plastic wrap until ready to serve. Don't make them too far in advance.

WATERCRESS TARTS

For maximum flavor, use very fresh watercress and serve tarts shortly after baking. The pastry is a variation on Simone Beck's *pâte à croustade*.

PATE A CROUSTADE
2 cups all-purpose flour
large pinch of salt
$\frac{2}{3}$ cup sweet butter, chilled and cut into
  15 equal squares
1 egg, beaten with 2 teaspoons water

FILLING
3 oz Gruyère cheese
2 bunches fresh watercress
2 eggs
4 tablespoons light cream
salt
black pepper

Make pastry in a food processor fitted with its steel blade or in the traditional way. Put flour and salt into the bowl and blend briefly. Add butter squares to bowl and blend, until the consistency of coarse crumbs is reached. Pour in egg and water and blend. If a food processor is being used the pastry will mass together after about 10 seconds. Transfer pastry to a floured board and work deftly into a slightly moist ball. Wrap in waxed paper and a plastic bag and refrigerate for several hours or overnight.

Watercress tarts

Bring pastry to room temperature, roll out thinly and line tart molds, round, square or boat-shaped – of either $1\frac{1}{4}$, $1\frac{1}{2}$ or $2\frac{1}{2}$ inches across. Use as many molds as you have in the first baking, then repeat the process until you achieve the right number of shells. Refrigerate on heavy baking sheets for half an hour.

Line each pastry-covered mold with a square of foil pressed well down. Bake in a preheated oven at 325°F for 15–20 minutes until the pastry has set and is just beginning to color. Let the shells cool slightly before removing them from the molds.

When ready to finish the tarts for serving, return the shells to the baking sheets. Shave tiny slices from the Gruyère, mince watercress leaves, beat together the eggs and cream and season well. Put a shaving of Gruyère into the base of each shell, cover with watercress, and very carefully spoon on the egg and cream mixture.

Bake the filled tarts for 10–15 minutes at 375°F, until the tops puff and color attractively. Serve warm. Makes 50–60.

SALADES FOLLES

With salads served as a main course, you can go slightly mad, as in salades folles, letting your imagination take over. There are a few rules for improvisation: ingredients should harmonize through the careful use of contrasting textures and striking colors, and not too much should be piled on the plate. In all other ways, though, let imagination be your guide. Here are some suggestions, with possibilities for several seasons.

MEDITERRANEAN SALAD

The Middle Eastern *baba ghanoush*, made with tahini (sesame paste) and broiled eggplant, and the provençal *tapenade* of black olives and anchovies have an alluring southern pungency. Belgian endive and the leaves of red chicory (arugula) are used to hold servings of each of these, to be scooped out and spread on toast.

TAPENADE
¾ cup small black olives, pitted
9 anchovy fillets
1 tablespoon capers, drained of their
 vinegar
½ teaspoon dry mustard
2 tablespoons lemon juice
1½ tablespoons cognac
olive oil
black pepper

BABA GHANOUSH
1 large or 2 medium-sized eggplants
2–3 large cloves garlic
2–3 oz tahini
juice of 1½ lemons
ground cumin
salt
black pepper

TO FINISH
1 head Belgian endive
1 head red chicory (arugula)
French bread
black olives for garnish

To make the *tapenade*, put the first six ingredients into a blender or the bowl of a food processor fitted with a steel blade. Blend to a purée and pour in enough olive oil to make a smooth, shiny paste, probably about ¼ cup. Grind in pepper, blend again. The *tapenade* can be stored in the refrigerator under a thin film of olive oil and plastic wrap for weeks. Bring to room temperature and stir well before serving.

For the *baba ghanoush*, roast whole eggplant(s) under a medium broiler, turning as the skin blisters and blackens all over. The flesh will soften. Let cool until the eggplant can be handled, lift off skin and wash flesh. Squeeze out its bitter juice, chop coarsely, and put into blender or food processor. Crush garlic cloves with the blade of a heavy knife and the aid of a little salt, add two to the eggplant, and blend. Add ¼ cup tahini, blend, add half the lemon juice, a pinch of cumin, salt and pepper. Taste and decide whether to add a third clove of garlic, more tahini, lemon juice, and cumin. Correct seasoning. The result should have a voluptuous, smoky flavor. Put into a small bowl, cover with plastic wrap, and let flavor develop for one or two days in the refrigerator. Bring to room temperature and stir before serving.

To present, trim, wash and dry both endive and chicory leaves of appropriate size. Scoop *baba ghanoush* into red leaves and *tapenade* into pairs of Belgian endive. Arrange leaves alternately on plates, slice French bread thinly, halve slices, and toast. Add toast to plates, garnish with black olives, and serve. Spread these creams on the toast – the *tapenade* quite thinly, as it's powerfully-flavored and salty – then eat the leaves. Serves 2.

FIGS AND GOATS' CHEESE

As fit for a sweet-and-pungent summer's dessert as for a one-course lunch.

1 round of fresh goats' cheese; if this
 cannot be obtained, substitute a
 crumbly farmhouse Lancashire,
 Wensleydale, or White Stilton
6 ripe figs
1 fresh lime
3–4 strawberries
fresh tarragon
superfine sugar

Cut round of goats' cheese into two semi-circles, slice each semi-circle thinly and arrange four or five slices overlapping down the center of each plate.

Cut stems from figs and slice figs into quarters; arrange slices either side of cheese. Cut wedges of lime and add two to each plate; cut stems from strawberries, halve, and put beneath cheese.

Scissor tarragon leaves, sprinkle along cheese, and serve. Squeeze lime, sprinkle superfine sugar, and combine flavors of strawberry, fig and cheese. Serves 2.

Clockwise from top right: Zest of chicken salad, Tic tac toe, Mediterranean salad, Brains and beauty, Figs and goats' cheese, Fusilli and sweet red pepper salad

Fusilli and sweet red pepper salad

FUSILLI AND RED PEPPER SALAD

1 large sweet red pepper
6 oz Mozzarella cheese
salt
olive oil
$\frac{1}{2}$ lb fusilli (corkscrew pasta)
vegetable oil
black pepper
3 fresh chicken livers, never frozen
3 small tomatoes, peeled, seeded and
    chopped
1 large clove garlic, peeled and
    minced
small handful of fresh garden cress

Broil and peel red pepper as in recipe for Zest of Chicken Salad. Slice in strips. Cut Mozzarella in tiny cubes. Bring a large saucepan of water to a boil, add salt and olive oil, boil pasta until *al dente* or just cooked.

While pasta is boiling, heat a thin film of vegetable oil in a small skillet, season cleaned chicken livers and toss in pan over a high heat for about 2–3 minutes until just pink inside. Remove from pan to cool.

When pasta is ready, drain thoroughly, return to saucepan, season liberally and toss pasta in a tablespoon of olive oil. Let cool for about 2 minutes and then toss with the diced Mozzarella. The heat of the pan and pasta will slightly melt

cheese, but if these are too hot you will end up with a stringy mess and have to dice the cheese all over again!

Remove pasta to a bowl, add tomato and garlic, scissor on cress, and toss.

Divide the mixture between two plates, leaving enough space for two lines of red pepper strips along each, as shown. Cut up the chicken livers and distribute over salads. Grind on pepper and serve. Serves 2.

ZEST OF CHICKEN SALAD

Roast chicken is well-steeped here in a wonderfully piquant Italian sauce.

1 roasting chicken $3\frac{1}{2}$–4 lb oven-ready
    weight
butter
dried tarragon
2 sweet red peppers
$1\frac{1}{4}$ cups homemade chicken stock
    (see page 100)
16 anchovy fillets
2 large cloves garlic, peeled and
    minced
1 tablespoon wine vinegar
3 tablespoons peanut oil
salt
black pepper
interesting salad leaves
cherry tomatoes or walnuts

Truss chicken, smear inside and out with butter and tarragon. Roast in a preheated oven at 375°F turning and basting frequently, until done (about 80 minutes).

Meanwhile, prepare the sauce. Roast whole peppers under a medium broiler, turning as the skins blister and blacken all over. Cool under wet paper towels to trap steam which will help loosen skins. Peel off all skin, cut peppers open and remove core and seeds. Cut up peppers and put into a blender or the bowl of a food processor. Add chicken stock, anchovy fillets and garlic and purée all to the consistency of a thickish sauce.

When chicken is roasted and partly

cooled, skin and shred the flesh from half of it (use the other half for something else). Put shredded flesh into a bowl and pour in enough sauce to coat chicken liberally. Refrigerate overnight, turning chicken in sauce occasionally.

To serve, make a vinaigrette with the vinegar, oil, salt and pepper. Wash and dry whatever leaves you like; turn in vinaigrette and shake off excess so that leaves are barely coated, and arrange them in an attractive pattern around each plate. Pile shredded chicken in the center of the leaves, add a little freshly-ground black pepper to the remaining red pepper sauce, and spoon a bit of the sauce over the chicken. Top with cherry tomatoes or with walnuts. Pass extra sauce at the table. Serves 2.

TIC TAC TOE

Smoked fish, avocado, wild mushrooms, and a crisp greenery are a persuasive mixture.

*2 oz slim green beans (ie, 24 perfect
    specimens), trimmed*
*2 oz smoked smelts, smoked eel or
    smoked herring fillets*
1 ripe avocado
juice of 1 lemon
*½ lb wild mushrooms; oyster
    mushrooms, chanterelles or ceps*
vegetable oil
*1 large clove garlic, peeled and
    minced*
*tarragon, sherry or elderflower
    vinegar*
salt
black pepper
1 tablespoon dry white wine
3 tablespoons peanut oil
a mixture of interesting leaves

Bring a saucepan of salted water to a boil and parboil green beans for 2–3 minutes, until just tender. Refresh in cold running water to stop cooking and set color. Drain and dry in paper towels.

Slice fillets of smoked fish into strips.

Cut avocado in half, remove seed, peel one half and hold it in a bowl of cold water laced with half the lemon juice.

Wash, drain, and cut up wild mushrooms, not too small since they shrink a lot in cooking. Heat vegetable oil in a pan, add mushrooms, and sauté over fairly high heat for several minutes. When cooked, add the chopped garlic and a good splash of flavored vinegar to the pan, add salt and pepper and remove mushrooms from pan to cool.

Make a vinaigrette with the white wine, peanut oil, salt and pepper. Wash and dry leaves. Turn leaves, beans and fish in the vinaigrette, shake off excess.

Arrange 12 beans and 6 strips of smoked fish in a criss-cross pattern, as shown, down the center of each plate. Pile the garlicky mushrooms either side of center cross, and arrange leaves in the four 'corners'. Remove avocado-half from water and lemon, slice thinly, turn in the remaining lemon juice and put slices to flank the mushrooms. Grind black pepper over and serve. Serves 2.

Zest of chicken salad

Tic tac toe

BRAINS AND BEAUTY

*2 sets calf's brains, or 3–4 sets lamb's
brains, depending on appetites*
$\frac{1}{4}$ cup wine vinegar
1 onion, peeled and sliced
1 carrot, peeled and sliced
1 large clove garlic, unpeeled
1 bay leaf
salt
3 peppercorns
10 slim asparagus spears
4 large, thick carrots
firm-textured bread, slightly stale
about 3 tablespoons butter
vegetable oil
3 tablespoons olive oil
black pepper
*1$\frac{1}{4}$ teaspoons mild Madras curry
    powder*
$\frac{1}{3}$ cup mayonnaise
2–3 tablespoons heavy cream
juice of 1 lemon
2 cup-shaped salad leaves

Brains and beauty

Soak brains for 1–2 hours in cold water and 1 tablespoon of wine vinegar; this will loosen the membrane of blood vessels in which each is encased.

While brains soak, fill a large saucepan with water, add onion and carrot, garlic, bay leaf, and a large pinch of salt. Boil for 15 minutes to make a court-bouillon.

After brains have soaked, carefully lift away their membranes. Wash off blood thoroughly and add peppercorns and 2 tablespoons of wine vinegar to the court-bouillon. Return it to the simmering point. Gently slide brains into the liquid.

Simmer 10–15 minutes; test by inserting a skewer into center of one brain, apply skewer to back of hand and if hot the brains are done. Transfer the brains and the court-bouillon to a bowl and let them cool in the cooking liquid.

Wash asparagus, cut off tough ends of stalks, and with a swivel parer, scrape off thick skin. Tie stalks in a bundle with string and bring a large pan of salted water to a boil. Lower the heat and simmer asparagus about 6 minutes or till they test done; drain, and refresh under cold water.

Quarter the 4 large carrots and carve into 16 small elongated olive shapes; wash and boil in salted water for about 3 minutes, until just cooked but still slightly crisp. Drain the carrots, refresh, dry and chill them, covered, until used.

Make croûtons by cutting thin slices of bread, then cut slices into thin fingers and cut fingers into tiny cubes. You will need 30–40 of these. Put butter and a little oil into a small skillet, melt butter over low heat, add cubes, and cook gently, tossing often, until croûtons become pale golden-brown. Remove from pan and cool.

Make a vinaigrette with 1 tablespoon of vinegar, olive oil, salt and pepper. Beat curry powder, salt, and pepper into mayonnaise, stir in heavy cream to taste and a few drops lemon juice to sharpen.

To assemble salads, halve asparagus stalks lengthwise, turn in vinaigrette and shake off excess, place seven of the most perfect halves, trimmed to fit, in a circle radiating from the center of each plate. Remove brains from court-bouillon, slice crosswise thinly and trim away any ragged edges. Turn the brains in lemon juice to keep white, shake off excess, and arrange between asparagus spears.

Fill two cup-shaped salad leaves – I've used red chicory (arugula) – with generous measures of curried mayonnaise and place in the center of each circle; slip seven of the best carrot olives underneath each leaf. Toss on croûtons and serve, dipping the various elements into mayonnaise as you eat. Serves 2.

GARLIC, STRONG AND SUBTLE

There is little I need say to introduce garlic, except that for devotees like me, a long braid of the season's bulbs is essential kitchen 'equipment'. In these recipes, garlic is variously used as a strong or elusive seasoning, as the significant ingredient of a soufflé, and finally, for true fanatics, as a highly desirable end in itself.

CAESAR SALAD

For this well-known Californian salad, the cloves are infused in olive oil, which is later drained and poured over croûtons and lettuce. The effect is subtle.

2 large cloves garlic, peeled and sliced
½ cup olive oil
day-old French bread
1 large head Romaine lettuce
6 anchovy fillets
½ teaspoon salt
generous grindings of black pepper
¼ teaspoon dry mustard
2 tablespoons wine vinegar
1 egg
3 tablespoons grated Parmesan cheese

Steep garlic for 24 hours in olive oil.

An hour or so before making salad, slice bread, minus crust, into enough cubes to make up 1 cup croûtons; dry these in an oven preheated to 300°F for 20–30 minutes or until turning golden-brown. Dribble hot croûtons with 2 tablespoons of the garlic oil.

Discard the ragged outer leaves of Romaine lettuce, tear the remainder across into manageable pieces, wash thoroughly, dry, and place the leaves in a salad bowl.

Drain anchovy fillets of their oil and chop finely.

Bring 3 inch depth of water to a boil in a small saucepan; in the meantime, scatter lettuce with salt, pepper, and mustard, spoon on vinegar and remaining olive oil, drained of garlic.

As the water boils, remove from the heat and lower in the egg. Cover pan and leave for 1 minute. Drain egg, run under cold water and break it over the salad, tossing leaves once more. Strew with croûtons, anchovy and Parmesan, toss briefly and eat. Serves 4 as a light lunch with good bread and a cool wine.

GARLIC SOUFFLE

Alice Waters' famous garlic soufflé from her *Chez Panisse Menu Cookbook*, has a roux and cream base, and though delicious, is extremely rich. I've worked out a version based on puréed cauliflower as support for the garlic. The result is bouyant while the flavor of the cauliflower is recessive.

1½ large bulbs garlic
olive oil
thyme
1 bay leaf
salt
black pepper
generous ½ cup cauliflower flowerets
1 tablespoon butter
2 egg yolks
¾–1 cup shredded Gruyère cheese
¼ cup grated Parmesan cheese
4 egg whites

Peel outer skin from garlic bulbs and break up into cloves, leaving these unpeeled. Put cloves into a small heavy saucepan, add water to cover, a dash of olive oil, a large pinch of thyme, a bay leaf, a grind each of salt and pepper. Cover the pan, bring water to simmer, and poach the garlic for about 15 minutes, or until the cloves test tender when pierced with a trussing needle.

Meanwhile, boil the cauliflower in salted water for 3–5 minutes or until cooked. Drain and let cool slightly then purée in a food processor until smooth. Season, then dry out in 1 tablespoon of butter by stirring for several minutes over a low heat. Transfer to a medium bowl.

When garlic is ready, drain well; as soon as you can handle it, peel off skins, cut away any brown ends and push the soft innards through a strainer into the same bowl as the cauliflower. The garlic will have lost most of its fire and become quite mellow.

Butter and lightly flour a 10 inch gratin dish.

Add egg yolks to the garlic base, season well and beat thoroughly. Mix the cheeses and have them to hand. Beat the egg whites to peaks. Stir a third of these into the garlic and yolks, pour back onto the remaining whites and swiftly fold all together, incorporating the cheese as you go. Spoon into gratin dish, spread the mixture smooth and bake on the top shelf of a preheated oven at 425°F for 15 minutes until soufflé has risen and its top has browned. The interior will remain a soft contrast to the darkened crust. Eat immediately as the soufflé quickly deflates. Serves 2.

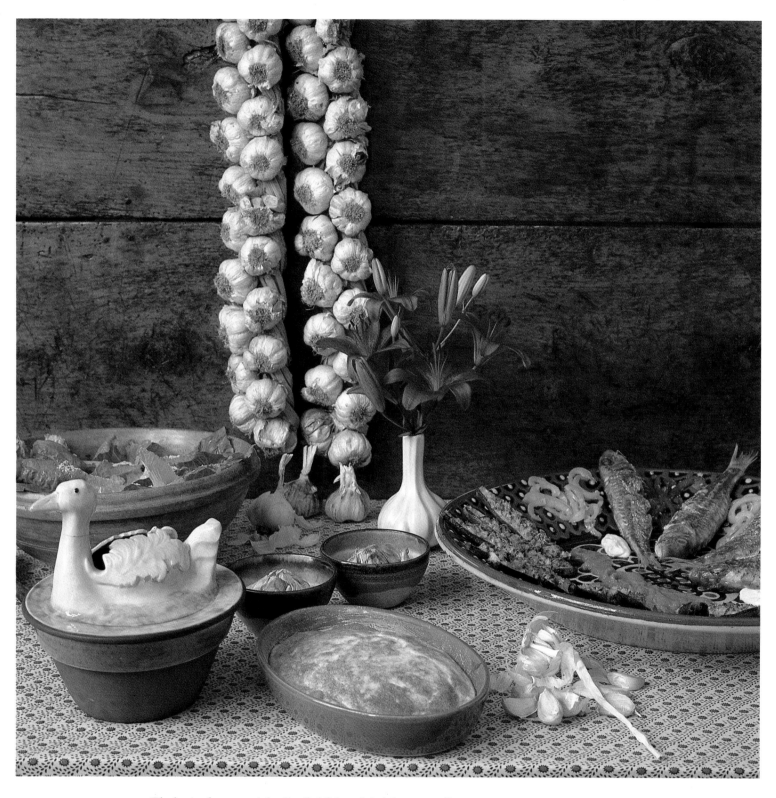

*Clockwise from top right: Broiled fish and Calabazines rellenos, Garlic soufflé, Baked garlic,
Cassoulet, Caesar salad*

CASSOULET WITH GREEN LENTILS

This is a classic, wintery dish from the southwest of France, made shockingly unorthodox to a native of Toulouse, Carcassonne, or Castelnaudary by the use of dark green Puy lentils, whose smoky flavor I prefer to the traditional navy beans. *Lentilles du Puy* hold their shape much better than red or yellow types and, like preserved goose, can be found in specialty food stores or gourmet markets. If you can't get goose, increase the weight of lamb and sausage.

1 lb lamb shoulder, boned weight
1 lb Puy lentils
small bouquet of parsley and 2 bay
 leaves
4 tomatoes, quartered and seeded
medium onion, peeled and stuck with 2
 cloves
1 lb Toulouse sausages (coarse-cut,
 pure pork)
freshly made bread crumbs
¼ lb salt pork or fat back
3 large cloves garlic
1 canned thigh of preserved goose
 *(*confit d'oie*)*
salt
black pepper

Cassoulet with green lentils

Roast the lamb in a preheated oven at 325°F for 25 minutes. Wash and drain lentils, place in a large flameproof casserole, cover with 6¼ cups water and bring slowly to a boil. Remove from heat and stir in bouquet, tomatoes, and onion, lay on sausages. Cover pot and bake in an oven preheated to 290°F for 1 hour, removing sausages after 40 minutes; prick these in several places to release fat, and let cool completely.

Meanwhile, make bread crumbs (I usually use about half a wholewheat loaf, minus crusts), slice lamb into ½ inch cubes, remove rind from the pork or bacon and cut flesh into dice. Sliver the cloves of garlic. Take the goose from its tin, scrape off fat (save this), and chop the

thigh, with skin and bone intact, into small sections. Skin and slice sausages.

Remove pot from the oven, drain the lentils, and reserve their liquid. Discard herbs and onion, press the tomatoes' flesh through a strainer into the lentil stock.

Clean the same casserole or take up another large one, and spread half the lentils over the base. Season well, add all of the meats, intermingled with garlic, season again and cover with remaining pulses. Moisten with 1 cup of the reserved liquid. Put on a good layer of bread crumbs and dot these with some of the reserved goose fat (or a little olive oil if not using *confit d'oie*). Bake, uncovered,

at 300°F for 2 hours. Twice during cooking, stir the crust, as it forms, into the lentils, moistening with reserved stock, adding a layer of bread crumbs and dotting with more goose fat at each time. Any fat which remains from the *confit d'oie* is excellent for making sautéed potatoes.

Eat bubbling hot and serve copiously for a weekend lunch, accompanied or followed by a green salad. Serves 6–8.

CALABAZINES RELLENOS

Otherwise known as stuffed zucchini, this Gibraltarian recipe is of Genoese origin. The traditional cheese ingredient has been Spanish ewes' milk *queso*, when available; hard goats' cheese, though, is a good alternative. I've added a tomato and cucumber sauce.

ZUCCHINI
8 medium zucchini, each 6–7 inches long
olive oil
3 large cloves garlic, peeled and minced
salt
black pepper
1 cup soft bread crumbs
milk
1 egg
small handful fresh chopped parsley
grated goats' cheese
pinch of dried oregano

TOMATO AND CUCUMBER SAUCE
½ lb cucumber flesh, peeled and seeded weight
salt
1 tablespoon butter
2 cloves garlic, peeled and minced
1½ cups drained canned Italian plum tomatoes
salt
black pepper

Broiled fish and Calabazines rellenos

Boil washed, unpeeled zucchini in simmering, salted water for 5 minutes; make sure you have enough water to cover the zucchini completely. Drain, refresh and dry. Cut away most of each stem, halve zucchini lengthwise, and carefully cut and scoop out flesh of the six best pairs, being careful not to tear shells. Invert shells onto paper towels to drain of excess moisture.

Finely chop the remaining halved pairs (minus stems) and the scooped zucchini flesh, put into a strainer, and squeeze away as much moisture as possible. Heat a splash of olive oil in a medium skillet and sauté the zucchini, with the minced garlic and seasoning, for about 5 minutes. Cool in a bowl.

Reserve a tablespoon or so of the bread crumbs, and soak the rest for several minutes in a little milk. Squeeze, and add most of these to the zucchini and garlic. Beat in the egg and parsley, grate in the goats' cheese to taste (it should be quite strong), season with oregano, salt, and pepper, and judge whether to add remaining bread crumbs. The mixture should be moist but not wet, and quite savory.

Dry the shells inside and out with paper towels and fill with mounded stuffing. Place the shells in a large, lightly-oiled baking dish with low sides. Strew tops with reserved bread crumbs and dribble with a little olive oil. Bake in a preheated oven at 425°F, for 20–30 minutes until the tops of the shells are browning. Serve with spoonfuls of sauce, made as follows.

Take cucumber flesh, chop coarsely, salt lightly and drain in a strainer for 1 hour to expel moisture.

Wash the cucumber, dry in paper towels and sauté in butter until half-cooked. Stir minced garlic into the cucumber, and after several minutes, add the tomatoes and break up with a wooden spoon. Simmer the sauce, uncovered, until most of liquid has evaporated.

Cool the mixture slightly and purée in a food processor, not so thoroughly as to lose all trace of the cucumber's texture. Season and reheat the sauce. Serves 4–6 as a vegetable.

BROILED FISH WITH SWEET PEPPERS AND GARLIC-CHILI MAYONNAISE

The contrasts of texture and temperature are good here: freshly broiled fish, just-sautéed garlicky peppers, pungent mayonnaise. As an alternative to red mullet, which is delectable but can be hard to come by, try sea bass or pompano.

MAYONNAISE
2 fresh chili peppers, plump if possible
2 large cloves garlic, peeled
salt
1 egg
1 tablespoon lemon juice
olive oil

FISH
6 red mullet (about 6 oz each)
salt
black pepper
olive oil

PEPPER GARNISH
2 medium-size sweet peppers, 1 red, 1
   yellow; halved, seeded, sliced
1 large clove garlic, peeled and minced
olive oil
salt
black pepper

Broil chilis until skins loosen and char; cool. Take the garlic cloves and break them down to a paste on a board with the aid of salt and a heavy knife blade.

Wearing rubber gloves if you think that the oil of the chilis will burn your fingers, skin, seed and slice them. Put one of these peppers with garlic into a food processor, steel blade in place.

Add egg, process for 30 seconds, add lemon juice, process for 10 seconds, and through feeder tube, slowly pour in olive oil, blending at high speed, until mayonnaise becomes creamily thick. Taste, and judge whether to blend in part of the second chili; mayonnaise should taste rather fiery but not aflame. Salt, if need be, and set aside.

Scale, draw and de-fin the red mullet, preserving the livers if you like them. Wash, dry, season, and oil mullet all over.

Thoroughly preheat broiler and broil mullet, 5 minutes per side, under high heat. Meanwhile, sauté sweet peppers and minced garlic in a splash of oil across one or two skillets until just tender. Season well.

Serve 1 mullet per person, flanked by the sweet peppers and a good spoonful of garlic-chili mayonnaise. Serves 6 as a first course.

BAKED GARLIC

The apotheosis. I think nothing quite equals cloves of tender garlic – cooked more slowly than in the Garlic Soufflé (see page 19) – squeezed onto buttered toast and well-seasoned.

1 bulb of garlic, with sizeable cloves,
   per person
salt
olive oil
butter
wholewheat bread
black pepper

Carefully peel outer skin from each bulb, leaving cloves attached to base with skins intact. Put heads base down in a baking dish with salt and a dribble of oil. Bake, uncovered, in a preheated oven at 300°F for 30 minutes.

Baste garlic, add water just to coat the bottom of dish, cover with lid, and bake for a further 45–60 minutes, or until cloves are soft.

Serve a bulb to each person, with plenty of hot, buttered toast; squeeze the contents of each clove onto toast, spread, and grind on pepper.

Baked garlic

TERRINE TECTONICS

These are six terrines, in the widest sense. Each has been molded into an earthenware dish or terrine, or a metal equivalent, and all but two have some connection with meat and poultry. The tomato molds and pear *bavarois* are included in this collection because of their use of gelatin.

TERRINE OF SWEETBREAD WITH WATERCRESS SAUCE

This is pale and elegant, a sweetbread surrounded by a forcemeat of veal and calf's brains, flavored with tarragon and served with a watercress sauce.

TERRINE
10–12 oz pork back fat, cut in thin sheets by your butcher
1 'heart' sweetbread about 11 oz
a set of calf's brains
salt
lemon juice
$\frac{1}{3}$ cup dry white wine
$\frac{1}{4}$ teaspoon dried tarragon
$1\frac{1}{2}$ lb stew veal, from shoulder
1 egg, beaten
black pepper
butter
6–7 large leaves from a round-heart lettuce
3 oz pork back fat
fresh parsley, chopped

SAUCE
2 bunches fresh watercress
sour cream
salt
black pepper

Line the base and sides of a 6-cup terrine (I use a rather wide bread pan) with a single layer of back fat in sheets, leaving some for the top.

Soak sweetbread and brains in several changes of cold water for 2 hours, to draw out blood. Rinse very well after soaking.

Put sweetbread into a pan, cover with fresh water, add salt and a dash of lemon juice, bring to a boil; lower the heat and simmer for 5 minutes. Remove sweetbread with slotted spoon, refresh and dry it, peel away fat, tubes, and outer membrane. Place between sheets of paper towels on a board, cover with another board and some heavy cans and weigh down for 2 hours.

Meanwhile, peel as much membrane as possible from the uncooked brains, simmer for 10 minutes in sweetbread's poaching liquid. Drain and cool.

Boil together wine and tarragon until reduced to 2 tablespoons. The flavor of the tarragon becomes pronounced.

Remove excess nerve and connective tissue from veal shoulder, cut in cubes, put these into the bowl of food processor with brains and process until smooth. Add cooled wine and beaten egg, mix and season well. Fry a little of this forcemeat in butter, and when cold, taste for seasoning; adjust salt and pepper if necessary.

Blanch, refresh and dry lettuce leaves, cut the 3 oz of back fat into lardons 3–4 inches long by $\frac{1}{4}$ inch thick. Roll lardons in chopped parsley.

Dry sweetbread, slice into 4–5 pieces, season these and wrap each in lettuce. Press forcemeat to fill a third of the terrine, lacing with half the lardons. Lay the sweetbread down the center. Cover the sides and top with the remaining forcemeat, interspersed with the rest of the lardons. Smooth the surface repeatedly with a wet hand, tap the container on a working surface to settle the contents, lay the top with a sheet or two of back fat.

Cover the terrine with a double thickness of foil, place in a bain-marie. Bake in a preheated oven at 350°F for about 2 hours, turning around once, until contents test hot through middle.

When terrine is done, remove from bain-marie and cover foiled top with a board or brick that fits into rim. Weight this, and when filling is cold, remove all but foil and refrigerate terrine in its pan, well-wrapped, for 4–5 days to mature flavors.

When planning to eat, prepare sauce by puréeing watercress leaves in food processor. Stir in sour cream to make a fairly loose consistency and season.

Cut terrine carefully, serve 1 slice per person, with an exotic leaf and some sauce. Serves 6–8.

Clockwise from top right: Chicken liver pâté with Calvados, Tomato molds and cilantro sauce, Terrine of guinea-fowl, Terrine of sweetbread with watercress sauce, Pear and caramel bavarois with pear sauce, Pâté de porc en brioche

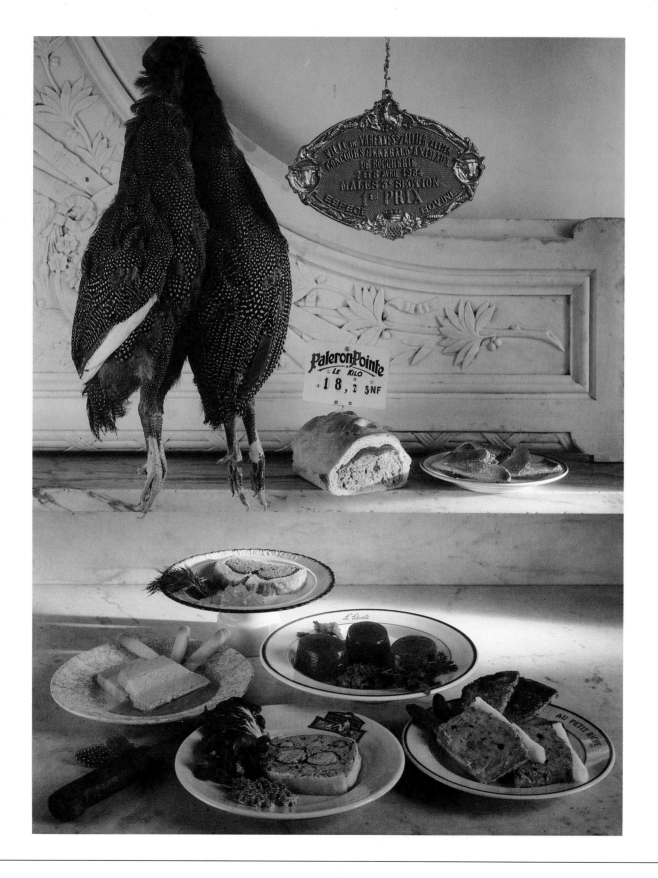

CHICKEN LIVER PATE WITH CALVADOS

Calvados and apple are the intriguing dimension to this delectable 'pâté', based on an invention of the late Michael Field. It was one of the first 'grown-up' things I learned to make, and remains top of my preferred list.

---

1 lb fresh chicken livers, never frozen
salt
black pepper
¾ cup plus 3 tablespoons sweet butter, softened
½ cup minced onion
1 large shallot, peeled and minced
½ cup chopped apple
¼ cup Calvados or applejack
2–4 tablespoons heavy cream
1 teaspoon lemon juice
clarified butter, to seal (see method)

Clean livers, cut away connective tissue and any discolored parts, dry. Cut each liver in half. Season with salt and pepper. Melt 2 tablespoons butter in a large skillet, add onion and shallot and sweat over low heat, stirring occasionally, until soft and lightly colored. Stir in apple, cook until easily mashed with back of a spoon. Transfer all to a food processor fitted with a steel blade.

Clean the pan, melt 3 tablespoons butter, and as foam from butter subsides, throw in livers. Toss for about 3 minutes over high heat until browned but still pink inside. Meanwhile warm Calvados and when livers are done, remove these from the heat, ignite spirit and pour it, flaming, a little at a time onto livers, shaking sauté pan until flames have died. Add the livers and Calvados to the apple and onion.

Moisten with 2 tablespoons of cream and blend at high speed, adding rest of cream if mixture seems too thick. Process until very smooth. Rub resulting paste through a strainer; let cool and return to processor. Add remaining softened butter. Blend completely, add lemon juice, salt and pepper to taste (remember that chilling will blunt flavor). Put mixture into a terrine of 3–4 cups capacity, smooth top, refrigerate till firm, and seal as follows. Melt ½ cup butter, spoon away foam and run the clear yellow liquid beneath (free of its milky solids) over the pâté. Refrigerate until set and let mature for 4–5 days before scooping out to eat with toast. Serves 6–8.

TERRINE OF GUINEA-FOWL

If you like game terrines, a good way to enjoy one out of season is to use guinea-fowl, which are now bred on farms, available the year round, and classed as poultry. The effect here is highly-flavored, with some truffle as an added flourish.

---

1 guinea-fowl, about 2 lb, dressed weight
port
Cognac
1 whole black truffle, not too small
1½ lb fresh pork sides, weighed without rind or bone
4 bacon rashers, unsmoked
¼ tablespoon coarse salt
8 black peppercorns
5 juniper berries
2 large cloves garlic, peeled and chopped
1 egg, beaten
enough bacon rashers to line and cover a 5-cup terrine
butter
1 bay leaf
lard

Roast the guinea-fowl in a preheated oven at 400°F for 10 minutes; cool. This will aid skinning.

Skin carcass and cut breast meat into enough thin strips to make up two layers in a 5-cup terrine. Put these to marinate with 1½ tablespoons each port and Cognac. Pare the truffle (reserve parings), cut in batons and add these to the marinade. Refrigerate overnight, turning occasionally.

Pull remaining fowl from bones, denerve it and chop flesh by hand, not too finely. Cut excess nerve and connective tissue from pork sides, cut up bacon; grind latter two in food processor to a coarsely-chopped consistency. Combine the three meats in a bowl.

Meanwhile, make a stock with the stripped carcass, skin, and giblets (minus liver) of the guinea-fowl by simmering all in lightly-salted water for several hours. Strain the stock and boil to reduce to 6 tablespoons, then cool.

In a mortar, crush salt, peppercorns, juniper berries, and garlic to a paste, add to the forcemeat with egg, chopped parings from truffle, 1 tablespoon port and 2 tablespoons Cognac. When the reduced stock is cold, work this in. Set to mature overnight in refrigerator.

Next day, line the terrine with bacon, drain guinea breast and truffles of their marinade and add the marinade to the forcemeat; make a test for seasoning as in the Terrine of Sweetbread (page 24).

When satisfied, press a third of the forcemeat along the base of the terrine and lay on half the strips of breast and truffle. Cover this with a third of the forcemeat, then the rest of the truffle and breast and finally the remaining forcemeat. Smooth with a wet hand, rap terrine on working surface, put a bay leaf in the middle, and add a slice or two of bacon.

Cover terrine with foil and its lid and bake in a bain-marie in a preheated oven at 325°F, for 1½-2 hours, turning around once, until the meat tests hot through the center. When the terrine is done, weight and cool as in Terrine of Sweetbread. Refrigerate overnight. The next morning remove the bay leaf and seal surface with melted lard. Refrigerate for a week to let the terrine's flavors mellow. Serve sliced with hot toast, butter, and gherkins. Serves 6.

TOMATO MOLDS AND CILANTRO SAUCE

These are for vegetarians who will eat gelatin, or for those who want something lighter than the previous recipes. I originally made this as one mold in a loaf pan with layers of different vegetables; the result collapsed into disaster on slicing. Individual molds, however, provided a rapid solution.

GELATIN

2 cans (28 oz size) peeled Italian plum
    tomatoes, with their juices
1 large onion, peeled and minced
2 carrots, peeled and minced
2 large stalks celery, with leaves,
    minced
1 bay leaf
pinch of dried tarragon
2 good pinches of paprika
2 teaspoons granulated sugar
½ teaspoon salt
1 tablespoon red wine vinegar
vegetable oil
1 celeriac, peeled
salt
lemon juice
6 sheets (2¾ × 9 inch size) gelatin
black pepper
20 cilantro leaves

SAUCE

2 bunches fresh cilantro
½ cup roughly chopped walnuts
2 or more tablespoons walnut oil
⅔–1 cup natural yogurt
salt
black pepper

In a large saucepan, simmer together all gelatin ingredients, up to but excluding oil, for 30 minutes.

Lightly oil 10 oval molds (3 oz size); chill until needed.

Cut the celeriac into $1\frac{1}{2} \times \frac{1}{4}$ inch batons, boil these for a few minutes in salted, acidulated water until cooked through; drain and dry.

Soak gelatin in water until soft.

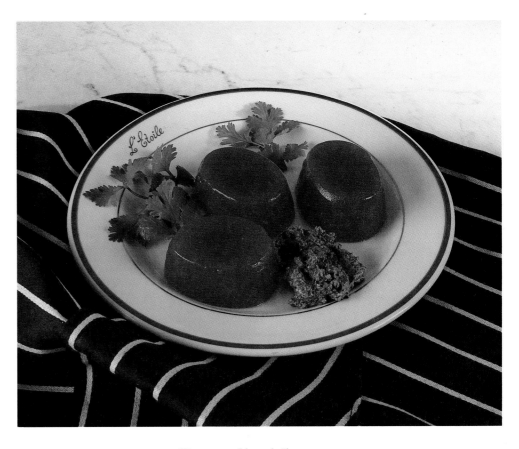

Tomato molds and cilantro sauce

Strain all juices from the finished tomato sauce, pressing solids firmly against strainer (use the solids as a soup base); you should have about 4 cups of liquid. Drain gelatin and dissolve it completely in this amount. Season to taste.

Cool gelatin mixture, stir it well, take off a small quantity and stir this over ice till thickening. Immediately ladle a thin layer into the base of each mold and refrigerate. Take 10 handsome cilantro leaves and put one face down into each mold; spoon on more thickened gelatin, let set, put a layer of four celeriac batons over the center of each (later, toss remaining celeriac in hot butter and eat as a vegetable). Finish each mold with two layers of gelatin that sandwich another cilantro leaf. Chill until firm; use any spare gelatin elsewhere.

Make a sauce by puréeing all but a handful of remaining cilantro leaves with walnuts and walnut oil; stir in yogurt to make a fairly loose sauce, add more oil and if need be, season.

To serve molds, run a blunt knife around the sides of each, dip molds briefly in hot water and invert. Present each with a spoonful of sauce and a shoot of cilantro. Serves 10.

PATE DE PORC EN BRIOCHE

This is easy and quite impressive: the center is quickly made of pork and liver, while the brioche is adapted from Simone Beck's supersonic *jet brioche*.

FILLING

½ lb ground pork liver
3 oz ground pork back fat
¾ lb pork tenderloin, ground
1 large onion, peeled and minced
butter
¼ cup red wine
2 medium cloves garlic, peeled
salt
3 tablespoons soft white bread crumbs
1–2 tablespoons heavy cream
fresh dill, chopped
black pepper
3 oz piece boiled fresh or pickled beef
*   tongue*

BRIOCHE

1½ cups strong bread flour, plus extra
*   for kneading*
pinch of salt
pinch of sugar
1 cake (⅗ oz) compressed yeast
2 tablespoons tepid milk
7 tablespoons unsalted butter
2 eggs
vegetable oil
1 egg yolk
home-made aspic (see page 47)
fresh dill

For the filling, have your butcher put the first 3 ingredients, separately, through the medium blade of his meat grinder, telling him that each weight required should be the total after grinding.

At home, take a large skillet, melt one-third of the back fat, add onion and sweat this slowly in fat till soft and colored. Add pork tenderloin and stir over a medium heat for several minutes, until greyish; add liver and cook until its red just goes. Remove from heat to a bowl.

Pâté de porc en brioche

Butter a 9 × 5 × 2¾ inch loaf pan. Meanwhile, reduce the red wine to a generous tablespoon. Add to the meat with the rest of the back fat, garlic cloves crushed in salt, bread crumbs, 1–2 tablespoons cream, depending on consistency of mixture (it shouldn't be too loose), lots of fresh dill, salt and pepper. Fry a little of the forcemeat in butter to test flavors; it should be quite savory.

Cut tongue into lardon-like strips and roll these in chopped dill.

Spoon pork mixture into a rectangle onto foil, lay the tongue strips over it, lengthwise, and form the whole into a sausage shape about an inch shorter than your pan. Wrap 'sausage' and refrigerate.

To make the accelerated brioche, sift together dry ingredients and stir yeast into warmed milk until liquefied. Melt and cool butter and beat with eggs

and yeasty milk. Work these well into the flour. Transfer the dough, which is soft and sticky, to a floured board and for 3–4 minutes scrape, knead, and manhandle it, adding more flour, until dough becomes elastic but is still rather yielding and only slightly sticky when it pulls away from your hand.

Form into a ball, lightly oil the top and put into a medium bowl set into a bain-marie whose water is kept at 95°F. Cover bowl with a plastic sheet and weight this with a bread board. Leave dough to rise until more than double in bulk (takes 60–90 minutes).

Meanwhile put sausage to firm in the freezer for 30 minutes.

When brioche has risen, deflate it on to a floured board, press it into an even rectangle, unwrap sausage, and place it in the center. Fold sides of brioche to meet around sausage and firmly pinch the seam. Fold over ends, cutting off excess dough there. Lower brioche into pan, with seam underneath. Make three holes along top, insert a small, rolled piece of cardboard into each as a 'chimney' for steam to escape, and build up a little circle of excess dough round the three cards. Cover all loosely with plastic wrap and let brioche rise, in a warm place, until it fills the pan.

When ready, brush dough with egg yolk beaten in a little water. Bake in the center of a preheated oven 425°F, for 20 minutes, then reduce the oven temperature to 350°F for 35 minutes more. Let sausage cool completely in pan, remove 'chimneys' and refrigerate.

To fill the gap between baked, chilled sausage and brioche, melt $1\frac{1}{4}$ cups of aspic gelatin; pour this into a bowl set over ice and stir liquid until it starts to thicken. Swiftly remove bowl from ice and spoon the aspic, via a funnel, into each chimney hole, tilting pâté in all directions to spread it evenly, until aspic will go no further. You will probably not use quite all of it. Refrigerate for several hours to set.

Unmold pâté, slice with a bread knife and present with chopped aspic and fronds of dill. Serves 8.

PEAR AND CARAMEL BAVAROIS WITH PEAR SAUCE

Stretch a point and call this dessert a terrine; the smooth caramel contrasts well with the grainy-textured pears and the sauce.

CARAMEL LAYERS
generous $\frac{3}{4}$ cup granulated
    sugar
$2\frac{1}{2}$ cups milk
5 sheets gelatin
8 egg yolks
$\frac{1}{3}$ cup plus 1 tablespoon heavy
    cream

PEAR LAYER
$\frac{1}{4}$ cup granulated sugar
$\frac{1}{2}$ cup Sauternes or similar sweet wine
1 firm pear (about 7 oz), quartered,
    peeled and cored
$2\frac{1}{2}$ sheets gelatin
1 generous tablespoon eau de vie de
    poire – or kirsch, if unavailable
6 egg yolks
$\frac{1}{4}$ cup heavy cream

SAUCE
$1\frac{1}{2}$ tablespoons granulated sugar
$\frac{1}{3}$ cup Sauternes
3–4 firm pears (totalling 18–20 oz),
    quartered, peeled and cored
eau de vie de poire
lemon juice

Butter a metal loaf pan ($9\frac{1}{2} \times 4 \times 3$ inches) and press a piece of waxed paper, cut to size, against the base. Refrigerate.

Make a caramel with sugar and a little water, bringing it up to a good color (about 370°F). Meanwhile, scald milk, soak gelatin and beat yolks with a hand-held mixer until thick.

When caramel is ready, remove from heat; cover hands, pour on a little of the hot milk. The mixture will froth wildly; beat well, carefully add remainder. Return milky caramel to heat, bring to boil to dissolve any sugar that has stuck to pan.

Beat this into egg yolks. Pour back into milk pan, beat mixture over a high heat, just bring to first boil, and immediately strain into a bowl. Drain gelatin and beat this into custard to dissolve it completely.

While custard cools, prepare the pear layer. Melt sugar in the Sauternes in a heavy saucepan. Poach the pear quarters, covered, in the wine-syrup until cooked. Meanwhile, soak the gelatin in water.

Drain pear quarters well, purée in food processor while reducing syrup to just under $\frac{1}{2}$ cup. Add to this the eau de vie de poire and the drained gelatin; beat to dissolve.

Put egg yolks into a large heatproof bowl, set this above a small pan of simmering water, and beat with electric mixer for about a minute. Slowly pour on wine-syrup and continue to beat until mixture is thick and expanded in volume. Remove bowl from heat, beat the contents till cool. Fold in puréed pear mixture.

By this stage the caramel custard should be cooled but not setting. Stir well, measure off a generous $1\frac{1}{4}$ cups, and when this is cold, use a fork to whip 2 tablespoons heavy cream to the same consistency. Fold the two together and quickly pour this along the base of the loaf pan. Refrigerate to set.

Place bowl containing pear mixture inside a larger bowl of ice and water and stir pear constantly until cool. Whip $\frac{1}{4}$ cup cream with a fork to same consistency, fold the two together and pour all but about $\frac{2}{3}$ cup of this in an even layer atop the firm custard. Refrigerate again and eat the maverick $\frac{2}{3}$ cup, on the spot, to keep you going.

When pear layer is firm, remaining caramel custard may have started to set; simply stir it over hot water until completely loosened but not warm. Fold with $\frac{1}{4}$ cup whipped cream and fill mold to the top. Refrigerate for at least 4 hours.

To make the sauce, dissolve sugar in wine as before. Poach the pears until just cooked, drain and purée. Then reduce the syrup to a tablespoon and add this to the purée with eau de vie de poire and lemon juice to taste. Cool and refrigerate until ready to serve.

To serve the bavarois, carefully run a blunt knife around inside of mold, dip this briefly into hot water and invert the contents. Peel off paper. Slice 'terrine' with a sharp carving knife, present 2 slices per person with a ribbon of sauce and some cigarettes russes. Serves 6.

NUTS GALORE

At the end of my first visit to Turkey, I brought back to England, my home at the time, bags of walnuts, pine-nuts, hazelnuts and pistachios. Although Turkish nuts, of excellent quality and concentrated flavor, are imported commercially to Great Britain, I was challenged by this private windfall and began experimenting. I also added nuts from elsewhere, like almonds, chestnuts and macadamias, all of which can be bought in different forms in our shops.

BANANA BREAD WITH MACADAMIA NUTS

A classic, made a little exotic by the addition of crushed coriander and a handful of Hawaiian macadamia nuts, with their subtly-sweet, rather smoky flavor. If macadamia nuts are not available, substitute walnuts.

BREAD
1 cup macadamia nuts, either salted or
  unsalted, as available, or walnuts
½ cup sweet butter, softened
⅔ cup packed dark brown sugar
2 eggs
3 ripe bananas
2 tablespoons sour cream
1 tablespoon lemon juice
1 cup all-purpose flour
1½ teaspoons baking powder
½ teaspoon baking soda
large pinch of salt
1 cup graham flour
¼ teaspoon coriander seeds

CREAM CHEESE BUTTER
½ cup sweet butter, softened
¼ cup cream cheese, softened

To prepare the bread, slice macadamia nuts into thirds and place on a baking sheet. Toast in a preheated oven at 350°F for 5–10 minutes, until nuts turn golden brown. Cool and set aside.

Butter a 9 × 5 × 2¾ inch loaf pan and line the base with buttered parchment.

Cream together the butter and sugar. Whip the eggs and beat into the butter. Mash the bananas thoroughly with a fork and add with the cream and lemon juice to the butter and egg mixture.

Sift together the all-purpose flour, baking powder, baking soda and salt. Combine well with the graham flour. Crush the coriander seeds with the side of a large knife blade and add to flours.

Beat the dry ingredients into the banana mixture, then fold in the macadamia nuts.

Pour the mixture into the loaf pan and bake in the oven at 350°F for 60–70 minutes or until the bread tests done. Cool in pan for 15 minutes. Invert, peel off the parchment paper and let cool completely.

The bread is moist, and good sliced fairly thick and toasted for supper, as a snack, or even at breakfast, accompanied by butter beaten with cream cheese until perfectly smooth, or put through a strainer if necessary.

WATER CHESTNUTS WRAPPED IN BACON

Not really nuts at all, but like nuts a kind of fruit, water chestnuts are imported in cans from the Far East, and can be bought from Chinese grocers. The crunch of chestnuts wrapped in hot, crisp bacon makes cocktail savories which guests eat as fast as you can cook them. They should not be served with a dip.

large can (about 19 oz) of water
  chestnuts
thinly-sliced bacon

Drain however many chestnuts you decide to use, dry with paper towels, cut in half across and in half again. Halve each bacon slice across its center, slice each half lengthwise into two equal strips.

Wrap a piece of chestnut in a strip of bacon and secure with a wooden cocktail pick. You can make about 120 mouthfuls with this quantity of chestnuts, preparing them in advance and refrigerating, or you can hold the uncut chestnuts in a bowl, refrigerated in their water, for a week or so, and make up small clusters as required.

To serve, broil first on one side and then the other until bacon cooks and crisps, then rush to eat them while still piping hot.

From top of left column: Banana bread with macadamia nuts, Hamsi tarator, Smoked salmon crêpes, Marron-caramel ice cream with hazelnut custard, Chicken liver pâté with cream, Water chestnuts wrapped in bacon, Roast chavignol on toasted rye and corn bread

SMOKED SALMON CREPES

A way of refreshing a popular first course, and of spinning a few slices into something substantial. *Fromage blanc* is a thick, skimmed milk soft cheese; if you can't get it, sour cream will substitute, but the result is richer.

*½ cup hazel and pine-nuts (pignoli),
    mixed*
1 cup fromage blanc
½ cup natural yogurt
garden cress or watercress
fresh chives
salt
black pepper
*8 slices best smoked salmon, Scotch if
    possible and very thinly cut*

Roast the whole pine-nuts for about 5 minutes in an oven preheated to 350°F until nuts turn golden-brown. If hazelnuts have not been skinned, roast in the same oven for about 10 minutes; the skin will flake and can be rubbed off. If the hazelnuts are already skinless roast for 5

minutes and then chop coarsely. Let cool completely.

Beat the *fromage blanc* until smooth, and beat in enough yogurt to make a rather loose, but not liquid, mixture. Add cooled nuts, some leaves of garden cress or of chopped watercress, some scissored chives, and salt and pepper to taste.

As the slices of salmon are probably narrow, overlap them in pairs to form four more or less square pieces. Put a large spoonful of *fromage blanc* mixture across one end of each square and roll up to form crepe, tucking 'selvage' underneath. These can be prepared hours in advance and refrigerated. The filling will seep slightly at either end, and you will have some left over after all four crêpes have been rolled. Reserve this.

Thirty minutes before serving remove crêpes from refrigerator and transfer to small plates. One per person is ample, as this is a filling dish. Decorate with chives and place a spoonful of the reserved *fromage blanc* mixture beneath each crêpe as a little extra sauce. Serves 4.

Smoked salmon crêpes

HAMSI TARATOR

This is a Turkish dish, *hamsi* being the Turkish word for anchovy, to which the Turks are devoted, and *tarator* a sauce for fish based on nuts and garlic, or sometimes garlic alone. I've used almonds here (ready-ground almonds from the supermarket, frowned on by some), and toasted them in the oven, which is not traditional but improves the flavor of the sauce. The whole anchovies which you'll find at the fishmarket (you may have to order them specially) may have been frozen and imported from Italy or elsewhere, but they work perfectly nevertheless.

1⅓ cups finely ground almonds
*2 thin slices bread, wholewheat if
    possible*
salt
2–3 large cloves garlic, peeled
olive oil
2 large lemons
black pepper
*32 whole anchovies, not drawn, heads
    and tails on*
vegetable oil
watercress

To make *tarator* sauce, place ground almonds on a heavy baking sheet. Toast in a preheated oven at 350°F for 10–12 minutes, stirring almonds around two or three times, until they have turned golden and begun to brown slightly. Cool.

Cut the crusts from the bread; white bread is the orthodox choice, but wholewheat or cracked wheat gives a more interesting texture. Soak in water and squeeze dry. Take 2 cloves garlic and with the aid of some salt, reduce them to a paste with the side of a knife blade. In a mortar or small, sturdy bowl, pound together almonds, bread and garlic. Add a little olive oil, the strained juice of a lemon, and a little water; beat to make a paste. Taste, and add more olive oil, juice of the second lemon (probably all of it), some more water, and the third garlic clove, peeled and crushed, if like me, you love garlic. Grind in salt and pepper. The paste should have the consistency of a fairly thick sauce; if it should start to separate, pound in some more soaked and squeezed bread. The final flavor should be sweetly almond and sharply lemon-garlic. This can be made in advance, covered, and refrigerated; bring to room temperature before serving.

This is a recipe for 4 people, and the notion of cleaning and boning 32 small fish may seem discouraging, but in fact it is an easy job which is quickly and deftly done.

Wash the anchovies. Hold each by the back of its head. Draw by running a small knife down the belly almost to the tail. Scrape out the innards with your thumb and pull back the head and gills, innards attached, snapping off the head where it connects with the backbone. Carefully open the fish out flat; the backbone will almost pop out. Grasp it and peel it off the flesh, taking side bones with it, and cut it away above the tail. Remove any visible small bones, trim fish if necessary, leaving tail intact. Rinse well and move on to the next fish. They can be prepared hours ahead of time and refrigerated, under foil, until you are ready to broil them.

To serve, put a round of sauce onto four small plates. Dry fish on paper towels, flap them shut, and brush both sides with a little oil. Salt and pepper them and broil 2 minutes per side. You will doubtless have to broil in two or three batches; keep fish warm in a very cool oven as they are ready.

Arrange 7 or 8 fish on each round of sauce and bring to table, garnished with watercress; have plenty of napkins and some finger bowls at the ready. With one hand, grasp a fish by the tail, have a teaspoon of sauce in the other hand, and take a bite of anchovy alternating with a bit of sauce. Serves 4 as a filling appetizer or the same number as an informal luncheon dish.

Chicken liver pâté with cream

CHICKEN LIVER PATE WITH CREAM

3 tablespoons dried currants
2 tablespoons shelled pistachios
1 lb chicken livers, fresh if possible
½ cup butter, softened
¼ cup brandy
¼ cup dry sherry
1 clove garlic, peeled and chopped
½–1 teaspoon salt
black pepper
pinch of ground allspice
pinch of dried thyme
pinch of dried basil
pinch of dried oregano
⅔ cup heavy cream
toast
butter

Wash currants and plump them by simmering for about 1 minute in boiling water. Drain and dry. Skin pistachios by blanching them for a minute in boiling water, draining, and rubbing away their skins in a towel. Toast the nuts in a preheated oven at 350°F for 5–7 minutes until they begin to color. Cool.

If the livers have been frozen, drain very well after thawing. Clean them, cut away connective tissue and any discol-ored areas and dry. Melt 2 tablespoons butter in a large skillet and toss livers over a high heat for about 3 minutes until cooked but still pink inside. Remove livers to a blender or food processor fitted with a steel blade.

Add brandy and sherry to pan juices, bring to a boil, ignite with a match and, gently shaking pan, flame away all the alcohol. Pour liquid into processor, add garlic, ½ teaspoon of salt, pepper, spices and herbs. Blend until smooth, let cool, add remaining butter, and blend again until very smooth. Add rest of salt if necessary, remembering that flavor mellows with chilling.

Remove pâté to a bowl. Beat cream to soft peaks, and fold, with currants and pistachios, into mixture. Pour it into a 4–cup terrine or if serving pâté in *quenelles*, into a medium bowl. Cover tightly with plastic wrap and refrigerate overnight. The flavor improves with age and is at its best three days after making.

If serving from terrine, make rounds or wedges of toast, butter them, and scoop out pâté with a small knife. But if wanting a less informal presentation, form one *quenelle* per person and serve on small plates with buttered toast.

To make these, have pâté at room temperature and three dessertspoons in a jug of very hot water. With your right hand, remove a spoon from water, shake off excess moisture, and immediately scoop out a rounded mass of pâté. Roll this mass repeatedly against side of bowl, turning pâté around and around in spoon to shape and compress *quenelle*. Transfer spoon to left hand; with right hand remove a second spoon from water, shake, smooth top of *quenelle*, and with a third hot, damp spoon, scoop *quenelle* smartly from first spoon and drop slightly above center of a small plate. Clean spoons and continue this process for the remaining portions. Put toast underneath. Serves 6–8.

MARRON-CARAMEL ICE CREAM WITH HAZELNUT CUSTARD

Puréed sweet chestnuts combine with caramel and an Italian meringue to make a light, fluffy and delicious dessert. Caramel – which lowers the freezing point of ice cream – the cooked meringue, and the farinaceous quality of chestnuts contribute to a lack of obvious ice crystals, though the cream is still-frozen.

ICE CREAM
1 can (16 oz) unsweetened chestnut
  purée
6 eggs
2 cups granulated sugar
1 tablespoon superfine sugar
2 tablespoons dark rum

CUSTARD
¾ cup shelled hazelnuts
1 split vanilla bean
2½ cups milk
8 egg yolks
½ cup superfine sugar
a dash of Kirsch

GARNISH
sprigs of fresh mint

To make ice cream, strain chestnut purée and beat it very smooth. Separate eggs.

Make a caramel with 1 cup of the granulated sugar and a little water, bringing it up to a good color (375°F). Meanwhile, beat yolks, with a hand-held electric mixer if possible, until thick and pale.

When caramel is ready, remove from heat and, covering hands with a cloth, add to it a little boiling water, which will cause it to roar up alarmingly. Beating egg yolks hard with electric mixer, pour in caramel. As you beat, it will dissolve into yolks and cause them to expand in volume. Beat until they are very thick and cold; then beat in the chestnut purée.

For the Italian meringue – egg whites into which a sugar syrup, cooked to the firm ball stage, is beaten – melt 1 cup granulated sugar with a little water. When it starts to simmer, beat whites to peaks, beating in a tablespoon of super-fine sugar at the end to stabilize them slightly. They should be ready as the syrup reaches 245°F. Using a large wire whip, beat the syrup in a rapidly falling stream into the whites and continue beating until whites are cold. A light, shiny meringue will result.

Fold this into the chestnut base, stir in rum and freeze overnight in one or two large plastic boxes.

To make custard, skin, roast and coarsely chop hazelnuts as in recipe for Smoked salmon crêpes (see page 32).

Infuse them, with split vanilla bean, in milk brought up to a simmering point, while beating yolks and sugar until thick and pale. Pour milk into yolks, beating fast. Put the mixture back into milk pan through a strainer.

Over a high heat beat vigorously until custard just boils. This happens suddenly; to prevent curdling, immediately remove from heat and strain into a bowl. Beat in hazelnuts, add a dash of Kirsch, wash vanilla bean and put it aside to dry. Cool and then chill custard.

Move ice cream from freezer to refrigerator about 30 minutes before serving. Pour a little custard onto dessert plates, pile on ice cream, and garnish with sprigs of fresh mint. Serves 8.

ROAST CHAVIGNOL ON TOASTED RYE AND CORN BREAD

In certain French restaurants for some years it has become fashionable to serve small roast or broiled goats' cheese on fried bread or toast. The cheese is usually a chavignol, known familiarly but inaccurately as a *crottin*, from the Berry district near the River Loire, and prepared in this way it is an interesting variation on the cheese course.

If you buy several chavignols from a good cheese importer, store them, if necessary, under olive oil in a jar. But be careful, after several weeks in oil they may begin to ferment, so don't plan to keep them too long before use.

This is a recipe best made for two as it's tricky and needs to be eaten piping hot. Toast from homemade bread and a garnish of walnuts and apple add new dimensions.

RYE AND CORN BREAD
2½ cups strong bread flour
¾ cup rye meal, stone-ground if possible
generous ½ cup cornmeal
1 cake (⅗ oz) compressed yeast
1 tablespoon salt, preferably rock salt
about 1¼ cups water
vegetable oil
½ cup shredded Cheddar cheese

TO FINISH
¼ small, tart apple
lemon juice
4 slices toasted rye and corn bread, as
  recipe
butter
½ cup broken walnuts
2 chavignol cheeses, 2 inches across
  × 1 inch deep, firm but not hard
  or dried out
black pepper

To make bread which is moist, close-textured and agreeably sour, mix the three flours in a large bowl and cream yeast in a little warm water. Put salt into a liquid measure with a tablespoon or two of boiling water, and stir until salt is dissolved. Add about 1 cup plus 2 tablespoons cold water.

Pour yeast liquid into center of flour, add some of salted water, stir, and mix in all but about 2 tablespoons of remaining water. Work ingredients with hands and judge whether to add more water, or if too wet, more bread flour. When consistency of dough seems right, elastic and not too damp, form a ball and knead vigorously on a board, flouring as necessary, for 5 minutes.

Wash and dry the bowl, pour in a drop of oil, smear one surface of dough with this, and turn it over; the oil will inhibit formation of a crust as dough rises. Put bowl aside in a cool place; slow raising makes for better bread. Cover bowl with a plastic sheet and weight this with a bread board. Let dough rise until triple in bulk, which takes 3–4 hours. At this point, punch down, knead briefly but thoroughly, clean bowl, oil it, and let dough rise again – it will take less time – under plastic and board. This double raising and slow ripening of gluten in the dough will result in a bread of good character.

When ready, oil two loaf pans of 3 cups capacity each (about $7 \times 3 \times 2\frac{1}{2}$ inches deep). Strew clean board with cornmeal, place dough on board, and by folding and kneading, work in cheese. Knead dough for 2–3 minutes after

cheese is incorporated, divide into two oblongs of equal weight, shape with folds underneath and place them in pans. Turn each oblong out and over to oil tops; return to pans. With scissors, make a cut the length of each loaf and widen cut with hands. Cover loosely with plastic and let rise until dough passes slightly over tops of pans.

Bake the loaves in center of a preheated oven at 450°F for 15 minutes, then reduce temperature to 375°F for 15 minutes more. Turn out loaves and return them, upside down, to the oven at 325°F for 10 minutes. Cool loaves on wire rack.

These loaves freeze well, slice thinly, and make excellent sandwiches.

To assemble this dish, pare, core and shred the apple quarter; immerse in lemon juice to prevent discoloration, then set aside while you complete the preparations. Cut four thin slices of bread, toast and butter these, and keep

them warm. Toss walnuts over medium heat in a little butter until browned; keep warm. Place cheeses (drained and well-dried with paper towels, if they have been stored in oil), on a heavy baking sheet in a preheated oven at 475°F, for about 3 minutes, or until melting around the edges. With a very sharp knife, cut each cheese into four or five slices, return them to oven for about 2 minutes. Cut toast in half down the middle, place four pieces on each of two small heated plates and, with the aid of a spatula, arrange the melted cheese on toast. Strew with nuts and some shredded apple, quickly dried on paper towels, grind on pepper and serve piping hot. Serves 2.

Marron-caramel ice cream

Roast chavignol on rye and corn bread

FRUITS OF THE WORLD

Here are fruits from several countries: domestic strawberries and raspberries, ripe Brazilian figs, Cape gooseberries (tomatillos), Italian pears, New Zealand kiwis – and more besides. Some are in guises as simple and refreshing as the terrine of orange gelatin. Others, such as the mango-studded Bavarian meringue, are more complex. Cherries are used for garnish, while wine has been turned into a sherbet that can lighten the end of a copious meal but is tart enough to revive the palate between courses.

In two of these recipes, I've recast old favorites; the Tarte Tatin is made with pears, and a rich chocolate mousse is served in *quenelles*.

BAVARIAN MERINGUE WITH RED-FRUITS SAUCE

This is a vanilla bavarois, or Bavarian cream, turned out on to a puff pastry base and covered with meringue. Red-fruits sauce flavoured with Kirsch, is served separately.

½ lb puff pastry made with sweet butter (see page 47)

BAVARIAN CREAM
5 sheets gelatin
2½ cups milk
2 split vanilla beans
7 egg yolks
7 tablespoons superfine sugar
Kirsch
1 mango, peeled
⅔ cup heavy cream

MERINGUE
4 egg whites
⅔ cup superfine sugar

RED-FRUITS SAUCE
¾ pint raspberries
¾ pint strawberries
¾ pint loganberries
juice of 3 large lemons, strained
superfine sugar
Kirsch

For Bavarian cream, oil interior of a loaf pan with good quality vegetable oil and line bottom with an oblong of waxed paper pressed well down.

Soak the gelatin in water to soften. Scald the milk with vanilla beans. Beat the yolks with sugar for 5 minutes until light and thick, beat in scalded milk, pour mixture back into the milk pan and beat over high heat until the first boil. Swiftly strain into a bowl, wash and dry vanilla beans. Drain gelatin, and beat this in to custard to dissolve it completely. Add about a tablespoon of Kirsch. Cut half the mango into slices, then cut the slices in small cubes.

Set the bowl of custard over ice and water and stir until cold. Remove the bowl from ice, half-whip the cream then return custard to ice, stir continuously and when almost set remove from ice and thoroughly fold in the cream. Cream and custard should be of the same consistency in order to blend properly. Add more Kirsch if necessary, but the flavor should be subtle. Add half the mango cubes, pour into the mold and place remaining cubes by hand into the bavarois so that the fruit is evenly distributed. Refrigerate for at least 4 hours, until well set.

For puff pastry base, roll pastry into a 12 × 7 inch strip (it will shrink considerably, particularly in the predominant direction rolled, on baking), place onto a heavy baking sheet, prick all over with a

fork and refrigerate for at least 1 hour. Bake in a preheated oven at 375°F for about 35 minutes, turning over after 25 minutes. The pastry should be deep golden-brown and well-risen. Cool.

Shortly before serving dessert, raise oven temperature to 450°F. Cover a heavy 12 × 9 inch baking sheet with foil, place pastry on foil, run a blunt knife round inside of bavarois mold, dip it briefly into hot water and turn out onto the puff. Peel off paper, trim pastry to edges of cream.

For meringue, beat egg whites to soft peaks, then beat in sugar by the tablespoonful until all the sugar is incorporated and meringue stands in stiff peaks. Using a spatula, thickly mask cream and visible puff pastry base with meringue, to insulate them from the oven's heat. Smooth surface and put all into oven for 3–5 minutes until the meringue has browned lightly.

Remove, with foil intact, to a flat platter, crinkle foil into a ruching all around to catch possible leaks from inside, and cut into ¾ inch slices with a very sharp knife.

For sauce, purée, in blender or food processor, the red fruits and lemon juice, plus the superfine sugar and Kirsch to taste. Put sauce through a fine strainer. Serves 6.

Clockwise from top right: Bavarian meringue with red-fruits sauce, Tart of kiwis and strawberries, Orange terrine with quenelles of chocolate mousse, Coeur à la crème, Toasted Sally Lunn, Claret sherbet, Tarte Tatin with pears

TOASTED SALLY LUNN WITH CHERRIES

Sally Lunn is a kind of light brioche. Its name is derived from either a corruption of *soleil lune* (sun and moon) or the name of an eighteenth-century cake seller in the English city of Bath.

SALLY LUNNS
1 cup milk
½ cup sweet butter
½ cup superfine sugar
2¼ teaspoons salt
1 cake (1 oz size) yeast
3 eggs, well-beaten
4½ cups strong bread flour
1 egg yolk

CHERRY GARNISH
½ cup fruity red wine
3 cups whole Bing cherries, stemmed and pitted
1 cup morello cherry preserves
lemon juice
superfine sugar

To make Sally Lunns, heat milk, butter, sugar, and salt to about 120°F, beat to melt butter and dissolve seasonings. Pour into a large mixing bowl. Dissolve yeast in a little warm water, stir into milk mixture with the eggs. Sift flour and by hand, beat 3¾ cups of it into bowl until blended with base. Add remaining flour and beat for 5 minutes by hand, turning bowl and constantly bringing dough in from sides. This is a soft, sticky dough which, with beating, becomes very elastic. Scrape side of bowl, cover with a plastic sheet and weight this with a bread board. Set aside in a cool place until dough is triple in bulk — a process which will take several hours.

Butter the interiors of three 4-cup Parisian brioche pans. Punch down dough, divide it into three equal portions (this may be difficult, as it is sticky and tenaciously elastic), and put each portion into a pan. Smooth over tops, cover with a cloth, and let rise in a cool room for an additional 1–2 hours, until blooming over tops of pans.

Brush each cake carefully with egg yolk beaten with a little water. Put the cakes into the middle of an oven preheated to 375°F. After 15 minutes switch oven down to 350°F and then watch from time to time, as the tops can burn easily. Cover with foil to prevent this if necessary.

After 30–35 minutes, test cakes with a trussing needle thrust into centers. If needle emerges piping hot, the Sally Lunns are done. If not, bake longer.

Remove each cake out of pan, invert on to a heavy baking sheet and return upside down to oven for 5 minutes to crisp bottoms. Cool right side up on cake rack.

Three Sally Lunns are too much for this particular recipe, so when cakes are cool, wrap one well and freeze it for future use.

To make the cherry garnish, reduce red wine in a small, heavy saucepan to a few tablespoons, add whole cherries, plus morello preserves. Cook over low heat, stirring occasionally with a wooden spoon, until preserves have melted. Add lemon juice, and sugar if necessary, to taste. It should not be too sweet. Remove cherries with a slotted spoon,

Toasted Sally Lunn with cherries

and reduce liquid until fairly thick. Slice Sally Lunns just over ½ inch thick, toast slices on both sides, butter one side lightly, and cut larger slices in half. Arrange on dessert plates, return cherries to their sauce, reheat, and spoon over toast. Serves 6.

TART OF KIWIS AND STRAWBERRIES

shortcrust pastry as Tarte Tatin
½ cup currant jelly
brandy
⅓ cup smooth apricot jam
¾ pint strawberries, uniform size
3 kiwi fruits
½ pint wild strawberries

Using two-thirds of shortcrust recipe described under Tarte Tatin, line a 9 × 1 inch flan ring set onto a heavy baking sheet. Refrigerate for 1 hour. Line pastry with parchment paper weighed down with baking beans.

Bake in a preheated oven at 350°F for 30–40 minutes, removing the paper and beans when the shell has set, leaving the pastry in oven until golden, and completely cooked. Let cool.

Bring currant jelly and a little brandy to the simmering point in a small, heavy saucepan, pass through a fine strainer and brush part of this glaze liberally over interior of pie shell, reserving remainder for top. Reheat to use.

Simmer apricot jam and a few drops of brandy in another saucepan, strain, and reserve. Reheat to use.

Halve strawberries lengthwise, peel and slice kiwis thinly, and together with wild strawberries, make an attractive arrangement to fill pie shell. Brush both kinds of strawberry with currant glaze, brush kiwis with apricot.

Assemble this tart within a few hours of eating, as moisture from the kiwis and strawberries progressively soften the crust. Serves 6.

TARTE TATIN WITH PEARS

An unorthodox version of a classic French tart, usually made with apples. As in the Pear and caramel bavarois with pear sauce, the grainy texture of pears is a good foil to the sweetness of caramel.

SHORTCRUST PASTRY
generous 1¼ cups all-purpose flour
2 tablespoons confectioners' sugar
large pinch of salt
⅔ cup sweet butter, softened
1 egg

CARAMEL AND PEARS
¾ cup granulated sugar
3–4 round medium-size pears, a little under-ripe, quartered, peeled and cored
3 tablespoons sweet butter
2 tablespoons superfine sugar
½ teaspoon brandy

To make shortcrust, sift flour, sugar and salt together onto a pastry board and make a well in the center. Put butter into the well, make a trough in the butter and break in the egg. With one hand, work butter and egg swiftly together until they form a sticky mass. Then, with a spatula, toss and chop flour gradually into butter and egg until it begins to look like pastry. With both hands, bring pastry together, add a few drops of cold water if necessary to make adhere, knead briefly and form into a homogeneous ball. Wrap in waxed paper and a plastic bag and refrigerate overnight if possible. Only about a third of this amount is needed for the Tatin; when ready to use, cut off this third, bring it to room temperature, and save remaining pastry for another use, like the kiwi and strawberry tart.

When ready to make the Tatin, have to hand a clean, straight-sided 8 × 1½ inch aluminum cake pan. Make a caramel with the granulated sugar and a little water, bringing it up to a good color (370°F). Pour carefully over the base of

Tarte Tatin with pears

the pan, tilting to cover completely. Cool in refrigerator until hard.

Slice each pear-quarter lengthwise into four equal parts, melt 1 tablespoon butter in a heavy skillet and toss half the slices, sprinkled with 1 tablespoon of superfine sugar, over high heat for 1–2 minutes until beginning to cook but still firm inside. Turn onto a wire rack over a bowl to cool and drain thoroughly. Repeat with remaining pear slices, sugar and 1 tablespoon butter. As pears are watery by nature, it is important for the success of this dessert that they are well drained.

When the caramel is hard and the pears cool, arrange the slices closely overlapping in two alternating circles on caramel, starting from outside of pan, with outside edge of fruit against bottom of pan. Melt the remaining 1 tablespoon of butter, add the brandy, and pour it over the pears.

Roll out pastry, cut into a circle that just fits inside pan, and place over fruit. Refrigerate for an hour.

Bake in the center of a preheated oven at 425°F for 35–40 minutes, checking after 20 minutes to see if pastry is browning too much; if so, cover with foil. The crust should be a deep golden brown and the syrup boiling and heavy

1THE BASICS

around edges of the pan when the tart is ready.

Cool tart for 15 minutes in pan, place a metal round from the bottom of a two-piece cake pan or a circle of heavy, foil-covered cardboard inside pan, and invert tart onto a cake rack set over a clean bowl to catch excess syrup. The pears will have absorbed the caramel and turned a mellow golden-brown.

Transfer the tart with its circular support to a flat serving plate, pull away support, and slice tart into six equal portions (which will be small, as this dessert is rich and sweet). Spoon some extra syrup, drained after baking, over each slice and serve with half-whipped cream. Serves 6.

CLARET SHERBET

Served without vine leaves, this sherbet cleanses the palate beautifully between courses of a large dinner. Make at least 36 hours in advance of serving, as wine-based mixtures take a long time to freeze.

1 cup granulated sugar
1½ cups water
3 sheets gelatin
4 cups good, inexpensive claret, such as Premières Côtes de Bordeaux, not more than five years old
juice of 1½ large lemons, strained
1½ egg whites

Boil the sugar and water for 10 minutes while soaking gelatin in a jug of water to soften. Drain gelatin, remove the hot syrup from heat and dissolve gelatin in it. Let cool completely.

Combine cold syrup, wine, and lemon juice, beat together and pour into deep plastic box. Cover with tight-fitting lid and place in freezer. After several hours, when mixture is semi-frozen, beat egg whites to soft peaks, fold and whip into wine-ice and re-freeze. After two hours, scrape sides of box and whip ice thoroughly. Repeat scraping

and beating at intervals during the day to encourage uniformity of texture.

When set, the sherbet will be a rather soft, crystalline mass. Scoop into grapes with a melon baller and fill six tall wine glasses. Put into refrigerator for 5 minutes, to frost glasses. Serve the sherbet without delay (as alcohol-based ices melt very quickly) on dessert plates garnished with black grapes and one or two vine-leaf shortbreads. Serves 6.

VINE-LEAF SHORTBREADS

½ cup sweet butter, softened
⅞ cup superfine sugar
1 egg
¼ cup milk
2½ cups all-purpose flour
2 teaspoons baking powder
large pinch of salt

Cream the butter using a wooden spoon until light, gradually beat in the sugar, creaming after each addition. Beat the egg to break up and beat into butter in two pours, then beat in milk. Sift together dry ingredients and beat into mixture. The dough should hold together well and be moist but not damp; if necessary add further drops of milk. Roll into a ball, wrap in waxed paper, and refrigerate until firm but not hard.

Break off pieces of dough, roll out on floured board to thickness of ⅛ inch, and using drawings of vine leaves as inspiration, cut free-hand leaf shapes – about 4 inches square – with a sharp knife. It may seem difficult at first to get a good likeness, but persevere.

Place leaves onto unbuttered heavy baking sheets. Bake in a preheated oven at 350°F for about 10 minutes until the edges are golden-brown. Cool for 1–2 minutes on the sheets before removing with spatula to wire racks. When cold, store carefully (they're quite fragile) in airtight cake tins until needed. Makes 24–30 leaves.

ORANGE TERRINE WITH QUENELLES OF CHOCOLATE MOUSSE

TERRINE
11–12 medium seedless oranges
4½ sheets gelatin
½ cup granulated sugar

MOUSSE
9 oz semi sweet dark chocolate
⅔ cup sweet butter
dash of dark rum
4 egg yolks
6 egg whites
scant ¼ cup icing sugar

To make terrine, use a small sharp knife to peel, segment and completely de-pith and de-membrane 6 oranges, putting segments onto a cake rack to dry out slightly. Squeeze juice from membranes of the 6 oranges, strain it, and make up liquid to scant 2 cups with strained juice of remaining 5–6 oranges. Soften gelatin in water.

Heat the juice with sugar and drained gelatin over a low heat until both are dissolved; remove from heat.

After the orange segments have dried for about 6 hours, oil the inside of a 7 × 3 × 2 inch loaf pan, line the bottom with a strip of waxed paper pressed well down. Carefully and closely overlap orange segments – being careful not to squeeze – in one layer the length of the pan. Melt orange gelatin and pour on just enough to barely cover oranges. Refrigerate until almost set, repeat one layer of oranges, pour on gelatin, refrigerate, and continue until segments are used up. Cover with gelatin to top of pan. Chill until set.

Meanwhile, make the mousse. Melt chocolate with butter in a small, heavy saucepan set, covered, into a larger pan of just-boiled water. When ready, beat smooth, remove pan from water, and beat mixture for 1–2 minutes to cool slightly. Add about a tablespoon of rum and the egg yolks. Beat again, to thicken and cool. When cool, beat egg whites to soft peaks, beat in icing sugar until firm peaks form. Beat about a quarter of the whites into the chocolate base to lighten it, then pour chocolate onto whites, folding them together quickly. Pour mousse into a wide mixing-bowl and refrigerate for several hours.

When ready to serve, dip terrine mold briefly into hot water, run a knife around sides, and turn out gelatin. Peel off paper. With a very sharp, straight knife, cut carefully into ½ inch slices, serving two per portion, side by side.

To make *quenelles* of chocolate mousse, have ready several dessert spoons and a jug of very hot water. With your right hand, dip one spoon into hot water, shake off excess moisture, and immediately scoop out a rounded mass of mousse. Roll this mass again and again against side of mixing-bowl, turning mousse around and around in spoon to shape and compress *quenelle*. Transfer spoon to left hand, with right hand dip second spoon into hot water, shake, smooth top of *quenelle*, and with a third hot, wet spoon, scoop *quenelle* deftly out of first spoon and drop onto dessert plate beneath orange slices. Place another *quenelle* beside first and continue. Serves 6.

COEUR A LA CREME WITH FRUIT

The cheesy acidity of yogurt is an important element in this deliciously light dessert.

1¼ *cups heavy cream*
1¼ *cups natural yogurt*
4 *egg whites*

TO SERVE
*figs, Cape gooseberries, or soft fruits
    like raspberries and strawberries*
optional: heavy cream, superfine sugar

Prepare six white-glazed, hole-pierced coeur à la crème molds by lining each with a square of muslin; the muslin should line the mold as smoothly as possible without crease or fold.

Whip the cream until stiff, beat the yogurt smooth and fold into the cream; beat egg whites to soft peaks and fold all together.

Spoon mixture into each mold until slightly too full; rap molds on the working surface to settle their contents, fold over each cloth to cover cream, and place molds on flat plates in the refrigerator or larder to drain overnight. The cream will set into compact heart shapes.

To serve, carefully fold back cloths and invert each mold onto the center of a dessert plate. Lift off mold, gently detach cloth, smooth any ragged edges, and serve with peeled, sliced figs and Cape gooseberries, or with soft fruits like raspberries and strawberries, and optionally, with unwhipped heavy cream and superfine sugar. Serves 6.

Orange terrine

Coeur à la crème

METHOD AND TECHNIQUE

I'm not an advocate of kitchens full of equipment. The best cooking, in my view, is done with a reasonable number of first-rate essentials like good pots, excellent knives, a reliable oven, and an ever-increasing knowledge of how they are best used. Techniques can be taught, but their mastery comes with practice. So in this chapter I'll run through a few fundamental procedures; also included are some basic recipes which are referred to throughout the book.

PIMIENTO SOUP WITH POLENTA AND AIOLI

A few years ago, I ate some of the most delectable food of my life in Berkeley, California, at the Fourth Street Grill and Chez Panisse, Alice Waters' restaurant. At Chez Panisse we had a lovely pimiento soup with *polenta* and *aïoli* and I came home determined to make my own version. Techniques in this recipe include: broiling peppers, emulsification by machine and an unusual way with *polenta*.

SOUP
4 cups minced onion
⅔ cup minced carrot
4 large cloves garlic, peeled
    and minced
2 tablespoons butter
2 tablespoons vegetable oil
1¼ lb tomatoes
salt
dry white wine
6 sweet red peppers or 'pimientos',
    total weight about 2 lb
7½ cups homemade chicken broth (see
    page 100)
black pepper

POLENTA
3 cups salted water
1 cup medium-grained polenta
    (yellow corn meal)
salt
black pepper

AIOLI
2 large cloves garlic
salt
1 egg
1 tablespoon lemon juice
olive oil

Make soup in one very large pot or two saucepans of 3 quart capacity each. Sweat the onions, carrots and garlic, covered, in butter and oil for 10 minutes, or until softened. Peel, seed and chop the tomatoes, add to the vegetables with salt and a good splash of white wine. Bring to boil, lower heat and simmer until the liquid is almost evaporated.

Meanwhile wash and dry the peppers, place under broiler about 1 inch away from high heat, and broil, turning with metal tongs or spoons, until skins blister and blacken all over. This charring brings out the smoky sweetness of the peppers' flesh.

Cool under wet paper towels to generate skin-loosening steam, and when cold, halve peppers lengthwise, cut out stems, drain juices, remove ribs and seeds. Peel off all the skin with a small knife, wash and slice peppers into saucepan(s). Add the broth, a little salt, bring to a boil, lower heat and simmer for about 10 minutes, until the peppers are tender. Cool a little, purée in blender or food processor, season, and cool completely.

To make *polenta*, bring salted water to a brisk simmer and very slowly add corn meal, beating to prevent lumps. When all the corn meal is in, stir well with a wooden spoon and cook gently for about 15 minutes, stirring frequently and thoroughly. The *polenta* is done when mixture comes away from side of pan. Season *polenta* and spread it evenly, ½ inch thick, with a wet spatula across a wooden board. Cool.

I don't like the tedium of mayonnaise-making by hand, and I refuse the labor of *aïoli* – the garlic mayonnaise – pounded and stirred in a mortar with pestle. Long live the food processor for production of rapid emulsions!

Have all the *aïoli* ingredients at room temperature, peel the garlic cloves and break down to a paste on a board with salt and the side of a heavy knife blade. Put into a food processor (or blender), add the whole egg, and process for 30 seconds, add lemon juice, and process for 10 seconds more. Through the feeder tube, very slowly add olive oil, blending at high speed, until *aïoli* looks like a medium-thick mayonnaise. Taste it for salt and transfer to a bowl.

To serve, slice *polenta* with a sharp knife into French fry shapes and toast these on two sides under a hot broiler till slightly charred. Reheat the soup, ladle into bowls, swirl through spoonfuls of *aïoli*, float on toasted polenta and serve immediately. Serves 7–8.

Clockwise from top right: Squash and lemon preserve, Caramelized apple with crisp pastry and Calvados sauce, London broil, Trout stuffed with julienned vegetables, Pimiento soup with polenta and aïoli

TROUT STUFFED WITH JULIENNED VEGETABLES

This subtle dish provides good practice in the techniques of boning a trout through its back and the cutting of fine julienne – thin strips – of vegetables. Adapted from a Gault-Millau recipe.

1 large carrot, peeled
1 small fennel bulb
½ lb button mushrooms
butter
vegetable oil
1 generous cup heavy cream
salt
black pepper
scissored fresh chives
chopped fresh fennel leaves
1 medium shallot, peeled and minced
⅓ generous cup dry white wine
⅓ generous cup homemade fish stock
  (see page 101)
4 trout, 10 oz each
dry white vermouth

With a long, slim knife, thinly slice the carrot, fennel and mushrooms. Stack several slices and cut in fine strips, reserving a number of the longest strips of carrot for use as decoration; blanch the latter for 10 seconds in boiling water, refresh, drain, and reserve. Wash remainder of julienne and sweat, covered, for 15 minutes in a little butter and oil in a large saucepan. Add ½ cup heavy cream, a little salt and simmer julienne, uncovered, until almost all cream is absorbed. Season well, add chives and fennel leaves to taste.

Put the shallot into a small saucepan with wine and fish stock. Simmer briefly, add the remaining cream and reduce by a third. Season the stock well and reserve.

Meanwhile bone each trout. With a small, sharp knife, cut down either side of dorsal (back) fin and in along the backbone to release the two fillets, working from the head almost to tail, without piercing belly.

Work the backbone and ribs free of flesh, and with a pair of scissors, sever backbone at the head and tail and remove. Cut out the side bones and pull out the viscera.

Pull back the trout's head, grasp each gill in turn and wrest it free. Snip off remaining fins and rinse fish thoroughly. Proceed with the other three. This is not a difficult technique and gets easier with each try; if you simply can't face it, ask your supplier to bone the trout by this method.

Dry and season them well inside and out and spoon a sensible amount of julienne into cavity of each fish, but do not overfill them. Put the trout into a heavy, oval, buttered baking-dish into which they will just fit in a single layer, spoon on remaining julienne, pour on cream sauce. Bake, uncovered, in a preheated oven at 425°F for 10 minutes or until fish have just cooked.

Transfer them carefully to a serving platter and keep warm; meanwhile reduce the sauce in a small saucepan until it lightly coats the back of a spoon. Season well, add a few drops of vermouth *just* for accent, then arrange the reserved carrot strips and some fresh chives along each fish, and serve the dish with a little sauce poured around and the rest passed separately. Serves 4.

Trout stuffed with julienned vegetables

London broil

LONDON BROIL

Flank steak is a cut eaten by few people other than Americans. The French, who know their way around obscure cuts use a near equivalent called *onglet de boeuf*. The uninitiated miss an excellent, long-fibered, very lean meat of reasonable price. The technique featured here is marinating, to give an already flavorsome choice some extra dimensions. Order the cut in advance from your butcher.

1 can lager beer
1 tablespoon clear honey
1 tablespoon dark soy sauce
1 tablespoon grated fresh ginger root
2 tablespoons peanut oil
2–3 scallions, minced
2 large cloves garlic, minced
½ fresh chili pepper, seeded
   and minced
handful of chopped fresh
   cilantro leaves
1½ lb flank steak, about ¾–1
   inch thick
salt
black pepper
Dijon mustard

Thoroughly mix the beer, honey, soy sauce, grated ginger, peanut oil, scallions, garlic, fresh chili and cilantro. Lay the steak in a glass or china container into which it fits snugly, cover with the marinade and turn over. Refrigerate the meat, covered, for two days, turning and basting the steak about every 8 hours or so.

When ready, bring meat to room temperature and thoroughly preheat broiler to high heat. Drain and season steak and broil it, about 1½ inches from heat, for 3–5 minutes each side. It must be very rare. Let it rest for a few minutes, then carve it, across the grain at an angle, into very thin slices. Serve accompanied by Dijon mustard. The meat has an elusive, sweet pungency imparted by its long marination. Serves 2–3, liberally.

CARAMELIZED APPLE WITH CRISP PASTRY AND CALVADOS SAUCE

A restaurant called Adlard's was opened a few years ago in Wymondham, Norfolk (England), by David Adlard and his American wife Mary. David was a chef with me at the Connaught Hotel in London, and he is an inspired cook, whose delicate apple dessert exploits two properties of the egg; whites as a binder for airy pastry and yolks whisked as the base of a sweet sabayon mousse. The resulting combination is delicious and unusual.

PASTRY
¼ cup sweet butter, softened
½ cup confectioners' sugar, sifted
¼ cup egg whites
½ cup all-purpose flour, sifted

APPLES
3 firm, sweet, eating apples, 3½oz
   each, halved, peeled and cored
Calvados or Applejack
light brown sugar
dry white wine

SABAYON
3 egg yolks
1 tablespoon dry white wine
1 tablespoon superfine sugar
½ tablespoon Calvados or Applejack

TO FINISH
confectioners' sugar

To make the pastry, cream the butter and sugar in a small bowl and when very light, slowly add the egg whites (if the mixture starts to separate, beat in a little of the flour); fold in all of the sifted flour.

Cover heavy baking sheet(s) with baking parchment and, using the base of a ramekin as guide, trace on the parchment a series of 2¾ inch circles. Drop spoonfuls of batter into these and spread very thin with back of a wet dessertspoon.

Bake in a preheated oven at 325°F for 10–12 minutes until the cookies are golden and browning at the edges. Remove carefully from paper with a spatula and allow to cool. The recipe makes about 22 discs; 12 are used here, and the rest are delicious as cookies.

To prepare the apples, slice halves thinly lengthwise, and keeping slices of each half together, place them inside-downward in an ovenproof dish. Sprinkle with a little Calvados and brown sugar, cover the base of dish with wine. Bake at 350°F for 15–20 minutes, or until the apples are cooked but not disintegrating. Remove from the oven, baste fruit with liquid and let cool completely.

Although a sabayon pot is certainly not an essential piece of kitchen equipment, whisking warm yolks across its rounded bottom ensures that none of the yolk congeals lumpishly into corners, and if you make a lot of egg-based sauces mounted over heat, the pot could be a useful investment. In any case, when ready to complete the dessert, beat sabayon ingredients together with a balloon whip in a heatproof bowl or the special pot. Set apples in their dish to heat at 325°F for 10 minutes, (in cooling, they will have absorbed surrounding liquid and thus acquired a marvelous flavor). Sift the confectioners' sugar over four pastry discs.

Set the bowl or pot over a pan of barely simmering water and whisk its contents well for 2–3 minutes, until the mixture forms a light, thick mousse. Watch carefully and don't overcook into scrambled eggs.

Pour sauce immediately onto four slightly warmed dessert plates. Fan the sliced apple across eight pastry discs and with these, construct four double-decker sandwiches, topping with sugar-dusted rounds. With a spatula, carefully place each stack of sandwiches in middle of sauce, and serve. The contrast of textures in this dessert is part of its attraction. Serves 4.

SQUASH AND LEMON PRESERVE

This recipe, from *The Wine & Food Society Menu Book*, which I wrote with my husband, shows how lemon curd can be transformed into something unusual by substituting the light crunch of squash for eggs. Using a jam funnel makes this an easier, neater task.

*1 very large, firm summer squash or 2
   smaller ones, to yield 1½ lb flesh
   after seeding and peeling
1¾ cups granulated or preserving
   sugar
6 tablespoons sweet butter
pinch of salt
grated zest and juice of 2
   large lemons*

Halve the squash across its middle, halve each half lengthwise, scoop out and discard seeds, pare off rind. Cut flesh into ½ inch dice and steam in several batches over boiling water until soft and translucent. Each round takes about 20 minutes.

Drain and dry squash thoroughly and purée it in a food processor – just enough to eliminate all lumps but not until ultra smooth. It should retain an interesting texture.

Transfer the squash to a heavy saucepan, add sugar, butter, salt and the grated zest and strained juice of the lemons. Bring to a boil, lower heat and simmer for 20 minutes, stirring the mixture occasionally to prevent sticking. Pot the preserve without delay into hot, dry, sterilized jam jars and cover immediately. Makes 3 small pots.

Squash and lemon preserve

A FEW BASICS

In addition to basic techniques, there are certain recipes which every cook will find useful to attach to the fundamental repertoire. The following recipes are important both in themselves and for completion of dishes described in the text: *beurre blanc* appears with Fish and vegetables in parchment (see page 66), puff pastry is part of Bavarian meringue (see page 36) and of Twist-of-grape Tarts (see page 105), while the aspic is a necessary element of the Pâté de porc en brioche on page 28.

BEURRE BLANC

*1 shallot, peeled and minced
¼ cup dry white wine
¼ cup white wine vinegar
salt
black pepper
1 cup sweet cold butter, cut in small
   cubes
lemon juice to taste*

Put the shallot, wine and wine vinegar, with a good grinding of seasonings, into a small saucepan with a heavy base. Boil and reduce the liquids until you are left with 1 tablespoon of liquid. Remove the pan from heat and quickly beat in 2 cubes of butter. As they melt, beat in another piece.

Continue in this way with the remaining butter, adding piece by piece and returning pan to the heat three or four times as you beat, letting each cube almost dissolve into the emulsion which is being formed before you add another. A foamy sauce will result.

Remove pan from heat when all butter has been absorbed, check seasoning, add lemon juice to taste; its presence should be subtle. Pour sauce into a warmed boat and serve without delay. Serves 4–6.

PUFF PASTRY

4 cups all-purpose flour, plus extra
½ teaspoon salt
2¼ cups hard, sweet butter
about 1 cup cold water

Sift the flour and salt into a bowl, cut ⅓ cup of the butter in cubes and cut these into the flour, using two butter knives. Pour in enough water to bind ingredients; you may need the entire 1 cup, but don't add it until you've judged how much the flour will absorb.

Make the pastry into a ball and knead this vigorously on a large floured pastry board for 5 minutes. This dough is called the *détrempe*. Reshape it into a ball and wrap it in waxed paper; refrigerate to relax for 1 hour.

Put the rest of the butter between two sheets of waxed paper and use a rolling pin to beat it into a slab of about 6 × 6 inches. Wrap and keep cool, in lowest part of refrigerator if necessary.

When the *détrempe* has rested, flour the pastry board again and roll the dough into a circle or square, keeping it slightly higher in the middle than at the sides. Put butter in the center, fold the *détrempe* around the butter to enclose it completely, and seal the dough with your fingers. Turn it over.

Flour the board and pastry and roll the dough into a rectangle of about 16 × 8 inches. Fold it in three from bottom to top, like a business letter. Give this a 90° turn so that one end of the letter is toward you, and flour it if necessary. Roll the pastry into a rectangle once more, fold it into three again, make two light dents in the side of the dough to indicate it has had two turns, and chill it for 1 hour, wrapped in waxed paper.

Give the pastry two more turns as above – always flouring it if the butter starts to break through, or resting it in the refrigerator if the dough becomes too elastic or the butter too soft. Make four dents to indicate four turns, wrap the pastry airtight and chill it overnight. Or if you wish to freeze it, wrap it for the freezer and do that.

When you are ready to make whatever is appropriate, thaw the pastry, if necessary; cut off the weight you will need, and give the dough its final pair of turns before rolling it out. Makes about 3 lb of pastry.

ASPIC

2 calf's feet
ingredients for basic meat broth (see Cold asparagus, spinach and basil Soup on page 102)
salt
black pepper
2 egg whites and their crushed shells
½ cup very lean ground beef mixed with a chopped green leek top and a handful of chopped fresh parsley
Cognac to taste

Order the calf's feet in advance from your butcher. Ask him to remove the bone from each foot at its joint and to split feet in half lengthwise.

Assemble ingredients for the broth. Scrub the calf's feet in cold water. Soak them in several changes of cold water for 8 hours. Rinse the feet, add them to a stockpot with the broth's meat and bones and proceed to make broth as in recipe. Strain and refrigerate as instructed. The broth should set to a firm jelly.

To use this jelly in something such as the Pâté de porc en brioche (page 28), it is necessary to clarify it. Scrape all fat from top of the bowlful of set broth and sponge away its traces with a paper towel wrung out in hot water. Melt the jelly, season it carefully, and measure the quantity of resulting liquid. For every 5 cups, assemble the specified amount of egg whites, shells, and beef.

Pour all but 1¼ cups of the liquid jelly into a very clean pot, and place this over a medium heat. Mix the beef and egg whites with the remaining 1¼ cups of jelly. As the liquid comes to a boil, beat in the beef and egg whites mixture and continue beating, slowly and thoroughly, until the broth comes to the first simmer.

The whites will be rising to the surface and the surface itself will rise to the top of the pot. Remove immediately from the heat and let stand for 10 minutes. Then bring contents of the pot just to a boil, twice more, without beating, leaving 10 minute intervals between each boil. The egg protein forms bonds with the stray meat particles in the liquid jelly and draws these out of solution; doing this in concert with the addition of the ground beef and aromatics will give the flavor a boost.

Line a large, fine strainer with a triple thickness of muslin and very gently ladle through the clarified aspic, keeping the base of the strainer well above the surface of the strained liquid. Let contents of the strainer drain undisturbed for 5 minutes. Discard whites and all the debris, check the seasoning of the aspic – which should be crystal-clear and of good color – and flavor to taste with Cognac, whose impact should not be overpowering.

When the aspic is cool, check its setting potential by pouring a depth of ½ inch into a chilled saucer. Chill in refrigerator for 10 minutes; the aspic should set firmly. Chop this and leave it at room temperature for 10 minutes more; if the pieces hold their shape, the aspic has set correctly. If not – a case which is highly unlikely – thoroughly beat a sheet or sheets of dissolved gelatin into the bowl of liquid aspic and continue testing.

Before the bowlful of cooled aspic has set, ladle it, in small quantities, into freezer bags, seal these, and freeze until ready for use.

STRETCHING THE HORIZONS

Traveling abroad brings spice, both literally and in the form of fresh ideas, to the cook's basic repertoire – inspiring an unusual new dish, or a way of enhancing a long-time favorite with alluring and novel ingredients.

In these chapters I explore the cooking of France, Turkey, and the USA, regions I know well and continue to search for intriguing gastronomic ideas. Italy, with her appealingly straightforward country food, makes a passing appearance, as do Bulgaria, Morocco, and Denmark, adding their diverse accents to an exotic collection.

The marketplace in an unfamiliar city is a wonderful source for discovery; but the cook's horizons can be stretched without once leaving home, by taking a new look at unjustly-neglected ingredients such as buttermilk, *polenta*, or chicken livers and remembering how good these can be.

COOKING IN PROVENCE

We usually spend a magical part of each summer in Provence, staying with friends near the square clock-tower of a hilltop village between Grasse and Cannes. The heat and the sounds, the garden full of flowers, the markets of Cannes, Nice and Menton where we find superb raw ingredients to turn into vivid outdoor meals – all of these things rouse us early each morning and send us, eventually, back home, unable to believe our time could have gone so quickly. These dishes are among my favorites.

A LUNCH-TIME SALAD

After a late-morning market visit, we often have a terrace lunch of fish or cold meat and a large salad of whatever we've been unable to resist buying. The favorite is sliced tomatoes strewn with basil leaves, without dressing, or a dish of just-cooked new potatoes. If we're feeling ambitious, however, we might stuff tiny round zucchini, or, as in this case, tomatoes. There is no recipe besides improvisation.

Take, say, one or two perfect tomatoes per person, peel them in just-boiled water, halve, and scoop out the insides. Crush several cloves of peeled garlic to a paste, with salt and the aid of a heavy knife blade. Combine with 1 part wine vinegar to 4–5 parts olive oil, salt and pepper, and a little peeled and grated fresh ginger root. Brush the tomatoes inside and out with some of this.

Take a few small eggplants (allow about 3 oz per tomato), slice unpeeled into ½ inch cubes, season, and sauté in a wide skillet with several tablespoons of olive oil until the eggplant is tender but still firm. Transfer to a bowl and sprinkle with dry white wine, coat with the vinaigrette you've just made, and cool.

In the meantime, trim, blanch and refresh slim green beans (in Provence, as elsewhere, the best ones, when not garden-grown, usually come from Kenya). Dry them, and toss in vinaigrette. Cube some firm goats' cheese and toast a small handful of pine-nuts under the broiler.

Cover a platter with lettuce leaves, lightly-dressed, and combine the eggplant with the cheese and nuts and a fresh herb like chervil. Season the mixture to taste, add more vinaigrette if needed and put this into the tomato halves. Arrange on lettuce and intersperse with the *haricots verts*.

'MERDA DE CAN'

These are green *gnocchi*, as made in Nice with Swiss chard leaves. The Niçois eat huge amounts of chard, and while I really prefer *gnocchi* of potato and flour only – see page 132 – these are an interesting variation and amusing to make. Serve as a dish on its own or as accompaniment to the Pintade en salmis.

½ lb Swiss chard leaves (use ribs to
   make a gratin)
salt
1 lb 10 oz floury potatoes
2 teaspoons olive oil
½ beaten egg
about 1½ cups all-purpose flour
black pepper
Parmesan cheese, freshly-grated
butter, heated

Remove any large veins from the chard leaves and boil in briskly-simmering salted water for 2–3 minutes, until tender. Refresh, squeeze as dry as possible and chop finely.

Meanwhile, boil the unpeeled potatoes in salted water until done; drain, and peel as soon as you can handle them. While still hot, purée through a food mill or ricer, and combine immediately with oil, egg, and chard.

With one hand, work about 1¼ cups flour into the potato base and knead this smooth. You may require more flour if the potatoes are particularly absorbent, but stop when the mixture feels soft, smooth, and still a little sticky. Season well, work in some Parmesan and form dough into rolls about as thick as your thumb. Leave to rest for 30 minutes.

Cut each roll into ¾ inch lengths, and between floured hands, roll the lengths into oblongs, tapered at each end. Poach in two pots of boiling salted water, not overcrowding *gnocchi*, until they rise to the surface. Drain carefully onto a hot platter, season, and pour on foaming butter and liberal Parmesan. Or if serving with guinea-fowl, baste *gnocchi* with a little of sauce.

Serves 4 as an unaccompanied dish, or 6–8 when escorting Pintade.

Clockwise from top right: Vin d'orange, Tarte aux prunes, Lunchtime salad, Pintade en salmis, Zucchini 'en spaghetti', Merda dé can

ZUCCHINI 'EN SPAGHETTI' LA MOURRACHONNE

This dish is exacting to make, but showy and delicious. Have at least one dress rehearsal and limit your numbers to four since it must be eaten without delay.

TOMATO SAUCE
1 cup chopped onion
2 large cloves garlic, minced
¼ cup chopped celery
¼ cup chopped carrot
1 tablespoon olive oil
1 can (28 oz) Italian plum tomatoes and their juices
3 tablespoons dry white wine
2 teaspoons granulated sugar
1 bay leaf
pinch of thyme
a few parsley stems
salt
black pepper

CREAM SAUCE
¼ cup butter
¼ cup minced carrot
1 large celery stick minced
1 shallot, peeled and minced
1 sprig of fresh thyme
1 small bay leaf
½ cup dry white wine
1¾ cups heavy cream
salt
about 2 teaspoons lemon juice
black pepper
fresh chives

TO FINISH
4 plump zucchini 3 oz each
1 tablespoon clarified butter from cream sauce recipe
about 8 large fresh basil leaves, shredded
salt
black pepper

The sauces and the preparation of the zucchini can be done in advance and refrigerated, while the finish and assembly should be carried out at the last minute. The flavors will benefit from this prior preparation.

To make the tomato sauce, sweat the first four ingredients with the olive oil in a medium skillet, covered, over a low heat, until the vegetables are soft but not colored. Add the remaining sauce ingredients to the pan. Break up the tomatoes with a wooden spoon, stir well, bring the mixture to boil and simmer briskly, uncovered, for 15–20 minutes, stirring occasionally to incorporate until the sauce is reduced to an interesting but still fairly liquid consistency.

Let it cool slightly, liquidize, and push the sauce through a coarse strainer to be rid of the seeds and debris. Check the seasoning.

The result is about 2½ cups of sauce; only a small amount of this is needed here, but the remainder can be frozen for repeats of this dish or used elsewhere. Cool and refrigerate the entire amount until required.

To make the cream sauce, clarify the butter, (see Chicken liver pâté with Calvados on page 26 for method) which will give you about 3 tablespoons of clear, yellow liquid. Take a small heavy saucepan, add a tablespoon of the clarified butter, plus the carrot, celery, shallot, thyme and bay leaf, stir, and place the pot over a low heat.

Cover, and let the contents sweat gently for 7–10 minutes until the vegetables are soft but not browning. Add the wine, raise the heat, and simmer briskly until about 1 tablespoon remains. Beat in the cream, a little salt, and boil lightly for 2–3 minutes.

Pour the sauce through a fine strainer – pressing the vegetables to extract maximum flavor – into another small saucepan. Add the lemon juice – probably as much as 2 teaspoons – plus salt and pepper to taste. Cool and refrigerate until just before you prepare the zucchini.

Trim the zucchini. If you have a mandoline, use it to slice the vegetables lengthwise into spaghetti-like sticks; otherwise, use a long, slim blade – like a carving knife – to cut the zucchini lengthwise into pieces ⅛ inch thick, and these, lengthwise again, into strands.

If doing this operation in advance, place the resulting zucchini 'spaghetti' in a bowl, cover with damp paper towels and refrigerate.

When ready to begin, put four 9 inch plates to heat in the oven, snip about 1 tablespoon of chives and shred the basil leaves and set aside. Place two small bains-marie to heat on burners, put the pan of cream sauce in one and a generous 5 tablespoons of tomato sauce in a pan in the other. Beat and gently heat both liquids thoroughly before finishing the zucchini.

Meanwhile, take a 12–13 inch skillet and heat in it 1 tablespoon of the clarified butter. When hot, add zucchini and toss or stir the strands over high heat – adding a *little* more of the butter if you think necessary – for 2–4 minutes until just cooked but still *al dente*. Season the zucchini strands well, and extinguish the heat beneath. Beat the chives into the cream sauce.

Immediately line up the four plates and in the center of each loosely pile an attractive nest of 'spaghetti'. Spoon round the cream sauce, drop a spoonful of tomato sauce into this pool, and deftly swirl each edge. Garnish the courgettes with basil and eat without delay. Serves 4 as a first course.

PINTADE EN SALMIS

One of our Provençal friends is Simone Beck, of *Mastering the Art of French Cooking* and two volumes of *Simca's Cuisine*, whose pastry and *jet brioche* I've adapted for use elsewhere in this book.

No one is a better cook than Simca, and this dish of guinea-fowl in a winy, smoky sauce is one which she taught to me and the friend in whose Provençal house we stay.

Zucchini 'en spaghetti'

Pintade en salmis

2 guinea-hens, about 2 lb each, dressed
  weight
1½ cups stock made from guinea-hen
  carcasses
salt
1 small carrot, peeled
1 small onion, peeled
about 5 tablespoons lard
2 medium onions, finely sliced
¼ lb salt pork or bacon
4 large cloves garlic, peeled and finely
  chopped
1 bay leaf
1 sprig of thyme
a few parsley stems
5 tablespoons all-purpose flour
3 cups dry red wine
1 clove
black pepper
thick slices of stale white bread
  without crusts
butter
small handful fresh parsley,
  chopped

The day before you plan to serve the birds, cut them in a total of eight serving pieces. Make a stock from their carcasses, using salt, the carrot and small onion.

Melt 1 tablespoon lard in a large, heavy skillet and lightly brown half the guinea sections on both sides. Remove and brown the remaining pieces, adding a little more lard if necessary. Reserve.

In a heavy, flame-proof casserole of a size that takes the poultry comfortably, melt 1 tablespoon lard, add the onions and the pork or bacon, cut into lardons. Brown both lightly over a low heat. Add 3 garlic cloves and the bay leaf, thyme and parsley stems.

Melt 3 tablespoons lard in a heavy medium saucepan, beat in the flour and let cook over a low heat, stirring, until the roux turns a nutty, golden-brown.

Off the heat, beat in the wine and the strained stock, and beat until smooth. Add the clove and a little salt, bring to a boil and simmer, half-covered, over a very low heat for 40 minutes, skimming regularly.

Arrange the guinea pieces in the casserole. Season and strain the mellowed sauce and add to the casserole. Cover with buttered waxed paper and the lid. Braise in a preheated oven at 375°F, for 35 minutes, turning and basting the birds once.

Remove the casserole from the oven, and either strain the sauce of its onion, or simply leave the pot to cool. When cold, cover and refrigerate overnight.

The next day, spoon the fat from the surface, add a few tablespoons of water to the pot, and gently reheat its contents, covered, over a low flame, for 10–15 minutes, or until birds are completely cooked through. Taste and correct the seasoning.

Meanwhile, cut the bread into cubes and toss in a little butter over a fairly high heat. Add chopped parsley and remaining garlic when croûtons are turning golden-brown.

Present the guinea-fowl on a hot platter, spoon over the sauce and garnish with croûtons. Serves 6–8.

TARTE AUX PRUNES

Being surrounded by excellent pastry shops, we sample their variety with dedication and have never been known to make a dessert. We particularly like the homely plum tarts of a pâtisserie in the village of Mouans-Sartoux, of which here is an approximate recipe. The flavor is sharp and sophisticated.

---

*10 oz rich shortcrust pastry, as for
  Tarte Tatin on page 39
1¼ lb tart dessert plums, ripe but firm
granulated sugar
ground cinnamon
juice of ½ lemon
butter
crème fraîche or cream whipped with
  lemon juice*

Roll out the pastry and use it to line a 9 inch flan ring set onto a heavy baking sheet. Chill the pastry for at least a half an hour before baking. Bake blind in a preheated oven at 350°F for about 25 minutes until golden and browning and almost completely done.

Wash and dry plums and halve them through their natural indentation; remove the pits and put the fruit, cut side up, in one layer across a baking dish. Sprinkle the plums liberally with sugar, some ground cinnamon, and the lemon juice. Dot the dish with butter and bake in a preheated oven at 375°F until the plums are tender but still hold their shape. Remove the plums from the oven and let them cool in their dish for 10 minutes. Take up halves with a slotted spoon and arrange snugly inside the tart shell, making a second layer with any extra plums which remain.

Simmer juices from baking dish into a syrup and pour this over the fruit; bake tart at 350°F for 10–15 minutes to finish cooking.

Let dessert cool for 15 minutes and serve warm, with *crème fraîche* or cream that's been fortified with lemon juice. Serves 6.

Tarte aux prunes

VIN D'ORANGE

This recipe was given to me by Madame Annette Bernhard, whose family lives perched dramatically beside the gorges of the river Loup, east of Grasse, in an area once thick with trees of *oranges amères*.

The blossoms of these trees were formerly used in perfumery and their fruits candied. Many local families still prepare the bitter-sweet aperitif described below. It is excellent iced and enlivened with Perrier. In colder climates, buy Seville oranges to make the drink in January, then store it away in bottles that are well stoppered, in a cool dark place until summer. Serve from an attractive carafe, with plenty of ice and Perrier to taste.

---

*2½ quarts still, dry rosé wine, like a
  Côtes de Provence
2 cups eau de vie de fruits (best
  bought on a trip to France)
3 bitter oranges, washed, dried and cut
  into eighths
pinch of nutmeg
2½ cups superfine sugar
Perrier water
ice*

Combine all the ingredients, except the Perrier water and ice, in one or more large airtight containers. Shake well, and leave at room temperature for 45 days, shaking occasionally.

Pour the wine carefully through a filter paper and strainer and ladle into bottles that can be tightly stoppered.

MARKET FORCES

I can't resist lingering in good fruit and vegetable markets; the best draw me back, time and again, to particular cities and quarters, and more than one dull town has been saved for me by seeking out its better efforts in the way of produce. These recipes accommodate ingredients from the comfortable onion to the more elusive blueberry.

CABBAGE POUCHES STUFFED WITH SCALLOPS AND FOIE GRAS

Fredy Girardet's book *La cuisine spontanée* gave me the idea of stuffing cabbage leaves on a smaller but snappier scale than that leaf's usual fate of ground beef, rice, or leftovers. The sweetness and varied textures of *foie gras*, scallops and carrot make an agreeable combination for eating in the early spring, when cabbage and fresh scallops coincide.

1 green cabbage, preferably Savoy
salt
6 large sea scallops with coral, never frozen
dry white wine
black pepper
1 large carrot, peeled and finely-diced
granulated sugar
$\frac{1}{4}$–$\frac{1}{3}$ cup sweet butter, cut in squares
3 oz pure foie gras, en bloc
1 shallot, peeled and minced
1 tablespoon heavy cream

Blanch 12 large and handsome cabbage leaves in boiling, salted water for 3–4 minutes until completely cooked. Refresh in cold water, dry well, and cut away thick part of each central rib.

Wash and dry scallops and slice the white muscles diagonally in small medallions. Cut the coral in halves or thirds, put the fish into a small, heavy saucepan and barely cover with white wine. Season, bring the wine to simmer and gently poach scallops for 2–3 minutes until *just* cooked. Drain the fish, reserving its liquid.

Simmer the carrot briefly with seasoning, a good pinch of sugar, a little butter and a spoonful of water until just done; drain the carrot, add its 'stock' to that of the scallops.

Cut the block of *foie gras* into $\frac{1}{4}$ inch cubes and set aside.

Spread eight of the best cabbage leaves onto working surface (reinforce each with an extra half-leaf if need be), mix the scallops, carrots, and *foie gras*, divide these among the eight, centering the mixture.

Season, wrap each leaf around its contents to make up a smart pouch. Put the eight packages, seam side down, into a low-sided baking dish into which they will fit snugly, place a scrap of butter on top of each, pour on a couple of tablespoons of the fish stock. Slide dish into center of an oven preheated at 425°F.

Reduce 6 tablespoons of the remaining stock to the volume of 2 tablespoons, add the cream, bring to a boil, and off the heat, begin to incorporate the butter, beating and returning the saucepan to the heat after each incorporation, as for a *beurre blanc* (see page 46 for recipe). When sauce is ready, season and keep warm until ready to serve.

The pouches are done after 15–20 minutes, when the contents are hot throughout; test with a knife or trussing needle. Serve 2 parcels per person, accompanied by spoonfuls of sauce. Serves 4 as an appetizer.

PEPPERS AND EGGPLANT

A delectable summery salad. The sliced eggplant are served warm and both vegetables are dressed with lemon juice and garlicky oil.

2 large cloves garlic, peeled and minced
6 tablespoons first-pressing olive oil
2 slim eggplant, about $\frac{1}{2}$ lb each
salt
2 yellow and 2 red sweet peppers, of good size and shape, with thick flesh
1 egg
black pepper
wholewheat bread crumbs, freshly-made
lemon juice
flat-leaf parsley

One day ahead, stir minced garlic into olive oil; cover and set aside at room temperature.

About 5 hours before eating, slice each eggplant across into $\frac{1}{4}$ inch rounds, no thicker, or the results will be tough. Strew slices with salt and weight under a large, heavy chopping board until shortly before the meal. The eggplant will lose a lot of brownish liquid.

Meanwhile, rub the peppers with oil and place under the broiler pan an inch or so from strong heat. Broil, turning peppers with spoons or metal tongs, until the skins blacken and blister. Remove from the heat and cool under wet paper towels to loosen the skin. When each is cool enough to handle, peel off the loosened skin, halve flesh lengthwise, cut out stems, drain away juices and scrape out seeds. Wash and dry peppers and slice in wide strips. Arrange these, inner surfaces downward, across one or two serving

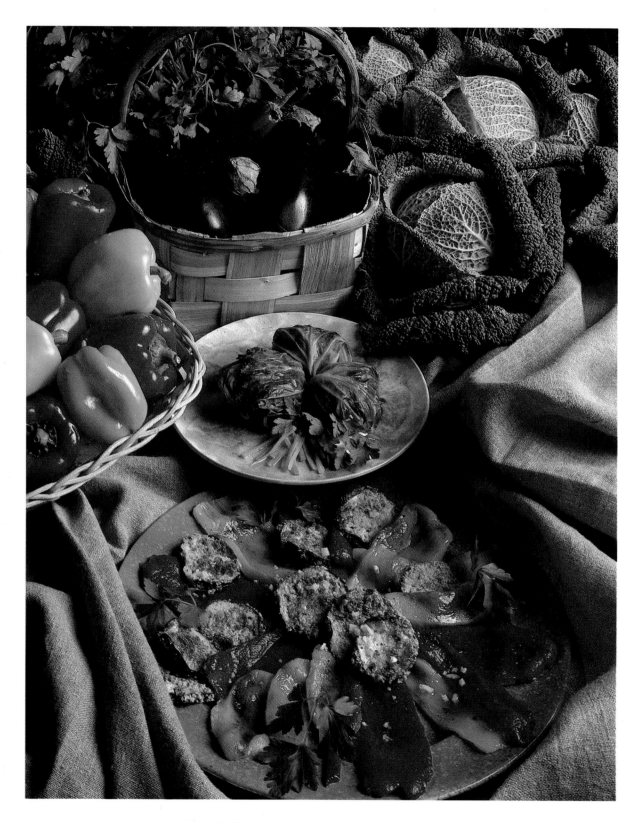

Cabbage pouches, Peppers and eggplant

platters remembering to leave enough space for the eggplant.

About 30 minutes before serving, thoroughly wash the eggplant and dry the slices on paper towels, but don't wring the eggplant slices or they will be as tough as cardboard when you chew them.

Beat the egg with ground pepper, then strew a lot of bread crumbs onto a plate. Dip the eggplant slices into the egg, then coat lightly with crumbs, and slowly broil on both sides, about 4 inches from a low heat, until the eggplant slices are tender inside and rather brown on the outside.

Keep warm in a slow oven until all of the eggplant is ready, then quickly distribute among the peppers on the serving platters. Grind on black pepper, dribble over lemon juice, spoon on olive oil and garlic mixture, add sprays of parsley and eat as soon as possible. Serves 4 as a substantial first course.

TOURIN BLANCHI AUX ESCARGOTS

Gilles Marre is a young French chef whose name will be celebrated. He has undergone ten years of preparation and training, including military service in the kitchens of the Elysée Palace and a period with Paul Haeberlin of l'Auberge de l'Ill in Alsace, whom Gilles considers as his mentor.

In 1984 'il s'est installé' as the French put it, in his family's Hôtel Terminus in Cahors, calling his restaurant Le Balandre, the canal barge. Here I've eaten two refreshingly excellent lunches, one as part of Cahors' Fête de la Truffe in January, where we started with Gilles' embellishment of the south-western onion and garlic soup known as *le tourin*.

I've juggled his amounts of milk and cream, as I find equal quantities of each too rich (though there's ample cream remaining); the *escargots* add smoky depths to the soup.

---

4 large white onions, about 2 lb 2 oz, peeled, halved and thinly sliced
¼ cup butter
1 large or 2 medium bulbs garlic, peeled
8 cups milk
salt
black pepper
grated nutmeg
72 escargots
3¾ cups heavy cream
3 egg yolks
fresh parsley, chopped
small croûtons

Sweat the onion with 3 tablespoons butter in a large, heavy pot with lid ajar. Halve garlic cloves, remove the slim green stem at the center of each, add the garlic to the onion and sweat, semi-covered, 4–5 minutes further to soften. Add a drop of water if necessary to prevent the garlic burning.

Pour in the milk, season, and grate on a little nutmeg. Bring liquid to simmer and leave barely to shudder, over a very low heat, for 30 minutes, stirring occasionally. Drain the garlic and onion (return milk to pot) and purée smooth in food processor. Beat purée back into the milk.

If the snails are canned, drain these of water, rinse well under running water – canned snails are very salty – dry and season; toss in 1 tablespoon butter to heat through, set aside to keep warm while completing the soup.

Beat the cream into the yolks while bringing the soup to first boil; remove the pot from heat and slowly beat in egg-and-cream to liaise the mixture, whisking after every addition.

Quickly roll the snails in parsley to coat evenly and divide among eight heated soup plates. Ladle in *tourin*. Strew with more parsley and croûtons which have been made by drying cubes of stale bread in a 300°F oven until the cubes turn golden brown. Eat without delay. Serves 8.

WARM SALAD OF PASTA, CORN AND POLENTA

½ cup medium-grained polenta (yellow corn meal)
1⅔ cups salted water
salt
black pepper
walnut oil
peanut oil
1 lb small, dried Italian pasta shapes; ideally in 3 colors
2 ears fresh young corn
green or purple basil

Measure the *polenta* and bring the salted water to boil in a small, heavy saucepan. Turn heat low and as water simmers, very slowly add corn meal, beating to prevent lumps. When all the corn meal is in, stir well with a wooden spoon and cook gently for about 10 minutes, stirring frequently and thoroughly. *Polenta* is done when it comes away from the sides of pan. Season and pour out, scraping pan sides, onto a wooden board. By means of a wet spatula, spread *polenta* into a flat square about ¼ inch thick. When cold and firm, slice into rectangles about the size of half a postage stamp.

Shortly before the salad is to be served, bring 2 large pots of salted water to boil, add a pour of walnut oil to one. Heat a large serving bowl in a low oven, take a wide skillet and pour into it a coating of peanut oil in which to cook the *polenta* dominoes (peanut oil will not give these an unpleasantly greasy coating). Drop pasta into the pot with the oil when the water is at full boil, stir well to separate, boil for about 10–12 minutes or until pasta is just past *al dente*.

Meanwhile, heat the oil in the skillet, add *polenta* slices and cook on both sides till a crisp but transparent crust forms on each. Drain on paper towels.

When pasta is about half done, plunge husked corn into a second pot and boil for the few minutes necessary to cook. Drain the ears of corn, and as soon as you can touch them, slice away kernels with a small, sharp knife. Put these into the heated bowl with a little walnut oil. Season, toss, and keep warm until ready to use.

When the pasta is ready, drain well, add to the warm corn with more walnut oil, season and toss; gently mix in cooked *polenta*, strew with basil leaves and serve. Eat this warm salad without delay. Serves 4–6.

PUMPKIN BRULEE WITH STRAWBERRIES AND RASPBERRIES

Pumpkin *brûlée* is the brilliant invention of American cookery writer Marion Morash: I've reinterpreted her recipe and serve spoonfuls of the custard accompanied by the crushed, sugared strawberries and raspberries. I think that the result is memorable.

2 cups heavy cream
2½ teaspoons dark rum
6 egg yolks
5 tablespoons superfine sugar
1 scant cup cooked pumpkin purée; if you can't find a fresh pumpkin with which to make your own, the canned variety is fine here
¼ teaspoon ground cinnamon
generous pinch of ground cloves
generous pinch of salt
½ cup packed light brown sugar

TO SERVE
fresh strawberries
fresh raspberries
confectioners' sugar

Scald the cream and rum while beating yolks with superfine sugar until thick and light. Combine the yolks with pumpkin, spices and salt and slowly beat in the hot cream. Pour mixture into a heatproof glass baking dish of 6 cup capacity and bake contents in a bain-marie at 350°F for 1 hour, or until the custard is set and a trussing needle thrust into center tests very warm. Cool and chill overnight.

To caramelize the top, sift on brown sugar, pressing it down to an even layer. Place dish inside a broiler pan filled with cold water and put the custard under a medium to low heat, about 4 inches away from source if possible. Watch the dish carefully and turn it as the sugar melts, blisters, and browns. Remove from the broiler, let cool for 15 minutes, repeat until brown has deepened and glazed. Try not to burn the sugar! Chill the *brûlée*, uncovered, for several hours. The caramel must not sweat or it will begin to soften.

To serve, bring the pumpkin mixture to room temperature, and with a fork, crush the strawberries and raspberries—also at room temperature—and dust them with sifted confectioners' sugar. Serve with piles of the mixed, sugared berries. Serves 6.

Salad of pasta, corn and polenta, Tourin blanchi aux escargots

RAFT OF PEARS AND BLUEBERRIES

Fresh blueberries have a short, late season; I can't get enough of them. The pastry for this 'raft' is made with cream cheese.

PASTRY
$\frac{7}{8}$ cup sweet butter
3 oz cream cheese
3 tablespoons sour cream
generous 1$\frac{1}{2}$ cups all-purpose flour
large pinch of salt

FILLING
2 lb ripe but firm pears, quartered,
    peeled and cored
2 tablespoons sweet butter
$\frac{1}{2}$ cup granulated sugar
3 tablespoons lemon juice
3 cups fresh blueberries
large pinch of ground cinnamon
large pinch of salt
$\frac{3}{4}$ teaspoon potatoflour or cornstarch
1 egg yolk

To make the pastry, beat together the softened butter, cheese and sour cream. Work in the flour and salt, form pastry into a ball, wrap, and chill for several hours.

Slice the quartered pear lengthwise – not too thinly – and toss, over a high heat, with the butter, 2 tablespoons sugar, and 1 tablespoon lemon juice until pears just barely resist a knife when pierced. Drain, save the juices and cool the fruit.

Put the blueberries into a saucepan with pears' liquid, the remaining sugar and lemon, cinnamon and salt. Cover pan and heat berries until just cooked and yielding their juice. Drain blueberries, add fruit to pears and cool. Take $\frac{2}{3}$ cup of the fruits' liquid and thicken over a low heat by whisking with potatoflour or cornstarch dissolved in a teaspoon of water. Combine with berries and pears.

Halve the pastry, roll out half into a narrow rectangle, heap fruit and thickened juices along the center. Paint the

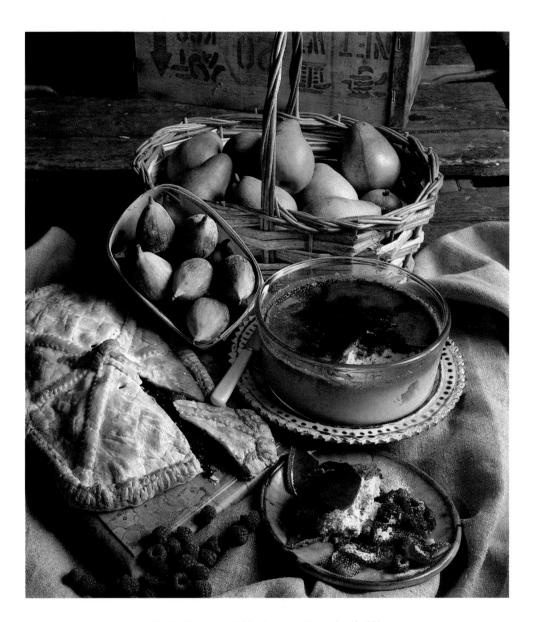

Raft of pears and blueberries, Pumpkin brûlée

edges with a little cold water, roll out remaining pastry and place over first half. Trim the borders and press close to the fruit with the tines of a fork. Paint the top of the 'raft' with water, re-roll the pastry offcuts and criss-cross three strips over the upper surface, pressing their ends into the border; turn this back onto itself and seal with a fork. Put a pastry knot into the center of cross and pierce a steam hole on either side.

Refrigerate raft for several hours before baking. Beat the egg yolk with a little water and just before baking, paint the raft with two coats of this egg glaze; cross-hatch the glaze with a fork then place the pastry on a heavy baking sheet. Bake the raft in a preheated oven at 425°F for 10 minutes. Reduce the oven temperature to 400°F for 25 minutes further. Serve warm, with cream or vanilla ice cream. Serves 6.

A SENSE OF SERENDIPITY

Each of these recipes represents something I have tasted, heard described, or in one case, merely glimpsed, during my travels of the past few years. The common thread has been the pleasure of sudden, sometimes unexpected, discovery and the interest in comparison of diverse cuisines.

GYUVECH

This is a Bulgarian dish whose origins are Turkish. I first ate it, as *türlü güveç*, in a working man's restaurant at Van, eastern Turkey, where lamb appeared amid the many vegetables. In both Bulgaria and Turkey the list of ingredients can differ from place to place depending on regional and seasonal variations.

In Bulgaria, cubes of beef, lamb, or pork may accompany ten or twelve vegetables, or as here, the vegetables may be on their own. In rural districts, lard might be the cooking fat, though most often sunflower oil, or oil-and-butter is the usual medium. Sometimes mushrooms are added, 'for grandeur', and at the right season, unripe grapes will be put to sharpen the mixture; a dash of vinegar is an occasional substitute for this ingredient.

One or two chili peppers are an optional extra, but leave these out if you don't like the heat. Ingredients and quantities should be regarded as flexible, and though the cooked result – ideally made in an earthenware casserole, the *gyuvech* – looks rather dull, it is delicious and satisfying.

Accompanying this dish are jars of *sharena* or 'colorful' salt, also known as *chubritsa*, meaning 'savory', after the herb which is the chief ingredient of this pounded blend of red peppers, mint, dill and savory with salt and pepper. Bowls of *sharena* salt appear on Bulgarian tables as relish for the hot bread which begins the meal.

---

1 eggplant, cut in small cubes
2 large potatoes, peeled and cubed very
*   small*
3–4 zucchini, thickly sliced
1 green pepper, seeded and thinly sliced
1½ cups shredded green cabbage
⅔ cup slim green beans, sliced
1 large onion, peeled and chopped
1–2 chili peppers, seeded and sliced in
*   thin rounds (optional)*
2 cups canned Italian plum tomatoes,
*   drained, chopped*
¼ lb fresh okra, if available
handful of fresh parsley, flat-leafed if
*   possible, minced*
1 teaspoon paprika
salt
¼ cup corn or sunflower oil
good dash of wine vinegar
black pepper if not using chilis
3 eggs

Place the eggplant, potatoes, zucchini, pepper, cabbage, green beans, onion, chilis and tomatoes into a large, heavy casserole – earthenware, for purists. Cut the stems from the okra and peel their caps without piercing the pods (or the sap will be released). Add the pods to the casserole. Add about half the parsley, the paprika and 1 teaspoon of salt. Pour on the oil and vinegar. Mix thoroughly with your hands and cover with a piece of buttered, waxed paper. Bake in a preheated oven at 375°F for 1½-2 hours, stirring two or three times and moistening the paper as you do so. When all the vegetables are cooked, taste and adjust the seasoning. Beat and season the eggs, add the remaining parsley and pour this over the vegetable mixture. Return to the oven for 5–10 minutes until the eggs are set. Present the *gyuvech* immediately, with hot bread. Serves 4–6.

PAPPA COL POMODORO

This is a Tuscan dish, a simple and agreeable peasant soup made of bread, tomatoes and water. The nicest I've eaten was actually in a restaurant, Le Cave di Maiano, near Fiesole, part of an immense and delicious meal, and this is more or less the recipe they gave me. Tuscan cooks use the local saltless bread which allows the flavour of their excellent tomatoes to predominate. Elsewhere, the *pappa* is worth making only with bread of good character that won't become a gluey swamp when moistened.

---

first-pressing olive oil
6 large cloves garlic, slivered
5 cups drained canned Italian plum
*   tomatoes*
10 oz good quality bread, several days
*   old*
3½-4 cups water
large bunch of fresh basil leaves,
*   shredded*
salt
black pepper

Run 2 tablespoons of oil around the base of a deep, heavy pan. Soften the garlic in the oil over low heat for about 5 minutes. Add the tomatoes, breaking them up with a wooden spoon, and simmer for 15–20 minutes until reasonably well cooked down.

Meanwhile, slice the bread with

Clockwise from top right: Tarte ovale, Pappa col pomodoro, Tarator, Tagine, Gyuvech,
Coeur de Camembert

crusts on, and break it into small pieces. Add to the tomato and cover with $3\frac{1}{2}$ cups of the water. Stir the mixture well and simmer for another 15 minutes, stirring occasionally, until the soup has become very thick. Add a little more water if you think necessary. Add the basil leaves toward the end of the cooking time and work them in. Season well.

I think the flavors and texture benefit when the *pappa* is made a day ahead, so cool and refrigerate. When required, reheat the soup, stirring and adding additional water only if necessary; the soup should not be thin. Ladle the soup into bowls, dribble olive oil over the surface of each bowl and eat very hot. Serves 4–5.

LAMB TAGINE WITH PRUNES

I seem to be in a minority of people who actually like Tangier, where I first ate this *tagine*, variously spiced and sweetened with honey and prunes. This tagine recipe is adapted from one of Paula Wolfert's, the American writer on Moroccan food.

1 shoulder of lamb
$1\frac{1}{2}$ large onions, peeled
2 tablespoons butter
good pinch of saffron threads
$\frac{1}{4}$ teaspoon ground nutmeg
$\frac{1}{4}$ teaspoon ground ginger
2 cups water
salt
1 tea bag
1 lb prunes
$\frac{1}{2}$ teaspoon ground cinnamon
2 tablespoons honey
$\frac{3}{4}$ cup whole blanched almonds
black pepper
small handful of fresh cilantro leaves,
    shredded

Ask your butcher to cut the lamb, on the bone, into 1-inch cubes. Finely chop the half onion, thinly slice the whole one.

Place the lamb in a deep, heavy pan or casserole with the butter, saffron (crumbled between index finger and thumb), nutmeg, ginger, and finely-chopped onion. Stir over a low heat to develop the aroma of the spices, but do not color the meat. Add the water, bring to a boil, lower the heat and skim the liquid. Add $\frac{1}{2}$ teaspoon salt, cover and gently simmer for $1\frac{1}{4}$ hours, stirring the lamb occasionally.

Meanwhile, use a tea bag to make a bowlful of strong tea and, while this is hot, immerse the prunes. Leave for 30 minutes or until the prunes have swelled just enough to cut out their pits, leaving each fruit whole.

When the meat has been simmering for $1\frac{1}{4}$ hours, add the cinnamon, honey and sliced onion. Cover and cook for about 30 minutes longer or until tender.

When the lamb is done, add the drained and pitted prunes and simmer the *tagine*, uncovered, for 5–10 minutes until the prunes are well-plumped. Meanwhile, toast the almonds under a preheated broiler.

Drain the meat and transfer to a serving dish. Drain and distribute the prunes among the meat and keep hot. Degrease the sauce and reduce it, over a high heat, to a coating consistency. Adjust the seasoning, which should be well poised between spicy and sweet, with pepper. Pour the sauce over the lamb and place on the top shelf of a preheated oven at 450°F for 2–3 minutes to glaze the meat and onions. Strew with the almonds and the shredded cilantro and serve. Serves 4–6.

TARATOR

During a week's trip to Bulgaria, I ate best in the staff restaurants of various state wineries. The Institute of Nutrition of the Bulgarian Medical Academy supervises the running of these, and the traditional Bulgarian cooking they serve is, in my experience, first-rate.

Since Bulgaria was part of the Ottoman Empire for nearly 500 years, some of the cooking, inevitably, derives from Turkey.

Such is the case with this cold yogurt soup which I've eaten both in Anatolia and at the Suhindol winery east of Sofia, the source of the recipe here. The name *tarator* is the same as for the Turkish sauce described earlier; a fact which I'm sure is attributable to the presence of walnuts and garlic.

4 cups natural yogurt
4 cups finely chopped cucumber
$\frac{1}{3}$ cup ground walnuts
2–4 large cloves garlic, peeled and
    crushed
2 tablespoons sunflower oil
$1\frac{1}{4}$–$1\frac{3}{4}$ cups water
salt
fresh dill, scissored, to taste

Put the yogurt into a large bowl and beat in the cucumber, walnuts, garlic and oil. Dilute with water to make a fairly liquid consistency. Add salt and dill to taste, beat well.

Refrigerate the soup for several hours to blend the flavors. Immediately before serving, float a few ice cubes on the surface. Serves 5–6.

COEUR DE CAMEMBERT AU CALVADOS

The idea for this graceful end to a meal was related to me by Philippe Olivier, *maître-fromager* of Boulogne, who says that formerly, in Normandy, it was not done to serve Camembert in its rind, in the same way as you would not pass around sardines in their can. Instead the *croûte* was cut away and the cheese was presented at the table wrapped with bread crumbs.

In this dish, warm apple sauce and Camembert touched with Calvados accompanied by Normandy cider to drink make a stirring combination.

APPLE SAUCE

1½ lb apples, a mixture of tart and
    sweet eating varieties, pared, cored
    and chopped
1 tablespoon sweet butter
¼ cup packed light brown sugar

CHEESE

1 Camembert fermier, unpasteurized,
    creamy and ripe to the center but not
    runny
Calvados
fine breadcrumbs, freshly-made from a
    wholewheat or cracked wheat loaf

TO SERVE

wholewheat or cracked wheat bread
naturally-fermented Normandy hard
    cider, chilled

Put the apples in a heavy saucepan with the butter, a little water and sugar to taste. The resulting sauce should not be too sweet. Cover and cook, stirring often to break down the apples, then beat into a smooth purée which holds its shape well. The sauce should retain an interesting texture and enough acidity to enhance the taste of Camembert.

Cut the entire rind from the Camembert. Pierce each side all over with a fork and pour on about 2 tablespoons Calvados. Press this into one surface with back of fork. Leave for 30 minutes, basting several times; turn the cheese over and repeat with more Calvados. After 30 minutes more, drain the cheese and cover completely with bread crumbs. Shake away the excess and pour on a little more Calvados.

Cut the cheese into six wedges and serve with warmed apple sauce, hot toast and chilled hard cider. Serves 2–4.

TARTE OVALE

I first saw this glorified jam tart in the window of a pâtisserie at Vienne, in the Rhône valley in France, but never tasted

Tarte ovale

it; I brought home the idea.

You need a firm pastry that requires no mold, and you may also find that quince jelly gives the perfect note of sweet, slightly exotic acidity.

PATE A CROUSTADE

2 cups all-purpose flour
large pinch of salt
⅔ cup sweet butter, chilled
1 egg, beaten with 2 teaspoons water

TO FINISH

⅔ cup quince jelly or a homemade
    quince jam
confectioners' sugar

Make the pastry by hand or in a food processor. Put the flour and salt into the bowl and blend briefly. Cut the butter into 5 squares, add to the flour and work for about 10 seconds until it reaches the consistency of coarse crumbs. Pour the egg and water through the feed tube with the machine on; the pastry will mass together after about 10 seconds. Transfer it onto a floured board and work deftly

into a slightly moist ball.

Wrap in waxed paper and plastic and refrigerate for several hours or overnight. Sieve the jelly or beat the jam until smooth, and reserve.

Bring the pastry to room temperature and roll out, between two sheets of floured waxed paper, to a thickness of about ⅛ inch. Cut out a 9 × 10 inch oval. Transfer to a heavy baking sheet. Re-roll the trimmings to the same thickness and cut into thin strips. Spread the jelly over the oval to within ⅝ inch or so of the edge, all around. Lay the strips of pastry across from top to bottom, fanning them slightly, and press them against the unjellied border. Trim any excess dough. With your fingers, roll the edge to form a rim. Refrigerate the unbaked tart for about 2 hours.

Bake in a preheated oven at 350°F for 30–40 minutes until the pastry is cooked and colouring. Turn around once during this time. The jelly will bubble up and out to some extent.

Remove the tart from the oven and let cool for about 10 minutes, then carefully loosen it from the baking sheet with a spatula. When cold, transfer to a serving platter, cover half of the tart with a sheet of waxed paper and sift a good coating of confectioners' sugar over the other half.

Present whole, and serve each person with a slice from both sugared and unsugared sections. Serves 4.

DELICACIES IN DISGUISE

Fresh chicken livers, a meal steamed in parchment, *polenta* with sausages, fresh figs and anything made with pig's ears are not commonplace, as far as I can tell, on today's dinner tables. I hope these recipes will encourage cooks to rectify this comparative neglect.

We photographed the results, in late spring, in a beautifully-tended version of an eighteenth-century English kitchen garden – this one a brick-walled half-acre in Warwickshire, looking from the greenhouse toward a fruit cage.

RADISH CANAPES, CROSTINI

Quickly-prepared mouthfuls served with drinks before dinner are not always considered worth the trouble, which is a great pity; radishes sliced onto buttered bread – a treasured snack of French children – and *crostini*, a hot Tuscan hors-d'oeuvre made with chicken livers, are two of my favorites. Try to persuade your butcher to get *fresh* livers. If you must use frozen ones, drain them very well after thawing.

RADISH CANAPES
1 narrow loaf of French bread
sweet butter
radishes
salt
black pepper

CROSTINI
10 oz chicken livers
salt
black pepper
olive oil
lemon juice

Cut French loaf into as many thin slices as you will want for the radish canapés, slice 14 or 15 further rounds for the *crostini* and put the latter to dry and lightly toast in a preheated oven at 290°F for about 20 minutes.

Butter untoasted slices, trim radishes, and slice and fan them across bread. Season.

When the toasts are slightly colored (finish them off under a low broiler if this is taking too long), trim, wash, and dry the livers. Season them, and sauté whole in a splash of olive oil over a high heat, tossing often, for about 3 minutes, until just cooked and still pink inside. Transfer to a bowl, squeeze on lemon juice, and quickly mash with a fork. Spread the purée onto toasts, grind on pepper, and serve *crostini* hot, accompanied by radish canapés.

POLENTA WITH SAUSAGES

A meal-in-one, this time a big robust dish from northern Italy, as described in Marcella Hazan's *Classic Italian Cook Book*; I've adapted her recipe somewhat. This is a different use of *polenta* from the way it has been presented earlier, though the basic idea is the same.

½ cup chopped onion
1½ tablespoons olive oil
1 large carrot, peeled and chopped
2 medium celery sticks, chopped
3 oz thinly-sliced pancetta *(cured belly pork in a sausage shape), cut into ½ inch strips*
1 lb luganega or other slim, sweet pork sausage
1½ cups canned Italian plum tomatoes with their juices
6 cups salted water
2 cups medium or coarse-grained polenta *(corn meal)*
salt
black pepper

Put the onion with olive oil in a large skillet and sweat, covered, until the onion is colored. Add the carrot, celery and *pancetta*, and sauté over medium heat for 3–4 minutes, stirring often.

Slice the sausage into 3 inch lengths, add to the pan and cook for 10 minutes, turning occasionally. Pour in the tomatoes and juice, and break up with a wooden spoon. Simmer for 30 minutes, stirring occasionally.

Meanwhile, bring the salted water to a brisk simmer and very slowly add the corn meal, whisking to prevent lumps. When all the corn meal is in, stir well with a wooden spoon and cook gently for 15–20 minutes, stirring frequently and thoroughly. The *polenta* is done when it comes away from side of pan.

Season and pour into a large, round, heated dish. Make a hollow in the center, pile on the sausages and add their sauce. Serve immediately, with a large green salad to accompany or follow. Serves 6.

Clockwise from top right: Polenta with sausages, Silk purse salad, Radish canapés, crostini, La terrine de Jeanne, Fish with vegetables in parchment, Figs in fruit salad

SILK PURSE SALAD

The French know how good this can be, but most British and Americans look at me aghast when they learn the main ingredient here. They are usually converted, though, after tasting the dish. Pigs' ears in fact combine crunch and a slightly tongue-like quality which is excellent sharply-dressed with pickled gherkins and celery; they also lack the glueyness of pig's feet. While wooing your butcher for fresh chicken livers, ask him to order this inexpensive cut of pork at the same time.

---

4 pigs' ears
salt
1 carrot, peeled
1 onion, peeled
1 clove garlic, unpeeled
1 bouquet garni
3 tablespoons lemon juice
2 tablespoons Dijon mustard
1 celery stick, minced
4 pickled gherkins, minced
2 shallots, peeled and minced
fresh parsley, chopped
fresh chervil, chopped
fresh chives, chopped
2 eggs
4 tablespoons olive oil
black pepper
lettuce leaves

Clean the ears, singe off hair, and wash. Coat with salt and refrigerate overnight. The next day wash and drain the ears and put them into a large pot with the carrot, onion, garlic and bouquet garni. Cover with water, bring to boil, skim and simmer half-covered for 2–2½ hours until the ears test tender. Let them cool in the liquid.

Make the dressing by combining the lemon juice and mustard with celery, gherkins, and shallots. Add a lot of chopped herbs. Boil the eggs for 3 minutes, scoop yolks into dressing, chop and add whites. Beat in olive oil, add salt and pepper to taste.

Drain and dry cooled ears, cut away the very cartilaginous ends, slice ears in half lengthwise, cut the halves across and then into thin strips. Toss with the dressing, taste for seasoning, and present on a bed of lettuce. Serves 4–6.

LA TERRINE DE JEANNE

Chicken livers again, tasting almost like *foie gras* along the center of a pork forcemeat. This is the recipe of Gisèle Mardon, a Frenchwoman who teaches cooking in London. Very easily made, this terrine is one for which fresh livers of firm texture and pale color are absolutely essential.

½ lb chicken livers, never frozen
1 tablespoon port
1 tablespoon Cognac
about 1¼ lb fresh pork sides, weighed
    after bones and rind have been
    removed
1 shallot, peeled and chopped
1 clove garlic, peeled and chopped
¼ teaspoon quatre épices (sometimes
    sold as Epices Marie or Epice
    Parisienne)
2 tablespoons chopped fresh parsley
salt
black pepper
butter
enough smoked bacon of good regional
    cure if possible, to line a 4-cup
    terrine
1 bay leaf
lard (optional)

TO SERVE
buttered toast

Trim livers and marinate in port and brandy, refrigerating overnight. The next day, trim the pork of excess nerve tissue, leaving you with about 1 lb of streaky meat. Grind this with the shallot, garlic, *quatre épices*, parsley, and a little salt and pepper. Drain the marinade from the livers and add marinade to the mixture. Test flavors by frying a small ball of this forcemeat in butter; add more seasoning if needed and test the flavors once again.

Soak the smoked bacon rashers in tepid water to remove any excess salt. Rinse well, dry, and stretch the rashers with back of a knife. Line a 4-cup terrine of attractive shape with overlapping slices of the bacon rashers.

Weigh forcemeat and press half into terrine; season livers and lay them on top in an even layer. Cover with rest of pork mixture, smooth and round with a damp hand, lay bay leaf in middle, fold over bacon from sides. Cover with foil and the lid, then place in a bain-marie. Bake in a preheated oven at 325°F for 1½ hours, turning once. A trussing needle plunged into center should test hot.

Remove the terrine from the oven and bain-marie with its foil intact, cover with 2 lb weight to compress the mixture. Cool, and chill, still weighted, overnight; remove weight in the morning, and leave uncut for 2–3 days to allow flavors to develop and mature.

To keep the terrine for a longer period, unmold it, scrape away and disgard the jelly, wash and dry its container and carefully replace the contents, minus the bay leaf. Seal the surface completely with melted lard and refrigerate. Serves 4–6, with buttered toast.

FISH WITH VEGETABLES IN PARCHMENT

I like to combine fish or poultry with vegetables and herbs and bake them together in parchment or foil; the result is a meal-in-one whose aromas burst forth as you tear apart the bag.

The quantities suggested are for amounts *per person*; multiply by any number up to four.

butter
three of the following fish: a few
  mussels in closed shells, 2 scallops
  with coral, 2 oz each of porgy,
  salmon, or halibut (without skin)
a few mange-tout peas, trimmed
salt
generous 1 oz slim green beans,
  trimmed
4–5 tiny new potatoes in skins
2 oz zucchini
fresh basil
fresh chervil
fresh chives
black pepper
beurre blanc

For each person cut a 14 inch round of baking parchment paper and butter one side. Scrub, beard and dry the mussels. Slice scallops into bite-size pieces, leaving coral intact; slice any other fish into same size.

Blanch the mange-tout in boiling salted water until half-cooked. Blanch the beans until *al dente*, drain, refresh, and dry. Boil the potatoes until done, cut unblanched zucchini into lengths.

Lay buttered side of the parchment on the working surface (greasing the exterior makes the paper less likely to tear accidentally) and arrange all the fish and vegetables over one half of the circle. Strew with shredded basil, scissored chervil and chives; grind on salt and pepper. Fold parchment across and roll edges tightly to make a sort of turnover. Staple edges at 1–2 inch intervals and just before closing the end of each turnover, insert a straw and blow to inflate the parchment. Staple the package shut. Place on a heavy baking sheet in a preheated oven at 375°F for about 15 minutes; the bag will puff and color.

Serve immediately in a hot soup plate. Tear open the bag and pour over a little *beurre blanc*, whose recipe is on page 46.

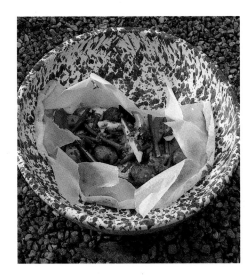

Fish in parchment

FIGS IN FRUIT SALAD

How to convince anyone that fruit salad has been neglected? I adore figs and their potential; like making their unskinned cross sections into patterns with other fruits, moistening everything with syrup and adding a herb or a few edible flowers. So I'll make this my last neglected dish and won't worry too much if the appellation has been stretched.

SUGAR SYRUP
½ cup granulated sugar
1 cup water
dash of lemon juice
small piece of dried tamarind fruit

SALAD
2 ripe but firm peaches
2 small oranges
4 figs
12–16 fresh strawberries
8 cherries

First, prepare the sugar syrup by dissolving the granulated sugar in the water and boiling the liquid for 1 minute. Add the lemon juice to sharpen and the dried tamarind fruit to give the syrup an agreeable tang. Cool and refrigerate

Figs in fruit salad

overnight and strain in the morning before use.

To make four individual salads, take the peaches, remove their skins in just-boiled water and gently poach in the strained syrup until a knife just pierces their flesh. Do not over-cook.

Let them cool while cutting the peel and pith from the oranges. Cut these into sections without their membrane and add their exuded juice to syrup.

Slice the figs across, and the strawberries from top to bottom. Pit and halve the cherries and slice the peaches.

Arrange all this fruit across four dinner plates. Spoon on a little syrup, cooled and strained once more (use the remainder elsewhere), surround fruits with edible flowers or herbs. Here I've added pansies, polyanthus, and the leaves and flowers of sweet cicely, an ethereal looking plant with a delicate sweet anise flavor.

These are some suggested combinations of various fruits with figs; figs and raspberries would be delectable on their own, or with sliced nectarines. Combinations of figs, plums and redcurrants are another possibility. Serves 4.

ANOTHER CULTURE

Yogurt is popular as never before, but buttermilk, its equally cultivated cousin, has become an undervalued relation. The family to which they both belong is that of the cultured milk products, which includes sour cream, smetana and various cheeses.

They are all formed by the introduction of benign bacteria which feed on lactose or milk sugar and produce lactic acid, which sours the milk and causes it to curdle. Different types of milk with various forms of bacteria, treated in differing ways, give individual results; the principle, however, is the same for all of them.

I love the silken-rich acidity of chilled buttermilk; to drink, to bake with, and to add focus to cool summer soups. Confusingly, little of what is sold in the supermarkets as 'cultured buttermilk' is the by-product of churning cream into butter. It is, in fact, milk from which the cream has been skimmed, soured by the introduction of a bacteria or lactic culture, and often thickened by the addition of separated milk solids.

There is a strong case for the real thing. In my experience it tastes better with its suave, satiny texture. The recipes which follow, however, are equally as good with true buttermilk or the cultured skim alternative and for practical purposes, I'll call both 'buttermilk'.

CHILLED CURRIED EGGPLANT SOUP

As I often demonstrate in these pages, the eggplant is a good vehicle for other flavors; here it is curry that adds an unexpected dimension. A flourish of buttermilk finishes it nicely.

---

scant 2 tablespoons butter
1 medium onion, peeled and sliced
1 teaspoon mild curry powder
1¼ lb eggplants
4 cups chicken broth, made as on page 100
salt
1½–2 cups buttermilk
juice of ½–1 lemon
black pepper
additional broth or buttermilk if necessary
fresh chervil
scallions

Melt the butter in a medium saucepan and sweat the onion until soft. Add the curry powder and stir over a low heat for about 1 minute.

Meanwhile, broil the eggplants until skin is charred and flesh is soft. Cut away stems and peel off skin; rinse flesh under cold water and squeeze away bitter juices. Chop the flesh and add it to saucepan with broth and a dash of salt; half-cover, and simmer soup for 5–10 minutes, until the vegetables are tender. Half-cool and liquidize until very smooth. Add 1½ cups of buttermilk and strained juice of the half lemon. Season and decide whether to add remaining buttermilk and lemon, and more seasoning.

Chill soup overnight; its flavors will mellow if left until the next day. Remove from the refrigerator 30 minutes before serving, thin with more broth or buttermilk if need be, check seasoning, ladle into bowls and garnish each with a sprig of fresh chervil and a section through the base of a scallion, its layers of skin curled by 30 minutes' immersion in cold water. Serves 4.

CHILLED SOUP OF YELLOW PEPPERS

Using almost exactly the same method, you can produce quite a different soup with sweet yellow peppers and without curry.

---

scant 2 tablespoons butter
1 medium carrot, peeled and sliced
1 medium onion, peeled and sliced
1 large clove garlic, peeled and crushed
1¼ lb sweet yellow peppers
3¾ cups homemade chicken broth, made as on page 100
salt
1½–2 cups buttermilk
juice of ½–1 lemon
black pepper
additional broth or buttermilk, if necessary
slim strips of sweet red pepper

Proceed as for eggplant soup, sweating carrot and onion with garlic – but without curry powder. Grill peppers as eggplants, skin. Halve lengthwise, cut out stems, drain juices, remove ribs and seeds. Rinse flesh in cool water, cut into strips and continue preparation as with eggplants.

Thin if required, check seasoning, ladle into bowls, and garnish with strips of red pepper, prepared as for flesh of the yellow. Serves 4.

From the top: Curried eggplant soup, Soup of sweet yellow peppers, Avocado and watercress salad

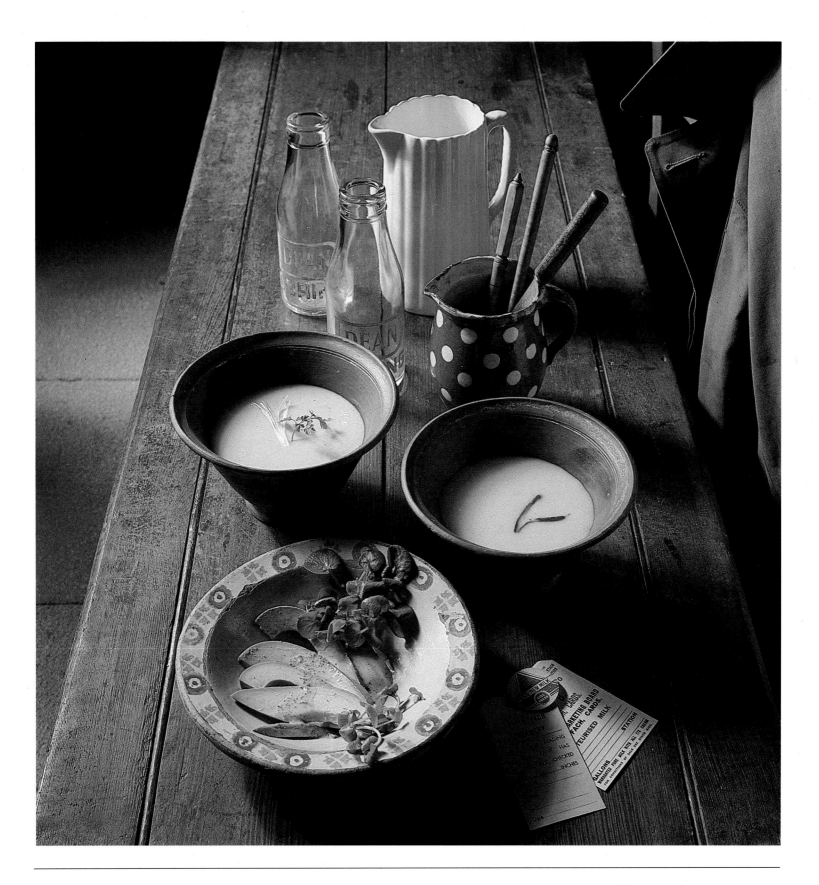

AVOCADO AND WATERCRESS SALAD, BUTTERMILK AND HERB DRESSING

I think that we don't often search for alternatives to the oil and vinegar sorts of dressings for salads. Buttermilk, enhanced with chives and the flair of mustard, sharpened with lemon juice and a touch of oil from toasted sesame seeds, does wonderful things for the long-familiar avocado. Add to this the pepper of watercress and you have a very striking salad.

1½ teaspoons sesame seeds
¾ cup buttermilk, chilled
watercress
fresh chives
pinch of dry mustard
salt
black pepper
lemon juice
2–3 ripe avocados

Lightly toast the sesame seeds under a preheated broiler set to a low temperature. Cool.

Put the buttermilk into a blender, add about 10 watercress leaves, some scissored chives, a good pinch of dry mustard, a grind each of salt and pepper. Blend until smooth and judge whether to add more of either herb, and/or mustard and seasoning. The dressing should be piquant without overpowering the subtlety of the buttermilk. Add a squeeze of lemon and blend the mixture again. Pour into a bowl and stir in the sesame seeds.

Halve the avocados, remove seeds and skins, and slice each half into a fan across a small plate. Lay a few attractive sprigs of watercress into the spring of each fan, grind pepper over avocado and spoon a ribbon of dressing across center of fan.

Serve without delay, with any additional dressing to accompany salad. Serves 4–6.

KAERENAELKS KOLDSKAAL

This is a cold Danish froth, to which I like to add a few cherries or raspberries when they are in season. The flavors should be fresh, so mix the various elements just before serving the drink.

---

4 cups cold buttermilk
grated zest and juice of 1 lemon
2 eggs
2 tablespoons superfine sugar
a small handful of fresh raspberries or
*   pitted cherries*

Whiz the buttermilk, lemon zest and strained juice in a blender. In a small bowl, beat the eggs and sugar until thick, add to the buttermilk with raspberries or cherries to taste, and purée. Makes 4 glassfuls.

BUTTERMILK ICE CREAM

⅔ cup sultanas
½ cup dark rum
6 egg yolks
1¾ cups superfine sugar
½ teaspoon salt
4 cups buttermilk
2 cups heavy cream
2 vanilla beans, split

Bring sultanas and rum to a boil, simmer briefly and leave fruit to cool.

With a hand-held electric beater, whisk the yolks, sugar, and salt until thick; combine the buttermilk, cream and vanilla beans in a heavy saucepan. Bring the liquid just to simmer and beat this into yolks. Return all to the pan and beat over medium heat until mixture thickens and *just* comes to a boil. Immediately strain into a bowl.

When custard has cooled, pour it into a deep plastic box, beat well, cover, place in freezer and leave, stirring and beating every hour. When ice cream is about half-frozen, work in sultanas and

rum, cover tightly and return to freezer; continue to stir about once every hour, until well on the way to setting.

Make 36 hours in advance as the alcohol in rum retards the freezing.

Serve scoops of the ice cream with a shortbread, or in tandem with slices of buttermilk cake. Serves 6–8.

BUTTERMILK CAKE

This is a classic American recipe which I've adapted from Flo Braker's version in *The Simple Art of Perfect Baking*, published in 1985 in New York. Buttermilk gives the cake a tender crumb.

2½ cups all-purpose flour
1½ teaspoons baking powder
½ teaspoon baking soda
¼ teaspoon salt
1 teaspoon vanilla essence
1 cup buttermilk, at room
temperature
¾ cup sweet butter, softened
1½ cups superfine sugar
3 egg yolks at room temperature
confectioners' sugar

Butter the bases and sides of two loaf-shaped cake pans, each 6-cup capacity. Line each base with a rectangle of buttered parchment paper cut to size. Dust sides and base with flour, and tap out excess.

Sift together the four dry ingredients, twice, and reserve. Stir vanilla into buttermilk and set aside.

In a large bowl, cream the butter until light, gradually beat in the sugar. Beat together yolks, beat these slowly into butter base.

Spoon a quarter of the flour mixture over the creamed mixture, beat this in. Add a third of the buttermilk and vanilla and stir well. Continue alternating dry and wet ingredients until all are incorporated, finishing with flour.

Spoon the batter into loaf pans and spread, using a dampened spatula and working from the centre outward to create a slightly raised area around the rim; this will help to offset the eventual high rise in cakes' center.

Bake in the center of a preheated oven at 350°F for about 1¼ hours, turning the pans round half way through baking. Cakes are done when they have risen well, each center bounces back when lightly pressed, and a fine metal skewer thrust into depths tests clean and hot.

Cool both cakes for 30 minutes before removing from loaf pans; peel away parchment paper, cool completely and store.

To serve, dust tops with confectioners' sugar and slice. Good with buttermilk ice cream (see recipe on page 70) or a glass of chilled wine, white and medium-dry.

Buttermilk cake, Buttermilk ice cream, Kaernaelks koldskaal

THE FOOD OF TURKEY

Turkey is almost entirely an Asian peninsula thrust west between the Black Sea rain which steeps thousands of acres of tea plantations, and Mediterranean semi-tropical heat where bananas and oranges prosper.

The Turks, who are self-sufficient in food, cook from the traditions of an empire which formerly stretched from North Africa to the Danube and the southern tip of Arabia. These are traditions that combine the epicurean customs of Byzantine and Ottoman court life with those of the nomad — a great variety of small items carefully prepared, very subtly flavored and quickly transported.

The Turks are discriminating, aware of nuance and the provenance of the best ingredients. They care greatly about the quality of drinking water, and will tell you without hesitation that there are fifty ways of preparing eggplants. As Turkish cooks are not given to experiment, many recipes have hardly changed for centuries, and regional dishes abound.

Ingredients for Turkish meals can be bought from supermarkets, Cypriot grocers, or gourmet food stores.

MEZE

Although meals in Turkey are a succession of individual dishes, various mouthfuls may be served all at once to start things off, olives, for example, or nuts, *pastırma* (dried, spiced beef), smoked swordfish, and cold stuffed vine leaves. Or serve diced white cheese, diced melon, *sucuk* (sausage spiced with paprika and cumin) and the three meze which follow.

MIDYE DOLMASI (STUFFED MUSSELS)

1 medium onion, peeled and minced
$\frac{1}{4}$ teaspoon crushed coriander seeds
2 tablespoons olive oil
$\frac{1}{2}$ cup short-grain rice
$\frac{1}{4}$ cup pine-nuts
salt
$\frac{1}{3}$ cup dried currants
3 tablespoons chopped fresh parsley
$\frac{1}{4}$ teaspoon turmeric
black pepper
30 large fresh mussels in shells

Sweat the onion and coriander seeds in the oil in a medium saucepan for 5 minutes over low heat, stirring occasionally. Add the rice, nuts and a pinch of salt, then sweat, covered, for 5 minutes more, stirring several times to prevent the rice from sticking.

Add the currants, parsley, turmeric and water just to cover. Cover and simmer until the rice is tender and water is absorbed. Season well and cool on a plate. The turmeric colors the rice a warm yellow.

Beard, scrape and wash the mussels. Cutting from the point of each shell's straight edge, prise open the raw bivalves and spoon some stuffing between each pair of flesh-lined half-shells. Close the shells, scrape away excess stuffing, and tie each mussel tightly across with string. Pack the bivalves into a saucepan, add salt. Weight with a small inverted plate, pour on water just to cover, bring the water to a boil, cover and simmer for 30 minutes. Cool and drain the mussels, cut the strings and arrange the shells attractively on a plate with other meze. Serve the shellfish cold each on its half shell.

ARNAVUT CIGERI (ALBANIAN LIVER)

$\frac{1}{2}$ lb lamb's liver
2 teaspoons paprika
2 tablespoons seasoned flour
$2\frac{1}{2}$ tablespoons olive oil
salt
black pepper
1 medium onion, peeled and thinly sliced
chopped fresh parsley

Trim and dice the liver, wash and dry it. Coat with half the paprika and all the flour; toss in a strainer to be rid of excess.

Heat $1\frac{1}{2}$ tablespoons of oil until very hot and toss liver in this for a scant minute over a high heat. Drain, grind on salt and pepper. Warm the remaining 1 tablespoon of oil in a small saucepan, stir in the remaining paprika and pour this over the liver.

Sprinkle the onion with salt and let it stand for 30 minutes. Work the salt into the onion; squeeze out the moisture, rinse very well and dry. This process lessens the impact. Serve liver cold, strewn with onion and chopped parsley.

Clockwise from the top: Içli köfte, Orange and sultana sherbets, Etli yaprak dolması, Cılbır, Patlıcan ezme, Arnavut cigeri, Midye dolması

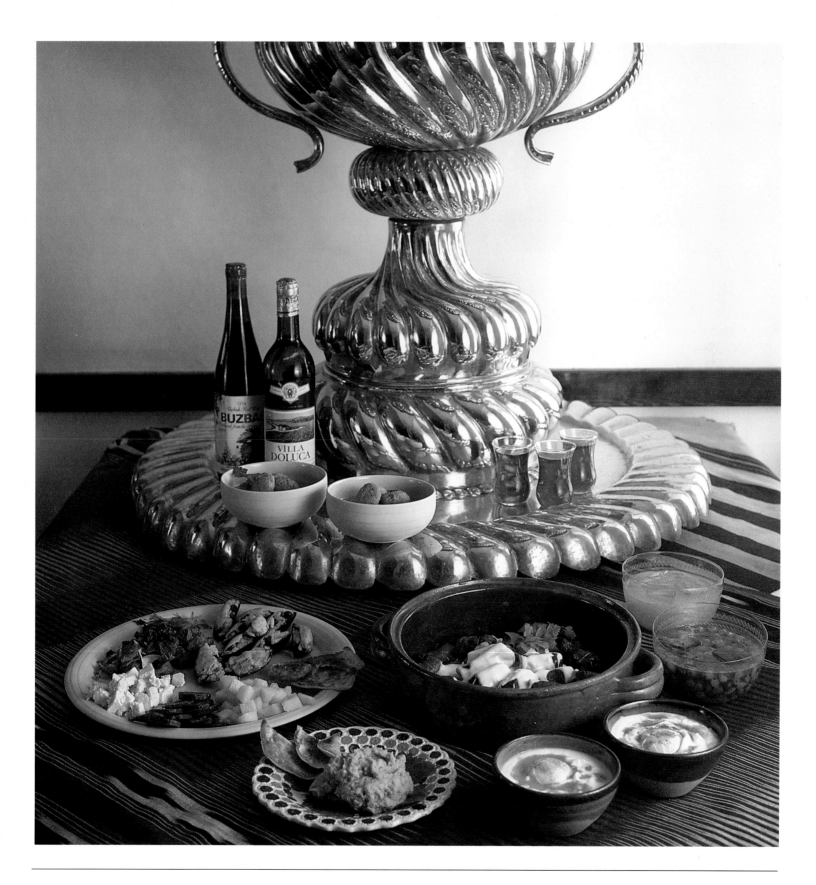

PATLICAN EZME (EGGPLANT AND CHILI PUREE)

1 eggplant, about $\frac{3}{4}$ lb
$\frac{1}{2}$ cup chopped onion
$\frac{1}{2}$–1 fresh chili pepper, split and seeded
small handful chopped fresh parsley
olive oil
2 tablespoons natural yogurt
salt

Broil the eggplant until its skin blackens and the flesh softens; cool, skin, wash the flesh and squeeze away all its bitter juice.

Combine the flesh in a food processor with the onion, chili (start with half, then add more to taste), parsley, 1 tablespoon oil, yogurt, and salt as needed. Purée the mixture, using a steel blade, until it is fairly smooth; the result should be hot but not overpowering.

Transfer to a small bowl, cover with a film of olive oil, and serve at room temperature with strips of split, buttered and toasted slices of *pide* or *pitta* bread. These *meze* serve 4–8 people depending on circumstances and appetites.

CILBIR

Another recipe using yogurt; the Turks eat a great deal of it, mainly made of milk from the goat, sheep or buffalo. Yogurt is combined here with freshly-poached eggs and topped by paprika and butter to make a mixture of hot and cold which is again unusual and delicious. The recipe comes from Konya, south of Ankara.

1 cup natural yogurt
2 small cloves garlic, crushed
salt
black pepper
2 eggs
2 tablespoons butter
$\frac{1}{4}$ teaspoon paprika

Combine the well chilled yogurt, garlic and seasoning; beat until smooth; divide the mixture between two small bowls.

Gently poach eggs while melting the butter. Drain eggs, trim off straying white, and slide each, 'sunny side up', into the yogurt. Stir paprika into butter and spoon this in zig-zags across each egg. Eat without delay. This is one of the most satisfying 'fast foods' that I know. Serves 2 as a filling snack.

ETLI YAPRAK DOLMASI

This recipe for vine leaves stuffed with meat and rice and served hot, as a single course, with yogurt sauce was given to me by Mrs Semra Yasal of London and Ankara. Such *dolma* are a part of home cooking; restaurants usually confine themselves to rice, currant and pine-nut stuffed leaves served cold and in small quantities among the *meze*. The same meat mixture can be used to fill sweet peppers, zucchini, eggplants or spinach leaves.

$1\frac{1}{2}$ (8 oz) packages vine leaves in brine

STUFFING
1 lb ground beef
$\frac{1}{2}$ cup short-grain rice
1 large onion, peeled and grated
$\frac{2}{3}$ cup Italian plum tomatoes, drained
    and chopped
$1\frac{1}{2}$ tablespoons tomato paste
1 tablespoon chopped fresh parsley
large pinch of dried oregano
large pinch of fresh or dried
    chopped mint
salt
black pepper
1 tablespoon butter

SAUCE
$1\frac{1}{4}$ cups natural yogurt
3 cloves garlic, peeled
salt
black pepper

To make the stuffing, combine all but $\frac{1}{2}$ tablespoon tomato paste of the first 10 ingredients; knead together well. Taste for seasoning; the mixture should be quite savory. Drain the vine leaves, and if tough, boil in water for 15–20 minutes to soften. Drain and cool.

In a deep casserole, heat the butter, the remaining tomato paste and the water; mix to a paste and cool.

Spread out one vine leaf, underside up, pinch off the stem, put $\frac{1}{2}$ tablespoon of stuffing at stem end, and roll leaf tightly, folding in sides. Repeat with all remaining stuffing. Pack the rolls into rows – open-side down – across the casserole, closely wedged so as not to unroll, making two compact layers on top of the paste of tomato and butter. Weight with a small inverted plate, pour on water just to cover, add salt, bring water to boil, and simmer *dolma*, covered, for 30 minutes.

To make *sarmısaklı yoğurt*, the garlic-flavored sauce; beat the yogurt smooth with a fork, crush the garlic to a paste with the aid of salt and the blade of a heavy knife, add to the yogurt and season well. Drain *dolma*; serve hot, dribbled with cold sauce. Serves 4 as a main course.

ICLI KOFTE

These meatballs of lamb and cracked wheat, stuffed with lamb and walnuts and served in a stock, look unglamorous, but if made with care, they are tender and delectable. The recipe is reputed to be Armenian, from the eastern part of Turkey, near Malatya.

Cracked wheat, or bulgur, has been boiled, dried and 'cracked' into fine, medium or coarse grains; it is used throughout the Middle East for many different recipes; it is the chief ingredient of *tabbouleh*, from the Lebanon. İçli Köfte are time-consuming to prepare but have a delicacy which makes the effort worthwhile.

1 lamb shoulder
salt
bouquet garni
1 small carrot, peeled
1 small onion, quartered
1 cup fine-grained bulgur
$\frac{1}{2}$ cup minced onion
black pepper

STUFFING
7 oz fatty lamb from shoulder
1 medium onion, peeled and minced
2 tablespoons butter
salt
ground cumin, to taste
small handful fresh chopped parsley
$\frac{1}{3}$ cup minced walnuts
ground cinnamon, to taste
black pepper

Have your butcher bone the shoulder and give you both meat and bones, or if skilled enough, do this yourself.

Make a stock by simmering the bones for several hours with salt, bouquet garni and a small carrot and onion.

Cut up the shoulder and take 1 lb of meat from it, free of all fat and connective tissue. Soak bulgur for 20 minutes in very hot water to cover. It will swell and soften. Grind the meat very, very fine and knead the minced onion into it by hand. Squeeze water from the bulgur; and when cool, knead with meat and a lot of seasoning. Work mixture on a board for 5 minutes.

To make stuffing, take the fatty meat from shoulder, without connective tissue and grind it finely (use any leftover lamb elsewhere). Sweat onion in butter for 5 minutes to soften. Add fatty lamb, break up with a fork, add salt and liberal sprinkling of cumin, and sauté, stirring, until lamb is just cooked. Drain, put in remaining ingredients; add more spices and seasoning if needed. The mixture should be highly flavored.

Let the stuffing cool while rolling the lamb and bulgur into 1 inch balls, using wet hands. Turn each ball around the tip of the thumb to make a deep, cup-like hollow, spoon in about $\frac{3}{4}$ teaspoon stuffing and close up the surface, smoothing with wet fingers. Shape the ball into an oval. Continue until all the raw lamb is used, and rest the balls in the refrigerator for several hours.

Remove the fat from the strained stock, add water to make up to $6\frac{1}{4}$ cups, season, and when ready to go, heat stock to simmering in one or two large saucepans. Add the meatballs and poach gently for 5 minutes, or until they float to surface. Divide köfte and stock among warmed soup bowls. Serves 4–5 as a main course.

ENVAI KHOSHABLAR

Here are two recipes from the mysterious *Turkish Cookery Book*, published in London in 1884 by one Turabi Effendi. The book is rare, and the identity of its author until recently unknown to the writer Alan Davidson, who owns a photocopy. The recipes are fascinating, clear and eminently usable. This pair of 'sherbets, or thin syrups with fruit in them', derive from a long tradition of cold, sweet drinks and fruit salads.

To serve 4, I make full quantity of the orange (without adding water or

Orange and sultana sherbet

extra sugar) and half the sultana, using granulated sugar for both $\frac{1}{4}$—$\frac{1}{3}$ cup sugar for $1\frac{1}{3}$ cups sultanas, and rose-water as a contrast to the first sherbet. Rose and orange-flower waters or essence can be bought from drugstores. Be sure to specify that you wish essences for cooking purposes.

PORTAKAL KHOSHABI (ORANGE SHERBET)

'Peel 5–6 oranges, and divide them in pieces; cut each clove or piece of orange in two, and remove the pips and the thin membranes from them; then put 4 oz of powdered sugar in a stewpan, with the juice of 2 oranges: if they are not sufficiently sweet, add more sugar; put it on a slow fire, and stir with a wooden spoon until it begins to boil; then take it off. When cold, pour in a glass bowl, and mix it with water to form a nice sherbet; then add the pieces of orange, with a few drops of the essence of orange-flower, and a few small pieces of ice, and serve.'

CHEKIRDEKSIZ UZUM KHOSHABI (SULTANA SHERBET)

'Get a pound of sultana raisins, take the stalks off and well wash them; put them in a stewpan with a pint of water, and set it to boil until they are swollen up; then take it off, and pass the liquor through a strainer into a saucepan, add sufficient loaf sugar, and boil until it becomes thickish, then remove it. When cold, pour it in a glass bowl, and moderate the sweetness with cold water, then put the boiled raisins in, with a few drops of the essence of orange-flower or rose, and a few small pieces of ice, and serve.

'All other raisins, currants, dried morella and other kinds of cherries, dried apricots, and dried plums of all kinds, may be done in the same way.'

THE SEASONS

Each year I look forward to the coming of a new season. While relishing the earthy spring freshness of new potatoes, I anticipate the sweet juice of mid-summer tomatoes. In September I think about wild mushrooms, while remembering that Christmas will bring on light, lemony fruitcakes and the fun of ornate pastries.

Spring is the time for these delicate new potatoes to be cooked simply, rolled in butter and seasoning and a chopping of fresh herbs; excellent in company with spring lamb or salmon steaks. Baby zucchini or miniature turnips are delicious treated in the same way. By the summer, those tomatoes taste wonderful when eaten out of doors, strewn with pungent basil and served as an escort for cold braised meat or a crackling and succulent grilled fish.

In the fall, mushrooms melt into sautés with spice spice and vegetables, following a soup that exploits the harvest produce. These are the weeks for grape-gathering, and wine adds interest to late-season dishes – a festive loin of pork, or a long-simmered stew in which the meat falls from the bone amidst wintery herbs and mellowed flavors. And then Christmas, with its fruitcakes and cranberries, is a time to relish the details of preparation that will fill your house with luscious scents of baking.

SPRING FEVER

What more need be said about spring; young vegetables, fresh tastes, early fruits, the clear pinks and greens that edge out lentil-brown? Let the food be witness for itself.

TOMATO AND COCONUT SOUP

This is an intriguingly delicate cold soup; the coconut flavor is elusive beneath the taste of uncooked tomatoes. The soup, however, must be only lightly chilled and should be eaten within a few hours of making. If refrigerated overnight, the various flavors of the soup wander disagreeably and results are not good.

8 tablespoons shredded coconut
5 cups chicken broth; homemade is
    essential here, and for method, see
    page 100
2½ lb ripe tomatoes, peeled, halved
    and seeded
2 generous tablespoons natural
    yogurt
salt
black pepper

Simmer the coconut in the broth for 5 minutes, then leave the broth to cool thoroughly. Strain the broth through a strainer lined with a double thickness of muslin. Scoop 2 tablespoons of the simmered coconut back into the strained broth, gather up the muslin and squeeze its contents hard over the liquid.

Liquidize the broth with the tomatoes until smooth. Add the yogurt and blend once again then check the flavors. Season to taste. Serve, lightly-chilled, within the next few hours while flavors are at their peak. Serves 6.

SALMON WITH RED WINE, IN PAPILLOTES

These salmon steaks are moistened with a light red wine then steamed in a paper envelope. The technique is similar to that used for a mixture of fish and vegetable on page 66. Drink the same wine as accompaniment; a good Beaujolais Villages, briefly-chilled, is ideal.

butter
4 salmon steaks, about 6 oz each
6 slim scallions, trimmed and
    thinly sliced
salt
black pepper
Beaujolais Villages or similar light red
    wine, chilled

Cut four 12 inch circles from baking parchment paper, and brush one side of each with oil.

Lay the sheets, oiled side down, on the working surface (oiling the exterior of the pouch supposedly makes it more difficult to tear accidentally). Put a small knob of butter off-center on each piece of parchment and place a salmon steak on top. Strew over some scallions and add a little more butter.

Season well, then spoon over each cutlet a tablespoon of the Beaujolais Villages. Fold over the *papillotes*, fold and roll edges together to a double thickness, stapling these all around. Just before closing the end of each envelope, insert a straw and blow to inflate the parcel – this creates greater space for moisture to develop and steam the salmon. Quickly staple the package shut to trap in the air. Place on heavy baking sheets. Bake in a preheated oven at 375°F for 15 minutes until the *papillotes* are

lightly browned and giving forth an alluring bouquet.

Serve immediately, each envelope on its own plate; slit and open the parcels at the table. Serve with boiled, buttered new potatoes and the chilled Beaujolais. Serves 4.

NEW POTATO SALAD WITH SPINACH AND SORREL

New potatoes are turned into a salad and combined with the sharp tastes of lemon juice and sorrel. It is difficult to give exact quantities for this; I usually make it by 'eye'.

Take 6–8 oz tiny new potatoes per person, scrub well but leave the skins intact. Boil the potatoes in salted water for 10–15 minutes until cooked. Meanwhile, trim the stems of young spinach leaves, add a proportion of sorrel – you won't need very much, as sorrel is deliciously, teeth-strippingly acid and shouldn't be overdone here – wash, then spin the greens in a salad drier to remove all excess moisture.

When the potatoes are ready, drain well and slice while still hot. Toss with a vinaigrette made from 1 part lemon juice to 4 parts olive oil, a large helping of Dijon mustard, plus liberal salt and black pepper. Add the torn-up leaves of wide-leaf parsley, or the coarsely chopped leaves of the curly variety, plus chopped chervil. Toss further.

Taste, season again and serve the potatoes without much delay in a nest of spinach and sorrel. Eat this as a first course or as part of a light lunch.

BLANQUETTE D'AGNEAU PRINTANIERE

A few years ago I watched Rex Barker – at that time chef of La Petite Cuisine cooking school, near London, demonstrate a classic spring lamb stew, and this is my adaptation of the one Rex showed us.

1 boned shoulder of spring lamb
4–6 cups light stock, made from
*   shoulder bones plus chicken pieces,*
*   plus aromatics*
2 medium onions, peeled and each
*   stuck with a clove*
2 carrots, peeled and quartered
bouquet garni
salt
3 tablespoons butter
¼ cup all-purpose flour
7 oz peeled baby carrots, in thin
*   sticks*
¼ lb haricots verts or mange-tout or a
*   mixture of both, trimmed*
7 oz button mushrooms
1–1½ tablespoons lemon juice
3 egg yolks
6 tablespoons heavy cream
black pepper
cayenne

Trim lamb of skin, connective tissue and excess fat, then cut into ¾ inch cubes. Make the stock with the shoulder bones, etc; degrease thoroughly.

Put the meat into a large heavy saucepan or flameproof casserole, cover with cold water, bring to a boil and simmer for 1 minute. Drain and rinse the lamb thoroughly in cold water. Clean the pan or casserole, replace the meat and add the onions, carrots, bouquet garni, 4 cups of the stock and a good pinch of salt. Half-cover the pan, bring the stock to a boil, skim and simmer over lowest heat for 1½–2 hours until the lamb is tender. Add more stock as necessary during the process.

When lamb is done, drain and reserve the stock; remove and discard the onions, carrots and bouquet garni. Clean the pan. Return the meat to the cleaned pan or casserole. In a medium saucepan, make a roux with 2 tablespoons butter and the flour. Cook gently, stirring, for 4 minutes. Add 4 cups of the reserved stock, and whisk until it comes to a boil. Gently simmer the *velouté* for 20 minutes, skimming regularly.

Meanwhile, cook the carrots in boiling salted water until just tender. Drain, refresh and reserve. Cook the haricots verts or mange-tout in the same way. Simmer the mushrooms with a knob of butter, 1 tablespoon lemon juice and water to cover for 5 minutes. Drain (use the mushroom stock in a soup, or add some to the *velouté*). Put all the vegetables with the lamb.

Beat the egg yolks with the cream, whisk in a little of the hot *velouté* to warm the mixture. Strain this back into the hot *velouté*, whisking smartly, and slowly heat, continuing to whisk, until the sauce simmers. The presence of flour will prevent yolks from congealing and the rich *velouté* should be of a smooth, medium consistency. Pour this enriched *velouté* onto the lamb and vegetables and reheat over a low heat on top of the stove, adding lemon juice, seasoning and cayenne to taste.

Serve immediately with hot, buttered green noodles. Serves 4.

Potato salad, Tomato soup, Salmon

SPAGHETTI WITH RED CAVIAR, LEMON AND CHIVES

A borrowed recipe, from a pair of gastronomic American pianists, Arthur Gold and Robert Fizdale, who published the ideas upon which I've based the version here about ten years ago in American *Vogue*.

This dish causes a sensation each time I serve it. No one quite believes that red caviar, which, as we know, is actually lumpfish roe, could be combined with lemon zest, chives and spaghetti! But the off-beat combination is always completely successful. Salt and fish meet lemon and the allium flavor of chives with conviction. Use wholewheat spaghetti for the interest of its color and texture.

$\frac{3}{4}$ *cup sweet butter*
6 oz red lumpfish roe
3 tablespoons heavy cream
3 tablespoons olive oil
salt
4 lemons
3 bunches very fresh chives
2 lb wholewheat spaghetti
black pepper

Allow the butter, roe and cream to come to room temperature. Bring a very large, deep pan of water to a brisk boil, add the olive oil and 1 tablespoon salt; put a large serving bowl to heat through in a low oven.

Meanwhile, grate the zest – without pith – from the 4 lemons. Scissor the chives into short lengths, combine the two and reserve.

Boil the spaghetti for 12 minutes or until *al dente*. Drain well. Add the butter and cream to the warmed bowl, swirl them around to melt the butter, and cover with the spaghetti. Toss well, liberally season with pepper, add a little salt and toss again. Place the zest, chives and roe on top, mix well and serve, eating without delay. Serves 8.

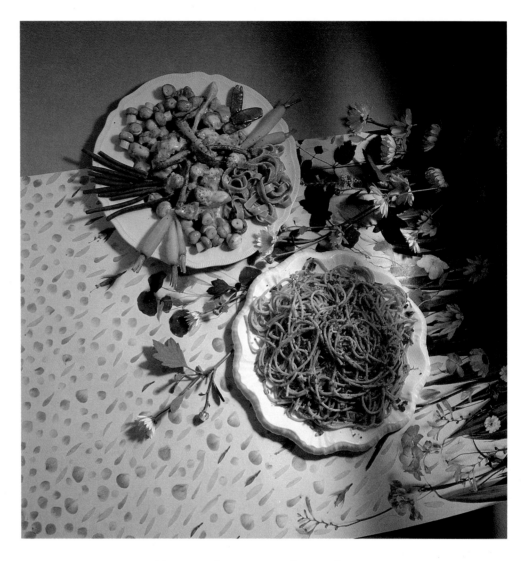

Blanquette d'agneau, Spaghetti with caviar

SPARKLING STRAWBERRY SHERBET

This delightful sherbet can be made with pink champagne or, as I do, with a sparkling Saumur Rosé, vinified by the champagne method; the wine should always be brut, or extra-dry. The mixture of *pétillance* with strawberry is arresting. Make this 48 hours ahead of serving, as the wine will slow its freezing considerably.

Serve this sparkling sherbet with the ginger cookies iced with a lemon glaze.

$1\frac{1}{4}$ *cups granulated sugar*
$1\frac{1}{2}$ *cups water*
$2\frac{1}{2}$ *cups sliced strawberries*
juice of $1\frac{1}{2}$ *small lemons*
$2\frac{1}{2}$ *cups sparkling Saumur Rosé or Champagne Rosé brut, well chilled*
1 egg white

Dissolve the sugar in the water and boil for 10 minutes until a sugar thermometer registers 220°F. Leave to cool completely.

Purée the strawberries in a blender or

food processor and combine with the lemon juice. When the syrup is cold, mix with the puréed fruit and carefully beat in the sparkling wine. Pour into a deep plastic box, stir again, cover and freeze. When the mixture has frozen to a slush, beat the egg white until soft peaks form and stir into the strawberry mixture. Freeze again, turning the sides into the middle several times during the process; this helps the distribution of the contents. The result, after 48 hours, will be a fairly loose sherbet of glittering paillettes, due to the quantity of wine. Serves 6–8.

GINGER COOKIES

You could eat these tempting cookies with the sparkling strawberry sherbet, with tea, coffee or a glass of milk. I like to spread half of them with a lemon glaze. Use pure vanilla, not 'flavoring' in this recipe.

¾ cup sweet butter, softened
¾ cup superfine sugar
1 tablespoon molasses
3 tablespoons light corn syrup
½ teaspoon vanilla essence
1¾ cups all-purpose flour, sifted
1 teaspoon baking soda
good pinch of salt
1½ teaspoons ground ginger
½ teaspoon ground cinnamon
¼ teaspoon ground nutmeg
¼ cup confectioners' sugar
lemon juice

Cream the butter with a scant ½ cup of the superfine sugar. Beat in the molasses, syrup and vanilla. Sift together the flour, soda, salt and spices. Beat the dry ingredients into the butter mixture and, using one hand, work them into a dough. Cut the dough in half and wrap the halves in waxed paper. Refrigerate for about 30 minutes.

Take one piece of dough and cut into large dice. Roll the dice into balls the size

Strawberry sherbet, Ginger cookies

of large marbles. Flatten each marble into a round about half its original height. Coat on all sides with some of the remaining superfine sugar.

Place the rounds, well spaced, on heavy baking sheets. Bake in a preheated oven at 375°F for about 12 minutes or until the cookies are a pale golden-brown with a slightly crazed surface. Make sure they are not over-baked. Leave the cookies on the sheets for a few minutes before removing to cool on wire racks.

Proceed in this way with all the dough, periodically sifting away loose crumbs from sugar meant for coating.

When cookies are cold, store half in an airtight tin, spread the other half with a glaze made from sifted confectioners' sugar mixed with sufficient lemon juice until the consistency is fairly runny. When the glaze has dried, store these cookies separately. They will become quite soft, due to the icing, while the plain ones will be firm but chewy; they should not be hard and dry, hence the importance of not over-baking. Makes about 48.

HIGH SUMMER

This is probably my favorite time of year for eating, particularly out of doors. With luck, the location will be close to the produce of a vegetable market, a fishmarket and a skilled butcher whose excellence allows cooks to do the minimum in the transformation of prime ingredients.

PORC A LA PERIGOURDINE

Elizabeth and Bill Kivlan, with whom we regularly stay in the South of France, are *fins becs*, and Elizabeth is an exceptionally good cook. If we're visiting them in July, she will sometimes make, for an outdoor evening meal, Elizabeth David's sumptuous recipe for cold loin of pork stuffed with truffles; accompanying this by haricots verts in a vinaigrette and tomatoes sliced and served with basil. This lovely *plat* is from *French Provincial Cooking*, and I've taken the liberty of adapting and rewriting it as I make it, using rosé wine as the cooking medium because I love the color of the jelly which results. Ask your butcher to prepare a piece of rib end of pork loin by removing bones and rind, leaving fat on and giving you both rind and bones with the meat.

2½ lb boned weight rib end of pork
1 large clove garlic
2–3 black truffles
salt
black pepper
2 cups dry rosé wine
⅔ cup water

Lay the pork on a chopping board, boned side up; cut the garlic and truffles into long, thick pieces, incise the meat along its length, and tuck the truffles and garlic well into the incisions. Season. Turn the pork over and tuck tapering end of meat beneath eye of the loin to form a long rolled shape; tie this with soft white string at ¾ inch intervals.

Place the pork (fat upward) with its bones in a deep, heavy casserole; cut the rind into strips and add these. It is the rind which yields enough gelatin to set the cooled cooking liquid into a light jelly. Bake, uncovered, in the lower third of a preheated oven at 325°F for 30 minutes until the exterior of meat has become well colored.

Pour in wine and water, cover casserole – leaving lid ajar – lower oven to 300°F, and allow pork to cook, basting occasionally, until it reaches an internal temperature of just under 170°F – test with a meat thermometer. This will probably take about 2 hours.

When ready remove pork from casserole, pour its liquid, twice, through a strainer freshly-lined each time with a double thickness of paper towels, and let stock drip through without squeezing the paper. Let cool, cover, and refrigerate both pork and the strained stock until the next day.

When ready to serve, lift fat from top of what is now the lightly-set jelly, carve pork into thin slices, removing string as you go. Haricots verts in a vinaigrette dressing, tomatoes thickly sliced with skins on, seasoned and served beneath leaves of basil make beautiful accompaniments.

Serve each person with appropriate pork, a small glass container holding jelly as garnish, and the beans, tomatoes and basil. Guests can remove and discard the fat from each slice as they eat. Serves 6, generously.

TOMATO QUICHE

When tomatoes are at their peak and have absorbed enough sun – preferably in a private garden or somewhere along the Mediterranean – to give them their height of flavor, I abandon my usual devotion to the canned Italian version and make this quiche from the fresh ones.

The pastry incorporates cheese and the combination of well-reduced, highly-flavored tomato with the rich taste of sharp Cheddar is to be recommended.

CHEESE PASTRY
1 cup all-purpose flour
pinch of salt
6 tablespoons sweet butter, chilled
¾ cup shredded sharp Cheddar
* or similar cheese*
1 egg, beaten

FILLING
1 tablespoon olive oil
1 small onion, peeled and
* minced*
2 large cloves garlic, minced
3 lbs ripe tomatoes, skinned, seeded and
* chopped*
1 bay leaf
sprig of thyme
sprigs of fresh parsley
2 eggs
⅔ cup heavy cream
a little milk
small handful of chopped
* fresh parsley*
salt
black pepper
½ cup shredded Gruyère or Emmental
* cheese*

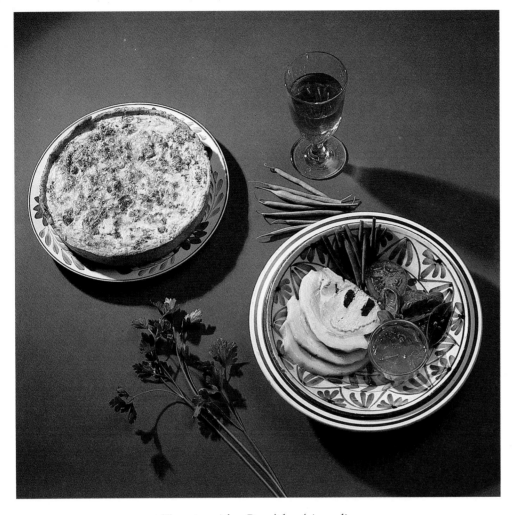

Tomato quiche, Porc à la périgourdine

pastry sets and starts to color. Allow to cool completely.

Spread the tomato over the shell, strew on shredded cheese, pour in the egg and cream and let the quiche bake at 375°F for 20–30 minutes until filling has puffed and begun to color. Cool the quiche for 10 minutes and slice. Serves 6–8 as a first course.

BROILED SARDINES WITH GINGER BUTTER

Quickly made for a summer's lunch; only the butter, laced with the grated gingerroot and lemon juice, needs advance planning.

6 tablespoons sweet butter, very soft
*   but not melting*
about 1¼ teaspoons lemon juice
piece of fresh gingerroot
salt
black pepper
8 fresh sardines, each 6–7 inches,
*   scaled, drawn, cleaned and dried,*
*   heads and tails intact*
olive oil

In a small bowl, beat the butter with a wooden spoon until very light, gradually beat in lemon juice until the flavor is quite sharp. Peel the gingerroot and grate in the flesh to taste; this should be assertive. Season the mixture well, shape the butter into a roll and chill until firm.

Season the sardines, brush them on both sides with oil and broil until the skin begins to char and the flesh has just ceased to be rosy at the bone. Serve with rounds of ginger butter that should melt over the fish. Serves 4.

To make the pastry, sift the flour with salt, cut the butter into small cubes and rub these in, add the shredded cheese and bind with beaten egg, adding a drop of water if necessary to make the pastry adhere. Roll the mixture into a ball, wrap it well, and chill for several hours.

Meanwhile, run the oil around the base of a wide skillet, sweat the onion and garlic until soft and turning color, add chopped tomatoes and herbs. Bring tomatoes to a simmer and let them cook over very low heat, stirring occasionally, until they are reduced to a purée which is almost dry. Be careful not to let it burn near the final stages. Stir constantly.

In the meantime, beat together the eggs, cream plus milk to lighten the mixture, some chopped parsley and salt and pepper to taste.

When the tomatoes are ready, remove the pan from the heat, fish out parsley, thyme and bay leaf; season and let cool completely.

Take pastry from the refrigerator, allow it to lose its chill, and roll it out to line a 9 inch flan ring set onto a heavy baking sheet.

Refrigerate until the pastry is firm. Line the shell with parchment paper or foil held in place by baking beans. Bake in a preheated oven at 350°F until the

CORN AND MINT SOUP

I like corn best on the cob; it was one of the great treats of my American childhood summers.

Corn soup, with mint added right at the end, so that the heat releases its burst of flavor as you begin to eat, is a more sophisticated pleasure for which it's useful to have several pairs of hands willing to sever the kernels from cobs.

This is one of the rare times when I'm happy to use a frozen vegetable; if the best ripe, fresh corn is not available, frozen kernels give a very good result.

1 large onion, peeled and thinly sliced
1 tablespoon butter
7½ cups homemade chicken broth; for method see page 100
3 cups cubed potatoes
4½ cups corn kernels, either cut from corn ears with a small knife so as to leave about ⅛ inch depth of pulp still adhering to the cob, or added frozen
salt
black pepper
1 bunch fresh mint

Sweat the onion in butter in a deep, heavy pot. When softened and colored, add broth, potatoes, 12 oz of the corn, a dash of salt. Simmer, half-covered, until the potatoes have cooked, which will probably take about 5 minutes.

Cool the soup slightly and liquidize until smooth, seasoning to taste. Return soup to the pot, add the remaining corn and just heat mixture through until the whole kernels are done – usually a matter of about 1 minute. This is a soup which tastes best when freshly-made.

While the combination is reheating, rapidly cut up enough mint leaves to strew across the surface of eight bowls; ladle in the soup, stir in the mint, and serve immediately. Serves 8.

SALAD OF MILLET AND HERBS

Being fond of salads like *tabbouleh*, made from the cracked wheat called *burghul* or *bulgur*, I began to experiment with millet. This is an undervalued grain which, steamed until it cracks and then mixed with a liberal amount of enhancing ingredients, becomes delicious.

It's important to give plenty of acidity – in the form of lemon juice, yogurt, sorrel, and a sharp herb like Mediterranean rocket, plus crunch in the shape of cucumber, radish, and oven-toasted pine-nuts – or the millet will stick in your throat like heavy porridge.

5 cups salted water
1 heaped cup whole millet grains
2 or more tablespoons lemon juice
about 1¼–1½ cups natural yogurt
½ lb piece of cucumber, peeled, seeded and finely chopped
¾ cup minced radishes
½ cup pine-nuts, lightly toasted
chopped fresh sorrel, rocket, chives, to taste
salad burne, lemon balm or similar leaf (optional)
salt
black pepper
crisp lettuce leaves

Corn soup, Millet salad, Broiled sardines

Bring salted water to a boil, add grains, well rinsed and drained, and let simmer rapidly for about 12 minutes, until millet just cracks. Drain into a large metal strainer and rinse under a stream of cold water.

Steam this strainerful, covered, over boiling water for about 15 minutes – making sure that the steam reaches all parts of the strainer's contents – until grains are cracked and very fluffy. Spread them onto a board to dry and when cool, rake your fingers through the mass to make sure there are no lumps.

Transfer the millet to a bowl, beat in 2 tablespoons of lemon juice and the yogurt; leave the millet to absorb this. The consistency should be a bit like that of good rice pudding. Let everything stand, covered, in a cool place, until the following day.

When preparing to serve the salad, stir in the cucumber, radishes, pine-nuts, chopped sorrel, rocket, and chives to taste, the whole salad burnet leaves or the torn leaves of lemon balm if you like, plus salt and pepper. Judge whether to sharpen with more lemon juice or to let down with more yogurt. The final consistency should be fairly loose, without runniness.

Pile the millet into a pyramid on a large platter or plate and adorn with a few attractive herbs. Fill a bowl with lettuce leaves and encourage guests to roll a bit of salad onto a leaf, and to eat each roll in two bites. Serves 6–8 as a first course.

FRUIT TARTS WITHOUT PASTRY

These are fun to make. The ingredients are whatever fresh fruits you like and find appropriate, plus the edible leaves of flowers like nasturtiums or scented geraniums. For each tart, you place a leaf or two on the plate from which the tart will be eaten, and then construct whatever arrangement appeals.

Here, for instance, I've used the leaves of the lemon-scented geranium, which are strong, so shouldn't be overdone. I've built the tarts in various combinations of orange with the peel cut off, fig and star fruit, all thinly sliced across; sections of small ogen melon, sliced across, skin trimmed away, center seeded; strawberries sliced from top to bottom, and whole raspberries.

The tarts should be assembled immediately before you expect to eat them, and served with a squeeze of orange or lemon juice, a sprinkling of sugar, and if you like, a spoonful of homemade *fromage blanc* which can be prepared as follows:

Warm 4 cups milk with $\frac{1}{2}$ cup buttermilk to blood heat 98°F, transfer to a bowl, and cool. Let stand at room temperature until milk sours and curdles, which can take up to 48 hours. When thickened, pour into a large strainer lined with muslin and let the whey drip from the curds for 5–6 hours. Strain this cheese and chill it until ready to serve. Makes about $\frac{3}{4}$ cup.

Fruit tarts without pastry

A GARDEN'S YIELD

I regret having neither herb, kitchen nor cottage garden, but perhaps I would spend too much time in whichever of these might be just outside the door. When gardening friends arrive with a basket of fresh parsley, potatoes and mint, with carrots that taste as though they've just been pulled from the ground and not molded in plastic, or with an extravagant cabbage looking too good to eat, I find it hard not to drop everything and begin cooking.

LAMB CHOPS WITH THREE PUREES

In this recipe you can either sauté two chops per person or buy two racks of best end and roast them.

EGGPLANT PUREE
2 eggplants, about 10 oz each
juice of 1 lemon
ground cumin
salt
black pepper
heavy cream

FENNEL AND APPLE PUREE
1¼ lb bulb fennel, with leaves
1 firm medium eating apple, cored and
*   pared*
about 2 tablespoons butter
lemon juice
salt
black pepper

GREEN BEAN PUREE
¾ lb young haricot verts
a small fistful of watercress
salt and black pepper
1 tablespoon butter
2–3 tablespoons heavy cream

TO FINISH
either 8 best end of neck of lamb chops,
*   trimmed of excess fat, rib bones*
*   shortened and pared of meat and fat;*
*   or 2 racks of best end, with*
*   backbone removed, with ribs*
*   exposed, trimmed, and*
*   cleaned*
vegetable oil
butter
salt
black pepper
watercress

All purées can be made in advance. Cut off tops of eggplants and roast them whole under a medium broiler, turning as skin blisters and blackens and flesh softens. Allow to cool until the eggplant can be handled, lift off the skin and wash flesh. Squeeze out all the bitter juice. Put the eggplant into food processor fitted with a steel blade, add lemon juice and purée until smooth. Add cumin to taste and season with salt and pepper. Allow to cool, cover and refrigerate. The purée will be very strong; adding cream when heating will temper this.

Trim fennel of its upper stems and any damaged outer parts, reserve leaves. Cut both fennel and apple into large dice and put these, with 2 tablespoons butter, a tablespoon of lemon juice, a little water and some salt, into a heavy, covered saucepan and simmer over a low heat for 5–8 minutes or until tender. Drain away excess liquid, and purée, with some fennel leaves, until smooth but retaining a certain texture. Season, cool and refrigerate.

Trim and, if necessary, string the haricot verts. Wash and boil them in a large amount of well-salted water, uncovered, until just tender; about 3–10 minutes, depending on the beans. Immediately drain and refresh them in ice water to stop cooking.

Remove stems from the watercress, wash leaves and blanch them for 1 minute in boiling, salted water. Drain and refresh in icy water and squeeze away excess moisture. Purée beans and watercress together until smooth. Remove from food processor and freeze the mixture. Put green purée to thaw at room temperature 2–3 hours before needed.

If using lamb in racks, about 1 hour before they'll be carved rub them with oil and salt and roast them in an oven preheated to 450°F for 15 minutes. Turn the heat down to 350°F and roast them about 30 minutes more for rare meat. Let racks rest in a warm place for 15 minutes before carving.

Heat the three purées simultaneously in small heavy saucepans. Add several tablespoons of cream to the eggplant, enough to mellow it to your satisfaction. Correct the seasoning. Dry the fennel and apple over the heat if necessary. Season and add extra butter, and stir in more fennel leaves if you like. Dry haricot verts purée for 1 minute on the heat, season, add butter and a little cream. Meanwhile, if serving lamb sautéed instead of roasted, sear chops in oil and butter for about 3 minutes per side until pink in the middle. (The two-rack method will give you more meat per head and require less attention than keeping an eye on sautéing chops).

To serve, carve racks and arrange three roast chops per heated dinner plate – or put two sautéed pieces on each – give everyone an ample spoonful of each purée, and garnish plates with watercress. Serves 4.

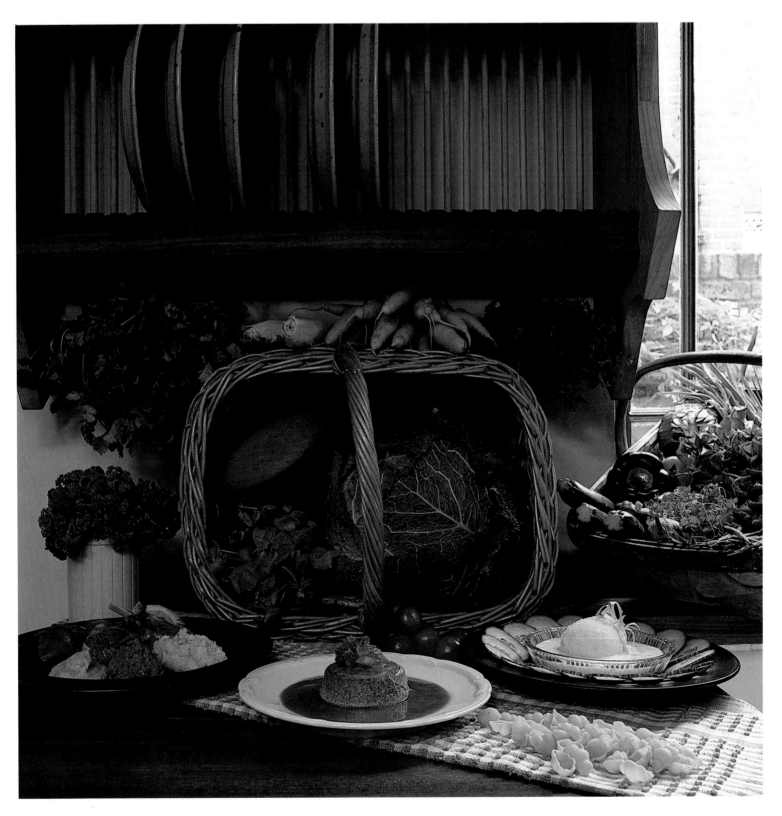

Lamb chops, Parsley custard, Cucumber and ginger sherbet

Cucumber and ginger sherbet

Mushroom and coriander soup

CUCUMBER AND GINGER SHERBET

This is a sweet-sour ice to be eaten as a summer appetizer or as a palate-freshener between courses.

SHERBET
2–3 cucumbers, 3 lb
5 tablespoons wine vinegar
2 teaspoons salt
$\frac{1}{4}$ teaspoon sugar
2 small scallions
$1\frac{1}{4}$ teaspoons grated ginger root
$\frac{1}{2}$ cup granulated sugar
$\frac{3}{4}$ cup water
2 sheets gelatin
$\frac{2}{3}$ cup natural yogurt

SAUCE
$\frac{2}{3}$ cup peeled, chopped and seeded
    cucumber
$1\frac{1}{2}$ cups natural yogurt
about 3 tablespoons lemon juice
salt
black pepper

GARNISH
sliced cucumber
6 small scallions

To make sherbet, peel, seed and roughly cut up cucumbers. You should then have about 8 cups of flesh.

Put cucumber into a large flat glass dish with four tablespoons of the vinegar, plus the salt and sugar and leave for 3 hours, basting regularly. Salt draws out the water; sugar and vinegar add flavor.

After 3 hours drain cucumbers (don't wash) and pat dry. Put into food processor with two trimmed and sliced scallions, ginger and remaining wine vinegar. Purée until smooth and chill thoroughly.

Meanwhile make a syrup by dissolving sugar in water and boiling the liquid for 1 minute. Soak gelatin until soft, drain and dissolve it in hot syrup off the fire. Cool.

Whisk together cucumber and syrup, judge flavor and freeze this in a deep plastic box, covered. After several hours, when semi-frozen, turn into food processor and quickly re-purée; add the yogurt, whiz, combine and refreeze.

Prepare this 24 hours in advance of serving but no earlier than that or the sherbet becomes too crystalline.

Make the sauce by beating the finely-chopped cucumber into the yogurt, add lemon juice and seasoning. Chill.

Some hours before serving, wash and trim scallions, cut their tops quite short and slash these several times above the bulb. Refrigerate in water to make tops curl. Put the sherbet into the refrigerator 1 hour before serving so that it's not rock-hard. Thinly slice unpeeled cucumber and wrap it in paper towels to preserve moisture. Scoop the sherbet into small dishes, spoon around sauce, add green onion, and serve on dinner plates with sliced cucumber. Serves 6.

MUSHROOM AND CORIANDER SOUP

By mushrooms I mean wild ones – if at all possible – in combination with the ubiquitous cultivated flats or buttons. The silky richness of a wild species gives this soup its special quality. I've made it with English ceps that I picked in a Surrey wood, and with imported oyster mushrooms – themselves cultivated, I suspect, but nonetheless distinguished – and have liked both versions.

I suggest finishing the soup with *crème fraîche*, the thick cultured cream of France for which I give a recipe below. Its soured tang works well here and, unlike 'sour cream', it can be boiled. If you don't want to do this, use regular heavy cream.

CREME FRAICHE
⅔ cup heavy cream
1 tablespoon buttermilk

SOUP
1½ large onions, peeled and thinly-sliced
5 cups homemade chicken broth, as made on page 100
scant ½ teaspoon coriander seeds, crushed
½ lb flat or button mushrooms, sliced
½ lb trimmed fresh wild mushrooms, such as morels, ceps, chanterelles or oyster mushrooms
salt
¾ cup pasta shells or other small macaroni
⅓ cup of the crème fraîche *or heavy cream*
black pepper
fresh dill
fresh cilantro

Prepare *crème fraîche* at least four days in advance of using, by heating the heavy cream to just less than 100°F. Transfer it to a bowl, add the buttermilk and mix well. Loosely cover the bowl and leave the cream at room temperature, undisturbed, to thicken and develop its acid tang. Depending on the weather, this will take from 1–3 days. Then chill the cream for another day until it becomes almost spreadable. The flavor is wonderful, and the cream will keep, refrigerated in a closed jar, for about 2 weeks.

To make the soup, add the onion to the broth and bring to a boil, then simmer for about 8 minutes, until the onions are cooked. Crush the coriander seeds in a mortar and add them to the slightly cooled broth, run it through the blender or food processor until the onions are puréed.

Slice and wash the cultivated mushrooms. Shake away excess moisture. Wipe the wild mushrooms well with a damp cloth unless they are very dirty and gritty, when they should be washed and well-shaken. Cut all types of wild mushrooms into chunks.

If using chanterelles, which give off so much water when heated that it would dilute the soup, put them, salted, into a heavy, lidded saucepan over high heat. Hold the lid down and shake pan to prevent sticking. As mushrooms heat they will expel their juice. When this boils, drain mushrooms and continue recipe.

Put all the mushrooms into the oniony broth, add salt, and simmer for 5 minutes.

Stir in the pasta shells and simmer, stirring occasionally, for 8–10 minutes until the pasta is cooked. Beat in ⅓ cup *crème fraîche* or heavy cream, simmer for 1 minute, taste the soup and then correct the seasoning.

I like to make this soup a day in advance and reheat it. The flavors pervade the pasta and make it seem like a third kind of mushroom. When serving, garnish each bowl with a sprig of fresh dill and a leaf or two of fresh cilantro. Serves 4–5.

HARLEQUIN QUICHE

SHORTCRUST
generous 1½ cups all-purpose flour
1 tablespoon confectioners' sugar
pinch of salt
⅔ cup sweet butter, softened
1 egg

FILLING
1½ cups very finely shredded red cabbage
salt
2 tablespoons vinegar
¼ lb zucchini
¼ lb carrots, peeled weight
3 shallots
2 tablespoons butter
black pepper
2 eggs
1 egg yolk
⅔ cup heavy cream
pinch of grated nutmeg
1 tablespoon chopped fresh chervil or chives
⅓ cup shredded Gruyère cheese

To prepare the shortcrust, sift the flour, sugar and salt onto a pastry board. Make a well in the center and put the butter into this; make a trough in the butter and break egg into it. With the fingers of one hand, work the butter and egg into a sticky mass.

Use a spatula to toss and chop the flour into this until pastry starts to form. Bring the pastry together with both hands, adding water if necessary to make it adhere, knead briefly and form into a ball. Wrap in waxed paper and a plastic bag and refrigerate several hours or overnight.

Bring the pastry to room temperature, roll out about two-thirds of it to line a 9 inch flan ring set onto a heavy baking sheet. Chill for 30 minutes. Bake blind in a preheated oven at 350°F for about 20 minutes or until the pastry has set and begins to color. Cool.

To prepare the filling, shred the cabbage very fine and boil it for 3–4 minutes in salted, vinegared water (vinegar is to set the color) until just tender. Drain and cool. Top and tail zucchini and, with the carrots, cut them into matchsticks 1 inch long. Peel and mince the shallots.

Melt the butter in a heavy saucepan, add the shallots and let them sweat, covered, for 3 minutes to soften; add the zucchini and carrots and let them cook gently, under buttered paper and a lid, stirring occasionally, for 6–7 minutes or until just tender. The three main vegetables should all retain a little crunch. Cool the three vegetables, combine with cabbage, and season.

Beat together the eggs, yolk, cream, nutmeg, salt and pepper to taste, with about a tablespoon of chopped chervil or chives.

Fill the quiche shell with the combined vegetables, scatter on the grated cheese, pour eggs and cream over the vegetables and bake at 375°F for 20–25 minutes, until the quiche is puffed and beginning to color. Serve hot. This can be made a few hours in advance and reheated for 10 minutes in an oven of the same temperature. Harlequin quiche serves 8–10 as a first course, or 6 as a main course with salad.

BALLOTINES DE VOLAILLE, SAUCE SABAYON

When I was a chef at Ma Cuisine restaurant in London, we boned chicken legs, stuffed them with crab and served each with a lobster sauce. It taught me that boning and stuffing a chicken leg need not be viewed with terror. It is quite easy and can utilize a variety of forcemeats.

The one here involves a chicken breast, with tarragon and nuts. If you chill the leg, it can be thinly-sliced and eaten like a rather elegant, nut-studded terrine. The sauce, based on a reduction of wine and chicken stock, is made on the principle of a sweet sabayon.

Ballotine de volaille

BALLOTINES
1 fresh roasting chicken 3 lb
1 carrot, peeled
1 onion, peeled and sliced
parsley stems
pinch of dried tarragon
salt
¼ cup pine-nuts or shelled pistachios or
    mixture of the two
1 egg yolk
1 tablespoon fresh bread crumbs
1 tablespoon chopped fresh tarragon or
    ⅓ teaspoon dried
4 shallots or scallions, minced
large pinch cayenne
black pepper

VEGETABLES
potatoes, carrots, small Belgian
    endives, or whatever is in season
salt
butter
sugar
lemon juice
black pepper

SABAYON
3 tablespoons chicken stock
3 tablespoons dry white wine
3 egg yolks
salt and black pepper
fresh tarragon as garnish

Remove both chicken legs from the point at which they join the bird's carcass. Take up one leg and with a small, sharp knife, begin to work the flesh away from the bone of the thigh joint, keeping the knife's edge against bone and not the flesh. Work down to the ball joint at the knee and work flesh free, without piercing it, freeing it from cartilage and moving down to free the bone and tendons from the drumstick meat.

With a large, sharp knife, chop off the drumstick bone above the foot and remove any trace of splinters. Keeping the foot intact during poaching secures stuffing and keeps ballotines in shape. Turn the leg skin side out. You should now have 1 pouch without holes and ready to receive the forcemeat.

Repeat the process with the second leg. Remove 5 oz skinless flesh from carcass (probably the value of 1 breast and wing) to make the stuffing. Detach second breast and wing as one piece and reserve.

Chop the remaining carcass into large pieces and with the leg bones, carrot, onion, parsley stems, pinch of dried tarragon and salt, make a good stock. Simmer this for 3–4 hours and top up with water as necessary. Poach the reserved breast and wing in the stock and use the second piece for something else. Strain the stock when ready, reserving a few bones from the pot.

To make the stuffing, skin pistachios, if used, by blanching them for a minute in boiling water, draining, and rubbing away the skins in a towel. Toast the pistachios and pine-nuts for 5 minutes in an oven preheated to 350°F until they begin to color.

Purée the 5 oz of raw chicken flesh, free of obvious nerve tissue, in a food processor, with the egg yolk. Remove to a bowl and add bread crumbs, tarragon, nuts, the minced shallots or scallions and liberal amounts of salt, cayenne and black pepper.

Open out each pouch, salt and pepper it, divide stuffing in half and with wet hands, stuff forcemeat well into each pocket. It will expand on cooking and fill leg to the foot. Fold the flap of thigh flesh snugly over the stuffing, round each form to give it a good shape and refrigerate covered with moist paper towels until ready to poach. The legs can be prepared the day before needed.

If you have chosen vegetables like potatoes and thick carrots to be cut into olives, turn them a few hours before cooking. Cut about four small carrot olives and two small potato olives per person and hold them in cold water until ready to use. Core and trim one or two endives per person and keep wrapped in dark paper in refrigerator. Combine three tablespoons of chicken stock and white wine, and reduce to two tablespoons for sabayon.

When ready to begin, put ballotines onto reserved bones in a medium saucepan, cover with stock that you've made from carcass and weight legs with a small, heavy saucepan lid. Bring the liquid gently to simmering point and poach legs in barely shuddering stock for 25 minutes.

Off the heat the ballotines can be kept hot in this broth, once poached, but try to have vegetables and sauce ready within 10 minutes of finishing chicken.

Cover the potatoes with fresh cold salted water, bring to a boil and simmer about 15 minutes, or until done. Hold in water if necessary. Cover the carrots with a little cold water, add a nut of butter, a little sugar and salt and simmer for 10–20 minutes, depending on age of carrots. The water should evaporate and the vegetables be glazed by the syrup formed with the sugar and butter. Drain away the excess water if necessary to achieve this. Toss carrots to coat them in glaze.

Poach the endives, covered with some lemon juice, a little butter, salt and sugar, for some 15 minutes or so; glaze as for carrots at end of cooking. Pepper each vegetable when ready. If others are used instead – green beans, pearl onions,

scallions or whatever – prepare and glaze them as above.

When ballotines are ready, remove their saucepan from the heat and rapidly make sabayon. Bring a pan of water up to just below a simmer while beating reduced wine and chicken stock with 3 yolks in a small heavy saucepan or heatproof bowl. Put this into hot water and beat yolks into a thick, frothy mousse – a matter of about 3 minutes. Remove the pan from water and beat

for a minute more then season.

Lift ballotines from their stock, gently cut away each foot, lightly dry ballotines of excess moisture and place each on a heated plate (save the stock since it makes an excellent basis for soup). Spoon on a pool of sauce, halve the endive lengthwise and arrange the rest of vegetables on the plate. Garnish the ballotines with fresh tarragon if available and serve with extra sauce in a warmed boat. Serves 2.

Harlequin quiche, Mushroom soup,
Ballotine de volaille, sauce sabayon

Harlequin quiche

Parsley custard

PARSLEY CUSTARDS, TOMATO AND PEAR SAUCE

This is for those gardeners with a glut of parsley and mint.

CUSTARDS
$\frac{1}{2}$ lb very fresh parsley, weighed
    with stems
70 small and very fresh mint
    leaves
salt
1 egg
3 egg yolks
2 tablespoons milk
black pepper
cayenne

SAUCE
8 oz can Italian plum tomatoes, with
    their juices
1 large, ripe, aromatic pear
lemon juice
salt
black pepper

GARNISH
1 small ripe tomato
sprigs of mint
sprigs of parsley

Butter two ovenproof ramekins of $\frac{2}{3}$-cup capacity each and line bases with buttered parchment cut to fit exactly.

Remove parsley stems, wash leaves and blanch these for about a minute in boiling, salted water. Drain and plunge leaves into very cold water. Wash the mint leaves and boil in the parsley's water for about 30 seconds. Refresh. Squeeze from both as much water as possible and purée them very finely in food processor. Using a wooden spoon, force this purée through a coarse strainer.

Beat together the egg, yolks and milk and add puréed herbs. Season well with salt, pepper and cayenne. Divide the custard between the ramekins and put them into a pan filled with enough water to come halfway up sides, bring water to just below simmer and poach custards in this bain-marie in a preheated oven at 310°F for about 40 minutes till risen slightly and cooked.

Meanwhile, open can of tomatoes and pour contents, including juice, into food processor or blender. Peel and core pear and add about $\frac{3}{4}$ cup of its flesh, blend thoroughly and add lemon juice to taste – probably about 2 teaspoons – along with salt and pepper. Strain this into a small bowl. The pear gives just enough of its flavor to be intriguing.

Peel and seed tomato, finely chop half of it. When custards are ready, run the blunt edge of a knife around circumference of each, turn out into the middle of two small plates and peel off paper. Run sauce – unheated – around the outside and top each custard with a little chopped tomato and a sprig each of parsley and mint. Serves 2 as a first course.

THE HARVEST, THE VINTAGE

Wine, like apples or wheat, is a cultivated crop, though the transformation of the grape into a noble vintage requires perhaps more sophisticated knowledge than the baking of loaves or an apple pie. A debatable point, no doubt! But during the period of the vintage, I long to taste some harvest foods, including the produce of the grape, and to sample the sort of dish that satisfies appetites sharpened by the shorter, brisker days of the fall.

GRATIN OF MILLET

This is another use for millet, that unjustly neglected cereal, on which I have also based the Salad of Millet and Herbs (see page 84). I have layered it here with tomato sauce and cheese to make a warming lunch or supper dish for the cooler days of fall.

I prefer to use canned Italian plum tomatoes when I cannot find good garden-grown varieties with a concentrated flavor. If you have the latter, however, do use them instead.

TOMATO SAUCE
1 cup minced onion
2 large cloves garlic, peeled and minced
$\frac{1}{4}$ cup chopped celery
$\frac{1}{4}$ cup chopped carrot
1 tablespoon olive oil
28 oz can Italian plum tomatoes and their juices
3 tablespoons dry white wine
2 teaspoons granulated sugar
1 bay leaf
pinch of thyme
a few parsley stems
salt
black pepper

MILLET
$7\frac{1}{2}$ cups water
salt
$1\frac{3}{4}$ cups whole millet grains, rinsed and drained
$\frac{1}{2}$ teaspoon dry mustard
1 tablespoon olive oil
2 egg yolks
1 cup shredded Gruyère cheese
grated Parmesan cheese
black pepper

TO FINISH
1 cup shredded Gruyère cheese
grated Parmesan cheese
black pepper

To make the tomato sauce, sweat the onion, garlic, celery and carrot in the olive oil in a heavy medium size skillet covered, over low heat until the vegetables are soft but not coloured. Add the remaining sauce ingredients, including a little salt to taste, breaking up the tomatoes with a wooden spoon. Stir well, bring to a boil and simmer briskly, uncovered, for 15–20 minutes, stirring occasionally, until the sauce is reduced to a slightly thickened but still fairly liquid consistency. Leave to cool slightly, then remove the bay leaf and liquidize. Push the sauce through a coarse strainer to remove the seeds. Season to taste. The result is about $2\frac{1}{2}$ cups of sauce. Measure out 2 cups sauce (using the remainder for other purposes).

Bring $7\frac{1}{2}$ cups water to a boil and add 1 teaspoon salt. Beat the millet into the boiling water and simmer rapidly for about 12 minutes until the grains just crack. Drain into a large colander and rinse under running cold water. Cover and steam the strainer of millet over a pan of boiling water for 15 minutes until the grains are cracked, fluffy and fairly dry.

Transfer the millet to a bowl and beat in the mustard, oil, egg yolks, Gruyère cheese and a liberal shaking of Parmesan. Season to taste and work the mixture well with your fingers.

With damp hands, rapidly spread this mixture evenly and about $\frac{1}{4}$ inch thick onto a large wooden board. Leave to cool completely.

Butter a 9×12 inch rectangular earthenware gratin dish.

Use a $1\frac{1}{2}$ inch round cutter to cut the cooled millet into rounds; lightly moisten the cutter as you work for ease. Line the bottom of the dish with millet off-cuts, which will probably disintegrate as you transfer them, but no-one sees this so it doesn't matter! Spoon 3 tablespoons tomato sauce over the millet in the dish. Sprinkle over $\frac{1}{4}$ cup Gruyère, some Parmesan and a grinding of pepper.

Working down the long side of the dish, overlap the millet rounds in rows from top to bottom. You will probably make five rows across. Add pepper, $\frac{3}{4}$ cup Gruyère and some more Parmesan. Pour the remaining sauce over the millet to cover. Sprinkle the surface with more of the Parmesan.

Bake in a preheated oven at 400°F for about 30 minutes until the millet is completely heated through. Leave to rest for 5 minutes before slicing. Serve with a green salad. Serves 4–6.

PORC MIREVAL

I spent a week during one recent autumn observing the harvest of the muscat grape – near Mireval, west of Montpellier, in the South of France – and eating wonderful food prepared by our hostess Anne-Marie Cazalis. I particularly liked Anne-Marie's adaptation of *porc à la normande*, in which she substitutes for Calvados or cider, the Cazalis' own Muscat de Mireval, the sweet golden fortified wine made at the local cooperative from Cazalis and neighbouring grapes. This muscat is, as far as I can tell, not available outside France, but Muscat de Beaumes-de-Venise, from east of the River Rhône, is a graceful alternative that is readily obtainable. The sweetly fruity wine, with the acidity of apples, gives just the right note to pork. You'll see that this is the same cut of meat as in Porc à la Périgourdine, but prepared to give a different effect.

For this dish ask your butcher for a piece of rib end of pork loin, rind and bones removed, meat to be rolled and tied at $\frac{3}{4}$ inch intervals. The finished, rolled weight should be a generous $2\frac{1}{4}$ lb, and the diameter about 3 inches.

---

3 oz piece salted pork sides, boned and rindless weight
butter
vegetable oil
1 large onion, peeled and diced
2$\frac{2}{3}$ cups diced tart apples
generous 2$\frac{1}{4}$ lb piece rolled rib end of pork loin
juice of $\frac{1}{2}$ lemon
salt
small handful of raisins
$\frac{1}{4}$ cup Muscat de Beaumes-de-Venise or Muscat de Mireval
$\frac{1}{2}$ cup heavy cream
1 tablespoon milk
black pepper

TO SERVE
long-grain rice, plain boiled

Choose a heavy, flameproof casserole into which the loin will fit comfortably, with room on either side.

Soak the pork sides for several hours to remove excess salt. Dry well and slice into short lardons.

Melt a knob of butter with a little oil in the casserole and sauté the lardons until just beginning to color. Add the onion and apple, cover and sweat until softened.

Remove from the casserole, add more oil and butter if necessary, and brown the pork loin lightly all over. Wipe the casserole clean with paper towels, replace the meat, fat side upwards, and add the lardons, onion, apple, lemon juice and a little salt.

Warm the casserole over a low heat. Partially cover and cook in the lower third of a preheated oven at 300°F for about $1\frac{1}{4}$–$1\frac{1}{2}$ hours, basting the meat occasionally with its own juices. Test pork with a meat thermometer; it should reach an internal temperature of 170°F. Add the raisins during the last 15 minutes of cooking.

Remove the meat from the casserole and leave to rest in a warm place for 15 minutes. Shortly before carving, add the muscat, cream and milk to the fruits and juices in the casserole to make the sauce. Simmer for several minutes until the alcohol evaporates and the sauce tastes sweetly piquant. Season.

Carve the pork thinly, removing the string as you go. Serve the sliced pork with the sauce on a bed of plain boiled rice. Serves 4–6.

PUMPKIN AND CHESTNUT SOUP

Earlier in this book I wrote with enthusiasm about a pumpkin *crème brûlée*; here the squash, or pumpkin is back in a savory role as part of an autumn soup. The unexpected ingredient is chestnuts; a little out of season now, but the canned French variety is fine for this purpose.

2$\frac{1}{2}$ cups cubed pumpkin or winter squash
1 can (8 oz) whole, unsweetened chestnuts, well drained
2 medium onions, peeled and thinly sliced
2 large cloves garlic, peeled and chopped
3 long inner stalks celery, sliced
7 cups well flavored chicken broth; for method, see page 100
salt
4 small tomatoes, about 14 oz, peeled, seeded and sliced
black pepper
$\frac{1}{4}$ cup milk
dash of heavy cream
fresh chervil leaves, if available
diced tomato flesh

Combine the pumpkin, chestnuts, onions, garlic, celery and broth in a large saucepan. Bring to a boil, add a pinch of salt and simmer, half-covered, for 10–15 minutes until the pumpkin and chestnut are almost cooked. Stir in the tomatoes and simmer for 5 minutes more.

Cool slightly, then liquidize until the soup is smooth, adding seasoning to taste. Dilute with the milk, and add the cream. Thin with more broth if necessary. Check the seasoning.

This soup is best reheated and eaten 24 hours after making. Serve in a tureen, garnished with chervil leaves and diced tomato flesh. Alternatively, use a hollowed-out, flat-bottomed pumpkin or winter squash; warm it first in a preheated oven at 350°F for 20 minutes. Serves 6.

Clockwise from top right: Pumpkin and chestnut soup, Porc Mireval, A sauté of mushrooms with zucchini and scallions, Cherry clafoutis

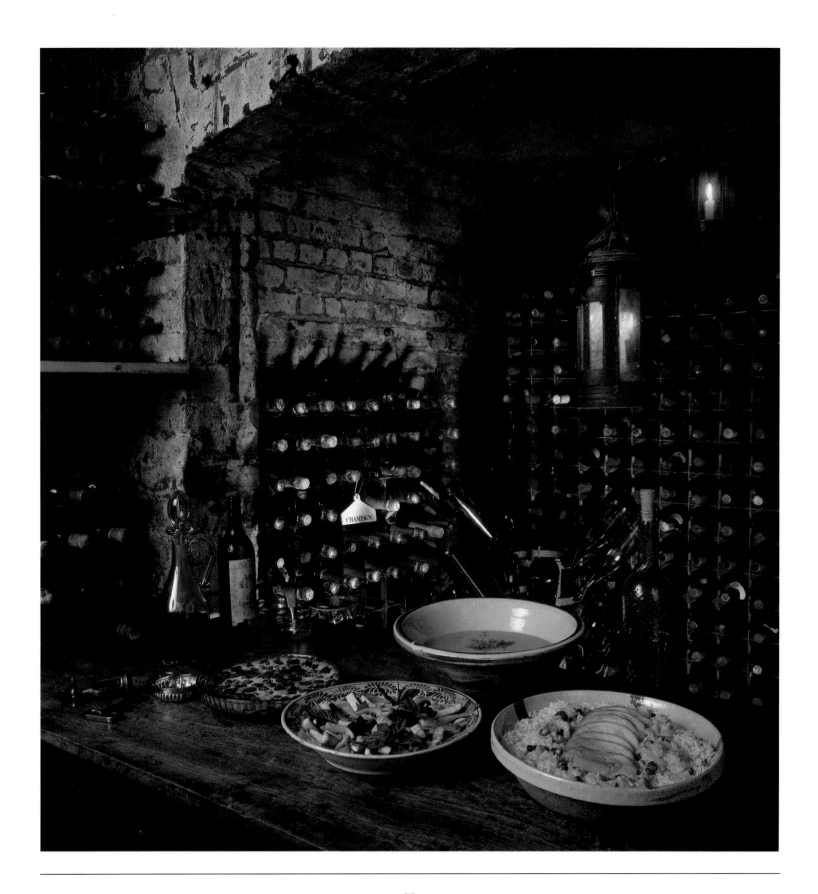

A SAUTE OF MUSHROOMS

This is a quick dish for lunch or supper, based on the field or the oyster mushroom or even the supermarket 'flat'. The ubiquitous zucchini and scallions give crunch; garlic, cumin and mint add interest.

butter
vegetable oil
½ lb slim scallions with bulbous
*   base, trimmed*
14 oz small zucchini, trimmed
2 large cloves garlic, minced
ground cumin
juice of 1 small lemon
salt
2½ cups diced field, oyster or flat
*   cultivated mushrooms*
fresh mint leaves, chopped
black pepper
whole mint leaves, for garnish
brown bread and butter

Melt a knob of butter with oil in two wide skillets.

Slash down into bulbs of the scallions but leave whole.

Cut the zucchini across into thirds, slice each third lengthwise into quarters and set aside.

Put the scallions into one skillet with half the garlic, a good sprinkling of cumin to taste, and a little lemon juice and salt. Cover and sweat the scallions until about half cooked.

Heat the butter and oil in the second skillet, add the remaining garlic, cumin to taste, the zucchini and salt. Put the mushrooms and remaining lemon juice in the first pan with the scallions. Increase the heat and stir the mushrooms to cook rapidly, tossing the zucchini as you go. The mushrooms will expel a lot of liquid.

When zucchini are done but retain some bite, the mushrooms should also be tender; drain away their juices (use these, for instance, in a soup). Combine the contents of both pans, add the chopped mint leaves and season to taste. Stir and toss together for a minute longer over high heat.

Serve the sauté quickly, garnished with whole mint leaves and accompanied by bread and butter. Eat without delay. Serves 2–4.

CHERRY CLAFOUTIS

This is an absolutely classic French country dish from the Limousin region, in the south west – cherries in a thick batter, sugared and flavored with Cognac. Thinner batters do not rise as well and allow the cherry juices to flow unattractively.

Strictly speaking, this fruit is not part of the early fall harvest. If there are late cherries around, however, or some imported ones available, or even if you have bottled your own in sugar syrup during July and August – as a Limousin cook might do – this is a lovely dessert to have right now.

3 cups ripe cherries
¾ cup all-purpose flour
1 tablespoon superfine sugar
large pinch of salt
2 eggs
⅔ cup milk
1–2 tablespoons Cognac

TO SERVE
granulated sugar
heavy cream

Remove the stems and pit the cherries; if using bottled fruit, drain well. Butter a shallow ovenproof dish, 9½ inches in diameter.

Sift the flour, sugar and salt into a bowl and break the eggs into the center. Beat the milk with 1 tablespoon Cognac and slowly add half the liquid to the eggs, gradually beating in the surrounding flour mixture. When half has been added, beat thoroughly until bubbles break on the surface. Beat in the remaining milk and beat until absolutely smooth. Cover the batter and leave to relax in a cool place for about 1 hour.

Beat again lightly and pour enough of the batter into the dish to cover the base. Arrange the cherries in one closely packed layer, pour on the rest of the batter and dribble over some more Cognac if desired.

Bake in a preheated oven at 350°F until the batter has risen and browned at the edges.

Leave to cool for 15 minutes. Sprinkle with granulated sugar, then slice and serve with lightly whipped cream. Serves 4–6.

BASIL-FLAVORED WINE JELLY

This is an old fashioned jelly, rarely seen now. I like it as an accompaniment to game birds, or with buttered toast at teatime. The basil leaves, infused while the juices and sugar are boiling, give it a subtle extra dimension.

3 lb ripe green grapes, weight without
*   stems*
1½ cups dry white wine
1½ lb tart cooking apples
1 lemon
2½ cups or more granulated sugar
10–12 fresh basil leaves
2 tablespoons Cognac

Put the grapes into a deep pan with the wine, then use both hands to squeeze and crush the grapes thoroughly. Bring the mixture to boil and simmer gently, uncovered, for about 30 minutes until the grapes are very soft.

Thinly slice the apples – unpeeled, cores and all – and the lemon and add to the wine; simmer for a further 30 minutes until the apples and lemon are thoroughly pulped.

Scald a jelly bag with boiling water, wring thoroughly when cool enough to handle and suspend above a large bowl. Pour in the mixture of wine and fruit,

Gratin of millet, Mushroom sauté

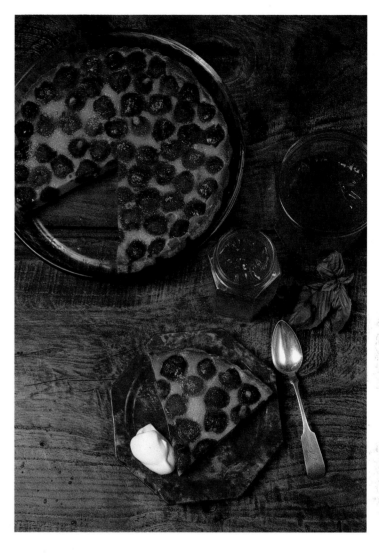

Clafoutis, Basil-wine jelly

and leave the juices to drip overnight, without squeezing the bag.

Measure the juices into a preserving pan or stainless steel saucepan, and for every $2\frac{1}{2}$ cups juice, add $2\frac{1}{3}$ cups sugar. Stir over a very low heat until the sugar is completely dissolved.

Tie the basil leaves into a muslin bag, add to the pan of wine and fruit juices. Raise the heat and let the syrup boil, without stirring.

Start testing for a set after 10 minutes of boiling. Chill a saucer, spoon on a little syrup, cool in the freezer, then run a finger over the surface; if a skin has formed that wrinkles when you push it, the setting point has been reached. If not setting, continue to boil until the test syrup wrinkles.

When the setting point arrives, take the pan from heat, remove the bag of basil, dip a large spoon into hot water and skim the surface of the jelly thoroughly. Add the Cognac and boil for 1 minute longer. Pot the jelly immediately in hot, dry, sterilized jam jars. Cover without delay.

Makes two 1 lb jars and one 8 oz jar

using 3 lb of grapes and $1\frac{1}{2}$ lb of cooking apples. The amount of sugar may vary depending on the pectin content of the fruits. Keep testing for set.

AUTUMN SOUPS

The weather of September and October can move unpredictably along the thermometer from hot to cold and back, so it is good to have a repertoire of soups which take heed of the temperature and the variety of available ingredients. For example, a cold purée of the last asparagus and basil, with spinach, for early in the season and a thick lentil, onion and sausage soup for the cold nights of October.

Six of these soups are based on one of three good, homemade broths, for which there is no instant substitute. The seventh is a hot tomato surprise beneath a dome of puff pastry called, in a loose reference to an old-fashioned cooking method, a 'huff'.

THREE-LENTIL SOUP

A nourishing meal of a soup, made colorful in the initial stages by three different kinds of lentil. The trick is not to cook the soup too much, so as to preserve the variety of its texture. The garnish of fried onion adds an interesting, slightly charred and caramelized sweetness.

¼ cup khaki lentils
¼ cup dark green (Puy) lentils
¼ cup red lentils
2 rashers bacon
1 thick carrot, peeled
1 large onion, peeled
3 large cloves garlic, peeled
1 celery stalk
7 tablespoons butter
vegetable oil
4 cups basic meat broth, as described for Cold Asparagus, Spinach and Basil Soup, page 102

2 medium tomatoes, peeled, seeded and chopped
2 small beef sausages
salt
black pepper
lemon juice
1 large onion, peeled and very finely sliced

Rinse and drain all lentils; soak khaki lentils in water to cover for 2 hours, green ones for 1½ hours, red ones should not be soaked at all.

Finely chop rashers of bacon, carrot, onion, garlic cloves and celery and sweat all of these, covered, for 10 minutes in 3 tablespoons butter and a little oil in a large covered saucepan.

Drain the lentils, add all three kinds to the saucepan and stir well. Add the broth, tomatoes and sausages. Do not salt. Half cover, bring them up to the simmering point and simmer for 20 minutes or until the lentils are cooked but have not started to disintegrate. Add salt and pepper to taste and a liberal squeeze of lemon juice.

Slice the sausages and serve soup garnished generously with fried onion slices, which you have prepared as follows:

First clarify the remaining butter. Clarified butter is less likely to burn at high temperatures. Melt the 4 tablespoons butter, allow to stand, then spoon clear, yellow liquid away from milky residue. Heat the clear liquid in a heavy, medium-size skillet and toss the onion in this clarified butter until brown and crisp. This takes quite a while to do properly. The onions should first be softened, then gradually colored until their flavor is highly concentrated. Season and drain on paper towels. Serves 4.

TOMATO SOUP-IN-A-HUFF

When the puff pastry dome is tapped open with a soup spoon, wonderful aromas fly up.

SOUP
2 large onions, peeled and minced
6 cloves garlic, peeled and minced
2 tablespoons butter
vegetable oil
¼ cup dry white wine
2½ lb ripe tomatoes
1 tablespoon granulated sugar
pinch of thyme
salt
1 tablespoon tomato paste
¼ cup heavy cream
black pepper
1 thick carrot, peeled
1 celery stalk
fresh chives

PASTRY
1 lb puff pastry, made with sweet butter; see page 47 for method
1 egg
light cream

Sweat the chopped onion and garlic with butter and a splash of oil in a medium-size skillet, covered, for 8–10 minutes, or until soft. Pour in white wine and reduce to about 1 tablespoon.

Seed and chop tomatoes, add to skillet with sugar, thyme and a little salt. Simmer for 20–30 minutes. The mixture should not reduce too much. Add the tomato paste and cook 1 minute longer.

Cool slightly, then pour into a blender or food processor, purée and season. Rub soup through a strainer; it will be quite thick. Boil the heavy cream to reduce it to 1½ tablespoons, add to soup. Correct seasoning, divide the soup among four tureens and allow to cool.

Meanwhile, slice the carrot and celery into thin strips, cut the strips into tiny dice and put a tablespoon of each into each tureen. Scissor on the chives and stir vegetables partly into soup.

When the soup is completely cold, divide puff pastry into four equal pieces. Roll out each piece $\frac{1}{4}$ inch thick, and, using a plate 2 inches wider than tops of tureens, cut out four pastry circles. Brush one side of each circle liberally with a wash made from an egg well-beaten with a dash of cream. Place the pastry egg-side-down on each tureen, and carefully but firmly press the pastry against china. Refrigerate for 1 hour.

Brush the pastry all over, including the sides, with the remaining egg wash. Bake in a preheated oven at 450°F for 15–20 minutes or until the pastry has puffed into a dome and is golden brown.

Serve immediately, encouraging people to break the crust into the soup as they eat. Serves 4.

Clockwise from top right: Carrot and tarragon soup, Tomato soup-in-a-huff, Fennel, bacon and haddock soup

FENNEL, BACON AND HADDOCK SOUP

Three flavors which marry unexpectedly well.

BASIC FISH BROTH
2 lb bones and heads from lean fish
  such as fluke, flounder or Pacific
  sole
1 large leek, cleaned and sliced
1 large onion, peeled and sliced
6 parsley stems
3 tablespoons lemon juice
1 large glass dry white wine
¼ teaspoon salt

SOUP
1 lb 2 oz bulb fennel, with leaves
2 onions (about 10 oz)
4 bacon rashers
½ cup butter
vegetable oil
6 cups basic fish broth (as above)
salt
10 oz haddock fillet
1¼ cup milk
¾ cup dry white wine
black pepper

TO GARNISH
small croûtons made from firm-
  textured, slightly stale bread
4 rashers bacon

Make a fish broth as for the Scallop Broth with Julienned Vegetables (see page 101) using the above quantities but less water. There is no need, here, to line the colander with muslin for straining, and don't worry about separating clear broth from sediment.

Reserving the fennel leaves, finely chop the fennel bulb, onion and bacon. Sweat in ¼ cup butter and a little oil in a large, heavy saucepan, covered, until soft, about 8–10 minutes. Add 6¼ cups broth, sediment and all, very little salt, and simmer for 10 minutes.

Meanwhile, poach the haddock in milk, covered, for 5 minutes. Cool.

Add the glass of white wine to soup base and simmer away alcohol for 2–3 minutes. Allow soup base to cool a little. Purée and correct seasoning, being careful with the salt.

Make croûtons by slicing the bread thinly, cutting the slices into slim fingers, and then the fingers into tiny cubes; you will need about 50 of these. Over low heat melt the remaining butter with a little oil in a wide skillet, add cubes and sauté gently, tossing often, until croûtons turn pale golden brown. Remove from the pan and allow to cool on paper towels.

Fry the rashers of bacon until crisp; chop and crumble finely. Remove haddock from milk and flake it.

To serve soup, reheat with haddock and 1 cup of the strained milk in which the fish was cooked. Do not allow this to boil or simmer, as the acid in the soup may curdle the milk and cause it to separate.

Ladle into bowls and garnish with croûtons, bacon and a few fennel leaves. Serves 6.

COLD PUMPKIN AND GINGER SOUP

An unusual and complementary mixture of flavors.

BASIC CHICKEN BROTH
1½ lb fresh chicken pieces, or half a
  boiling fowl, with excess fat
  removed
2 carrots, peeled
1 onion, peeled and sliced
1 celery stalk
6 parsley stems
1 bay leaf
pinch of dried thyme
½ teaspoon salt

SOUP
2 cups chopped onion
3 cups cubed pumpkin or winter squash
  flesh

6 cups basic chicken broth
salt
2 pieces fresh gingerroot, each about
  the size of a thumb
black pepper
3–4 tablespoons heavy cream
pistachio nuts, shelled, skinned and
  finely chopped

Make the broth by placing the chicken pieces or boiling fowl, cut into manageable sizes, into a large, heavy saucepan or stockpot of 4-quarts capacity.

Cover well with water, bring the water slowly to a boil and skim thoroughly. Add the carrots, onion, celery, parsley, bay leaf, thyme, and skim again as the water returns to boil. Add the salt, lower the heat and half cover the pot with a lid. Barely simmer for 3–4 hours, topping up with water as necessary.

Strain the broth through a colander lined with a double thickness of muslin, degrease with paper towels, or cool and refrigerate, removing solidified layer of fat when ready to use.

For the soup, simmer the onion, pumpkin, strained broth and a little salt for about 10 minutes, until the vegetables are just cooked.

Cut away the skin of one gingerroot with a small, sharp knife, and finely grate 1 teaspoon's worth; add some of this to the soup and purée, in two batches if necessary, in a blender or food processor, adding salt and pepper to taste. Add the heavy cream, and more ginger to taste. Its flavor should be evident but not overpowering.

Chill the soup for 2–3 hours. Stir well to reintegrate the cream, before ladling into cups or bowls.

Garnish each serving with more fresh grated ginger and pistachio nuts. Serves 5–6.

SCALLOP BROTH WITH JULIENNED VEGETABLES

This is an elegant, subtle soup and an effective means of making the most of an expensive shellfish.

BASIC FISH BROTH

3 lb bones and heads from lean fish such as fluke, flounder or Pacific sole
2 leeks, cleaned and sliced
1 large onion, peeled and sliced
8 parsley stems
4 tablespoons lemon juice
2 large glasses dry white wine
½ teaspoon salt

SCALLOP BROTH

1 small sweet red pepper
6¼ cups basic fish broth
1 thick carrot, peeled
a few button mushrooms
1 small leek
8 or 9 scallops (depending on size of muscle), with coral, bought in shell if possible; ask your supplier to clean them
½ cup dry white wine
salt
black pepper
gin

Make the basic broth by washing bones and heads thoroughly of blood and removing gills. Chop them into convenient sizes. Put them into a large saucepan or stockpot of 4-quarts capacity with the leeks, the onion, parsley and lemon juice. Cover well with water.

Bring to a simmer over a low heat, skim thoroughly, add wine and salt and simmer, uncovered, for 30 minutes. Strain the broth through a colander lined with a double thickness of muslin. Add a few more drops of white wine, let cool and refrigerate for 1–2 hours. The fine particles suspended in the broth will settle to the bottom of bowl. Disturb as little as possible.

Meanwhile, roast the red pepper under a preheated medium broiler, turning as skin blisters and blackens all over. Cool under wet paper towels which will help loosen skin. Peel off all the skin, cut pepper open and remove core and seeds. Slice the pepper into very thin strips of about 1½ inches long; set these aside as garnish.

When ready to proceed, carefully ladle 6 cups clear broth away from its sediment and pour into a large saucepan. Make a very, very fine julienne from thin slices of carrot, mushroom tops, and inner part of the leek – you should have about 2–3 tablespoons of each type of julienne – and add to the broth. Place this over low heat.

Take cleaned and washed white muscle and coral of scallops (it is not worth making this from frozen scallops; buying them in shells is a guarantee that freezing has not occurred). Keep the corals whole and slice the muscles diagonally into thirds or quarters, depending on size.

Put into another saucepan, heavy and of medium capacity, with the white wine and grindings of salt and pepper. Cover the pan, set over a very low heat and poach scallops in the wine for 2–3 minutes or until just cooked. They must not boil or cook too long or they will toughen and lose all appeal. When done, carefully transfer the fish with a slotted spoon to the saucepan containing the broth, which should be heating without simmering.

Add a splash of gin to the wine in which scallops were poached, and rapidly boil this down to 1½ tablespoons. When the broth has been heated through and is just about to simmer, strain in the reduced liquid. Correct seasoning and ladle broth with its vegetables and fish into cups or bowls. Garnish with strips of red pepper.

This broth is also very good if cooled and refrigerated for several hours, garnish and all. The broth jells slightly and the result is delicate. Serves 5.

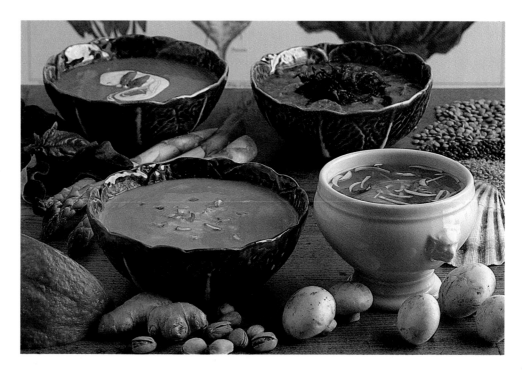

Asparagus soup, Three lentil soup, Scallop broth with julienned vegetables, Pumpkin soup

CARROT AND TARRAGON SOUP

BASIC CHICKEN BROTH
1½ lb fresh chicken
2 carrots, peeled
1 onion, peeled and sliced
1 celery stalk
6 parsley stems
½ teaspoon dried tarragon
½ teaspoon salt

SOUP
2 cups onion, thinly sliced
2 cups carrots, chopped
¼ cup butter
vegetable oil
7½ cups chicken broth (as above)
2 tablespoons long-grain rice
bunch of fresh tarragon
1 teaspoon granulated sugar
salt
black pepper
2 tablespoons butter

Make the chicken broth as described in Pumpkin and Ginger Soup (see page 100) but substituting tarragon for bay leaf and thyme. Cover chicken well with water, bring slowly to a boil and skim before adding vegetables and tarragon. Barely simmer for 3–4 hours, topping up with water as necessary.

To make the soup, sweat the onion and carrots in ¼ cup butter and a little oil in a large heavy saucepan, covered, for 8–10 minutes or until the onion softens. Add the chicken broth, rice, fresh tarragon, sugar and a pinch of salt. Bring to boil and simmer for 15–20 minutes, or until rice and carrots are cooked.

Cool slightly, purée in a blender or food processor, adding salt, pepper and two or more tablespoons of fresh tarragon leaves, to taste. Blend well. If the resulting purée is too thick, add a bit more broth to thin.

Reheat soup with 2 tablespoons butter, garnish bowls with fresh tarragon, and present. Serves 6.

COLD ASPARAGUS, SPINACH AND BASIL SOUP

BASIC MEAT BROTH
¾ lb beef shank
¼ lb veal trimmings, if available
1 lb veal bones, cut into manageable pieces (if veal bones are unavailable, substitute a chicken carcass)
2 carrots, peeled
1 onion, peeled and sliced
1 large clove garlic, unpeeled
1 celery stalk
6 parsley stems
1 bay leaf
pinch of dried thyme
½ teaspoon salt

SOUP
1 tablespoon butter
1 tablespoon flour
5 cups basic meat broth, heated
1 celery stalk, chopped
salt
1¼ lb green asparagus
1 cup fresh spinach leaves, well washed
6 large basil leaves
black pepper
3–4 teaspoons lemon juice
seasoned whipped cream
about 15 small basil leaves

To make the broth, place the beef, veal and bones in a large, heavy saucepan or stockpot of 6–8 pints capacity. Cover well with water, bring water slowly to the boiling point, and skim thoroughly. Add the carrots, onion, garlic, celery, parsley, bay leaf, thyme, and skim again as water returns to boil. Add a little salt. Lower heat, half-cover pot with a lid and barely simmer for 4–5 hours, topping up with water as necessary. This should give a full-flavored broth of good body.

Strain broth through a colander lined with a double thickness of muslin. Degrease with paper towels, or alternatively cool and refrigerate, then remove the layer of fat which has solidified at the top.

To make the soup, melt butter over a low heat in a heavy saucepan, blend in flour, beat for 1 minute and, off heat, pour in hot broth all at once, beat vigorously and bring to boil, beating. Add celery and a pinch of salt. Lower heat and let liquid barely simmer on side of burner for 30 minutes, skimming off the skin which will form regularly.

Meanwhile, peel and trim the hard stems of the asparagus stalks. Remove the tips and blanch these for 1 minute in boiling, salted water; drain and refresh them under cold water to halt cooking. Add stalks to soup base and simmer for 15 minutes. Add the asparagus tips and spinach leaves (minus stems), simmer for 3–4 minutes or until both are just cooked, add large basil leaves and simmer 1 minute longer.

Cool the soup slightly, then pour it into a blender or food processor fitted with a steel blade and purée, adding salt and pepper. Rub the soup through a strainer, correct the seasoning and add lemon juice; just enough to sharpen flavor slightly. Allow to cool, then chill for about 2 hours; if chilled for too long soup based on broth which contains a lot of natural gelatin, will set like a mousse.

Garnish each serving with a swirl of seasoned whipped cream and 2 or 3 small basil leaves. Serves 4–5.

CHRISTMAS FESTIVITIES

Winter brings the dazzle of Christmas, with its dinner parties, children's beanos, and specially sumptuous teas. Here are some ornaments, some enhancing details like Picasso's cookies, the Earl Grey's truffles and jam tarts in miniature, that will add their sparkle to your entertainments.

MARBLE CAKE

A classic mixture of chocolate and lemony swirls.

1 cup sweet butter, softened
grated zest of 1 large lemon
1¼ cups superfine sugar
3 eggs
generous 1¼ cups all-purpose flour
large pinch of salt
2 teaspoons baking powder
about 2 teaspoons milk
2 tablespoons unsweetened cocoa

Butter two loaf pans of $7\frac{1}{4} \times 3\frac{1}{4} \times 2\frac{1}{2}$ inches and line bottom of each with a strip of buttered parchment.

Cream the butter with lemon zest, gradually add superfine sugar; add eggs and beat by tablespoons into base until really light and fluffy.

Sift together the flour, salt and baking powder; sift them again over the creamed ingredients and fold all together lightly and deftly; add a drop or two of milk if necessary to make the batter a heavy dropping consistency.

Portion off one-third of this batter and combine well with sifted cocoa. Spoon a layer of the lemony base evenly over the bottom of each pan, followed by a layer of chocolate, then lemon, then chocolate. Run a butter knife back and forth through the length of each pan to marblize the batter, then cover the batter completely with the remaining lemon base.

Bake in a preheated oven at 350°F for 45–50 minutes or until cakes test done. They will rise high and crack down the center. Cool on wire racks for 10 minutes while still in their pans. Remove from pans, peel off the paper and allow to cool. These cakes will keep for about a week stored in an airtight container. Makes 2 small loaves.

CROSS TARTS

These are miniature versions of an old-fashioned type of jam tart, once very popular and, in the north of England, quite complex.

Strips of pastry divide each tart into sections, each ready for a different jam, or as here, two contrasting ones. Some cooks devised star patterns and, showing off, put in thirteen different flavors, others stuck to simple crosses or ran a whirl of pastry around the middle. A cunning way of turning remnants of jam to advantage.

SHORTCRUST PASTRY
2 cups all-purpose flour
3 tablespoons icing sugar
large pinch of salt
pinch of ground nutmeg
1 teaspoon baking powder
¾ cup sweet butter, softened
yolks of 2 hard-boiled eggs, sieved
1 egg

TO FINISH
jams, in contrasting colors

To make the shortcrust, sift the flour, sugar, salt, nutmeg and baking powder onto a pastry board, make a center well and place butter in the well. Form a trough in the butter, add the sieved yolks and break the egg into this.

With one hand, deftly work the butter, yolks and egg into a sticky mass, then use a spatula to toss and chop flour gradually into butter and egg until it begins to resemble pastry.

Use both hands to bring the pastry into shape, add a few drops of water if necessary to bind. Knead briefly and form into a ball. Wrap the pastry in waxed paper and plastic and refrigerate for several hours or, better still, overnight to facilitate easy handling.

Bring the shortcrust pastry to room temperature, roll out and line small circular tins of about $2\frac{1}{4}$ inches in diameter. With a sharp knife or a pastry cutter, cut narrow strips of dough and fit them across each other on top of the pastry linings, pressing strips gently into place to form divisions.

Chill the tarts for at least 30 minutes, then bake on baking sheets at 350°F for 15–20 minutes, or until golden, with browning edges. Cool the tarts and remove them from tins before filling with the assorted jams.

I filled these tarts, when cold, with currant jelly and orange marmalade. I think that for this size it is more attractive to use two contrasting colours rather than a mixture of four. But there is no reason not to make up different combinations of two; black currant with strawberry, plum with raspberry and so on, thereby creating a decorative and colorful array.

These tarts are best if made within a few hours of serving. Makes about 20.

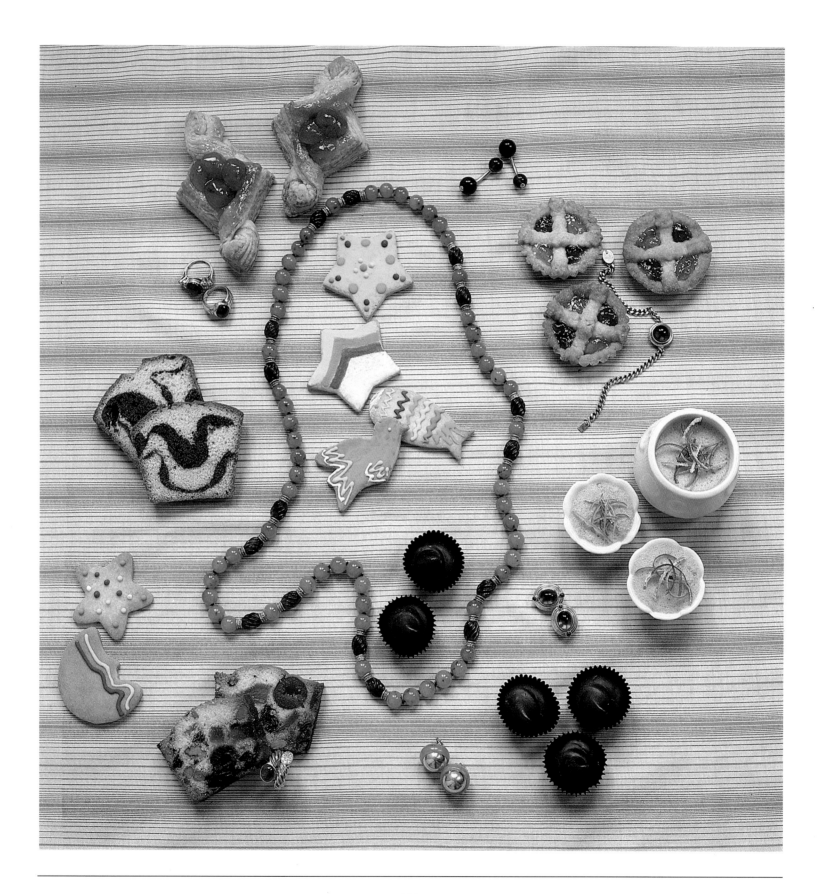

TWIST-OF-GRAPE TARTS

A simple technique gives unusual results.

$1\frac{1}{2}$ lb puff pastry made with sweet
    butter, see page 47 for method
1 egg
small bunch of black or green grapes
lemon juice (optional)
$\frac{1}{2}$ cup apricot jam

Roll the puff pastry to a thickness of about $\frac{1}{8}$ inch, and with the aid of a pastry cutter, cut out 4 inch squares (use offcuts to make something else such as palmiers). Fold each square into a triangle and make a sharp cut $\frac{3}{8}$ inch in from edge of each short side to within $\frac{3}{8}$ inch of the point where the two halves of pastry meet. Unfold the entire triangle, and fold each pointed strip of thin pastry across the center to the opposite side.

Make an egg wash with the egg beaten with a little water and use it to anchor each strip. The twist is now formed and should be symmetrical – if not, trim as necessary. Prick the center of each twist with a fork and chill, on baking sheets, for at least 30 minutes.

Paint the angled strips with a little egg wash. Bake in a preheated oven at 375°F for about 25 minutes until well risen, cooked through and browning. Cool completely.

While the tarts are baking, peel the grapes with a small, sharp knife, halve them and remove the seeds. If preparing

Clockwise from the top: Twist-of-grape tarts, Cross tarts, Pumpkin mousse, Earl Grey's truffles, Fruit and nut cake, Picasso's cookies, Marble cake

in advance, sprinkle with lemon juice and refrigerate.

When the tarts are cold, scoop some of the pastry from each centre if you think there are too many layers. Simmer the apricot jam with a little water, strain, and paint inside of each tart with this glaze.

Fill with well-dried grape halves. Brush grapes and surrounding pastry with glaze and serve as quickly as possible – within at least 2 hours of assembling, as the fruit and apricot will soften the pastry. Makes 10–12 tarts.

PICASSO'S COOKIES

A treat for children to make and paint, these are shortbreads cut into all sorts of shapes, then painted and piped with various brightly-colored icings. Time-consuming but absorbing work.

COOKIES
$\frac{1}{2}$ cup sweet butter, softened
$\frac{3}{4}$ cup superfine sugar
1 egg
about 2 tablespoons milk
$2\frac{1}{2}$ cups all-purpose flour
large pinch of salt
1 teaspoon baking powder

ICING
2 egg whites
a few drops of lemon juice
$2\frac{1}{4}$ cups confectioners' sugar
yellow, red, blue and green food
    coloring

For the cookies, cream the butter until light, gradually adding sugar until well integrated. Beat egg and add to butter in two pours, beat in 2 tablespoons milk. Sift the dry ingredients and beat thoroughly into the creamed base. The dough should be moist but not damp – if necessary add a few more drops of milk. Roll the dough into a ball, wrap in waxed paper and refrigerate until firm but not hard.

Break off pieces of dough, roll out on a floured board to slightly more than $\frac{1}{8}$ inch thick and with various shaped cutters, stamp out stars, fish, birds, half-moons, mushrooms, pigs; whatever appeals.

Place the cookies on heavy baking sheets. Bake in a preheated oven at 350°F for about 10 minutes until the edges are golden brown. Cool for 1 minute before removing from sheets with a spatula and placing on wire racks to cool. They can be stored in airtight containers for weeks, if necessary.

To make the icing, put the egg whites into a very clean bowl with lemon juice, and beat whites, electrically if possible, at a high speed until frothy. Gradually sift in the confectioners' sugar and beat until whites are thick, smooth, and standing in peaks when beater is removed. This will take 5–6 minutes. Put aside, covered with a damp cloth, until ready to use.

Make up 10 or so small piping bags from parchment paper, keeping the tips tiny. Have ready some small paint-brushes and some cups of water.

Put quantities of icing into little bowls or teacups. Keep one part white and mix drops of various food colorings into others until desired primary colors have been reached. Experiment!

To paint, thin some of icings with water so that various glazes, including white, can be brushed onto cookies. To pipe, fill bags two thirds full of unthinned color, fold the tops down, cut tips slightly (keeping openings small), and use, renewing bags when necessary. There are no rules here, except to let various layers and adjoining colors dry sufficiently before painting or piping over them, and to rinse brushes thoroughly when changing colors. When finished, allow the cookies to dry for several hours before serving or storing in an airtight container. Makes 48–60.

THE EARL GREY'S TRUFFLES

Made with a *ganache* of chocolate, cream and egg yolk, these have the haunting aftertaste of Earl Grey tea.

¾ cup heavy cream, very fresh
2 tablespoons sweet butter
1½ teaspoons Earl Grey tea
10 squares (10 oz) semisweet dark
    chocolate
1 egg yolk
cocoa (optional)
confectioners' sugar (optional)

In a small, heavy-bottomed saucepan, bring the cream to a boil with the butter; add tea, stir, cover, and leave to infuse, off the heat, for 10 minutes.

With a large knife, thoroughly chop chocolate. Strain the cream through a fine tea strainer and discard the tea; wash and dry the pan, return cream to it and bring it again to a boil. Off the heat, add chocolate, stir, cover pan, and leave the chocolate to melt for 4–5 minutes. Add the egg yolk and, with a wooden spoon, beat the mixture smooth. Pour into a wide, medium-size bowl and leave this *ganache* to cool. It will probably take about 30 minutes.

Prepare about 30 candy papers – chocolate brown are the most appropriate in color – to receive the truffles, and fit a nylon pastry bag with a plain ½ inch tip.

Using a hand-held electric mixer, beat cooled *ganache* at high speed for 3–5 minutes. It will lighten. When it forms very, very soft peaks, stop beating and immediately pile into prepared bag; pipe the chocolate into candy papers.

If you find the *ganache* too liquid to pipe, remove from the bag and beat it further. If, on the other hand, you have beaten it too much to achieve a stylish result, simply stir the mixture in a small, heavy saucepan over a very low heat until it returns to liquid form, turn into a clean bowl, beat, and try again.

If, however, your *ganache* should

Earl Grey's truffles

prove to be totally uncooperative, which can happen with this temperamental substance, all can be salvaged by letting it stand until firm enough to shape with the hand. Then spoon small, compact nuggets of *ganache* onto a plate or tray covered with unsweetened cocoa sifted with a little confectioners' sugar. Dust your fingertips with cocoa-sugar mixture and deftly roll each nugget into a ball, roll again in cocoa, and place in prepared paper cases.

These truffles can be stored in an airtight tin for up to a week if refrigerated. Eat about 30 minutes after removing from the refrigerator, because they soften quickly. Makes 20–30 chocolates.

FRUIT AND NUT CAKES

These are loaves of a Christmas cake-like nature, the batter a mixture of equal weights of butter, sugar, eggs and flour, just enough to bind the abundance of fruit and nuts. It is worth using the very best ingredients: Smyrna raisins if you can get them; slices of candied citron (not the cheap 'mixed peel' sold in supermarkets); a combination of red, green and white candied cherries if available. This quantity makes 4 small loaves, but you can use a 8–9 inch high-sided round pan instead if you prefer.

1⅓ cups Smyrna raisins, measured after
    pitted (or best available pitted or
    seedless raisins)
6 oz candied pineapple rings
4 oz candied citron slices
2 oz crystallized ginger
8 oz whole candied cherries – ideally, a
    combination of colors
2 oz walnuts, very coarsely chopped
2 oz pistachio nuts
generous 1½ cups all-purpose flour
large pinch of salt
1 cup sweet butter, softened
grated zest and juice of 1 lemon
1¼ cups superfine sugar
4 large eggs
4 tablespoons Cognac and more for
    ripening (optional)

Butter four loaf pans measuring approximately 7¼ × 3¼ × 2¼ inches, or a larger round pan if you wish, line with a double thickness of buttered baking parchment paper. Cut this to extend at least 2 inches above rims to protect the tops of cakes from excessive browning.

Pit raisins if need be, and coarsely sliver the pineapple, citron and ginger. Combine in a bowl with the cherries and nuts. Sift the flour with salt, and sift some of this over the fruits and nuts, turning them in the flour to separate the elements of this sticky mixture.

Cream the butter with the grated lemon zest, gradually adding all the sugar until butter is well aerated. With an electric mixer, beat the eggs for 10 minutes, until thick and light, and with a wooden spoon beat eggs gradually into the base. Beat remaining flour into base alternately with Cognac and lemon juice, until the batter is of firm dropping consistency. Stir in the floured fruit and nuts.

Divide the batter among the four pans, and with the back of a damp spoon, make a smooth hollow down the center of each so that cakes rise evenly. Put the pans into an oven preheated to 290°F, with a water-filled roasting tin on lowest

Fruit and nut cake

shelf to keep them moist. They will bake in 1¾–2 hours (a single 8–9 inch circular pan will take just under 3 hours) and are done when the tops turn a pale golden brown and a trussing needle thrust into center tests clean and hot.

Cool the cakes on wire racks, in pans, for about 30 minutes, then turn out, and remove parchment paper. If not to be ripened, the cakes can be eaten straightaway, or kept for about one week in an airtight tin.

But these cakes are lovely when soaked well with Cognac top and bottom, wrapped snugly in parchment paper and then with foil, stored for a week in a Scotch tape-sealed tin, then rebrandied and rewrapped once a week for about a month. They can then be kept for a long time in a closed and sealed container. Makes 4 small loaves or 1 large fruit and nut cake.

PUMPKIN MOUSSE WITH CANDIED PEEL OF LIME

A frothy mixture of eggs, pumpkin, cream and spices. The mousse contrasts well with the snap and tang of its lime garnish. Although the ingredients are almost identical to those of the Pumpkin Brûlée on page 58, the effect when eating is interestingly different.

MOUSSE
4 sheets gelatin
½ cup dark rum
4 eggs
⅔ cup superfine sugar
1 cup fresh or canned pumpkin, smoothly puréed
scant ½ teaspoon ground cinnamon
scant ½ teaspoon ground ginger
¼ teaspoon ground cloves
¼ teaspoon nutmeg
¾ cup heavy cream

CANDIED PEEL
1¼ cups granulated sugar
2 cups water
2 limes with very green skins (if limes unavailable, use lemons)
superfine sugar

To make the mousse, soften the gelatin in a jug of water, drain and dissolve in rum that has been gently warmed in a small heavy saucepan on top of a very low heat.

Place the eggs in a medium-size heatproof mixing bowl set over a small saucepan of simmering water. Using a hand-held electric mixer if possible, beat the eggs at high speed, gradually adding superfine sugar. Beat for 5–6 minutes or until the eggs grow very light, thick, voluminous and rather warm. Take the bowl from the heat and beat contents until almost cool.

Beat the pumpkin briefly to loosen its texture and fold, with the spices, into the egg base. Ensure that the gelatin-rum mixture is liquid, and strain this into the egg and pumpkin.

Fold everything together thoroughly but with a light hand so as not to break down the volume. The base will probably now have cooled completely, but if not, let it stand the few minutes necessary to achieve this before mixing in the whipped cream.

Whip the cream into very soft peaks (it should have the same consistency as the eggs and pumpkin) and fold into base. Spoon or pour the mousse into pots

or ramekins and chill for 3–4 hours. Serve on the day made.

While mousse is chilling, prepare the candied peel. Make a syrup by dissolving the granulated sugar with water in a heavy saucepan over a low heat. When the sugar has become completely liquid, boil the syrup for 1 minute longer.

Wash and dry the limes, and with a small, sharp knife, peel off the zest, without its bitter white pith, and cut into matchstick slivers; boil these in the syrup for 5 minutes then lift out with a fork or slotted spoon and allow the candied peel to cool, scattered on a plate and free of excess syrup.

When the peel is cold, sprinkle superfine sugar on another plate and roll half the peel in this, shaking away the excess crystals. If you like, prepare peels the day before they are needed. The syrup, well-diluted with lime or lemon juice and water, can then be made into a refreshing cool drink.

Remove the mousse from the refrigerator about 30 minutes in advance of serving, and at the last minute, garnish each pot with a combination of both sugared and unsugared peels. Makes enough for 16–20 small porcelain pots or ramekins.

Pumpkin mousse

WINTER WARMTH

An increasing number of people in English-speaking countries are renouncing meat and poultry, for a variety of reasons. I have never eaten these daily, but would hate to forgo the pleasure of them completely.

Recently I have begun to revive and diversify some old favorites like stewed oxtail and poached chicken. I've also been experimenting with grains and pulses, rediscovering the comfort of a good barley soup and the savor of kidney beans. For me, the prospects for cooking with meat and poultry looks more interesting all the time.

BARLEY AND BLACK BEAN SOUP

This is a robust mixture, not without finesse, which can be served as a meal-in-one if escorted by toast, cheese and possibly a green salad.

5 cups basic meat broth,
   see page 102
½ cup black beans
½ cup barley groats (not pearl
   barley)
butter
2 oz salt pork
1 cup minced onion
salt
black pepper
1½ cups finely sliced mushrooms
3 egg yolks
⅔ cup heavy cream
2–4 tablespoons milk
fresh parsley, chopped

Make the broth as described on page 102, browning the beef, veal trimmings and bones, carrot and onion first in a little oil in the saucepan to give a good color.

Rinse black beans and soak them overnight. Rinse barley and soak for 2 hours. Soak pork for 1 hour to remove excess salt. Drain and grind.

To make the soup, melt a little butter in a heavy saucepan, add the pork and onion. Sweat these over a low heat until onion is translucent.

Drain the beans and barley, add to pan with broth. Bring this to a simmer and skim. Boil the soup briskly for at least 25–30 minutes, stirring occasionally, until the beans and barley are tender. Taste for salt near the end of cooking; if pork is still quite salty, you may not need this.

Meanwhile, season and sauté the mushrooms in a little butter over a high heat for several minutes until cooked. Drain their expelled liquid into the soup for added flavor.

Beat together the egg yolks, cream and 2 tablespoons milk. When barley and beans are ready, add mushrooms to soup and beat a little of the hot liquid slowly into egg and cream to warm them. Beat this back into the soup and stir constantly over a low heat until yolks have thickened the mixture; don't let it boil. Thin a little of the mixture with milk if necessary, taste and season. Ladle into bowls and garnish with parsley. Serves 4–5 heartily.

OXTAIL STEW

This is my husband's recipe and I must admit he always makes it better than I do! The secret, he says, is to use up bottles of oxidized wine in the preparation, but I doubt that's all there is to it. The results are wickedly delicious.

6 large pieces oxtail, about 3 lb in total
1 bottle full-bodied red wine
1 large carrot, peeled and halved
1 bay leaf
2 large pinches dried
   mixed herbs
flour
salt
black pepper
vegetable oil
1 large onion, minced
½ cup red kidney beans
2 tablespoons brandy
tomato ketchup
2 oz chorizo or other dried, spiced
   sausage
parsley sprigs

Marinate the oxtail overnight in wine with the carrot, bay leaf and herbs, turning the meat periodically to allow the flavor of the marinade to fully penetrate the meat, tenderizing as it marinates.

Remove the pieces from the marinade, dry them and roll in flour seasoned with salt and pepper. Brown the oxtail all over, with a little oil, in a skillet.

Take the meat from the pan and sweat the onion in the oil left behind until the onion turns golden. Deglaze the pan with a little marinade, and put the onion, all of the marinade and the oxtail into a heavy casserole. Add a dash of salt. Bring the liquid to simmering point on top of the stove. Partially cover and poach in a preheated oven at 300°F for 3–4 hours, turning the meat occasionally until the flesh is tender and falling from the bones. Cool the meat slightly in its winy stock, drain and cool completely. Strain the stock. Cover and refrigerate overnight.

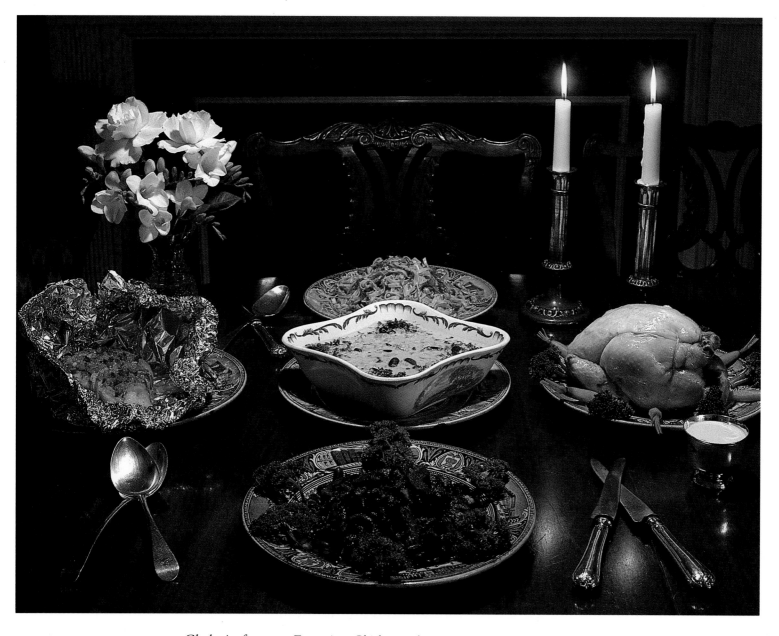

Clockwise from top: Fettuccine, Chicken with ginger, Oxtail stew, Veal cutlets,
Barley and black bean soup

Rinse and drain the kidney beans and soak them in water overnight. Bring the beans to a boil and boil hard for 15 minutes, then simmer for 20–30 minutes further, or until tender. Cool.

Remove the meat from the refrigerator, wipe away excess fat and slice the flesh into bite-size pieces. Put these into a saucepan with the oxtail's stock and heat. Add the brandy, a little ketchup, and a few spoonfuls of water if the sauce is very concentrated. Thinly slice *chorizo*, add with the drained beans and heat all thoroughly, seasoning with salt and pepper. Check flavors, which should be rich and dark. Add a drop more brandy and extra ketchup – and even more water – if necessary.

Simmer for several minutes and serve garnished with parsley and accompanied by boiled, buttered rice, potatoes or noodles. Serves 4.

FETTUCCINE WITH HAM AND AN EGG SAUCE

This dish is a herby pasta with ham, eaten at room temperature, its sabayon sauce flavored with ham poaching liquid. If fresh fettuccine are unavailable, do of course substitute the best dried noodles you can find.

5 oz smoked ham slice
2¼ cups
⅔ cup dry white wine
2 large cloves garlic, crushed
1 long strip lemon zest, pith removed
2 large parsley sprigs
½ cup whole blanched almonds
salt
olive oil
6 egg yolks
black pepper
¾ lb fresh green and red fettuccine or dried of whatever shade
fresh dill and chervil, or 2 other complementary herbs, coarsely chopped

Trim the ham of fat and place in a small saucepan with water, wine, garlic, lemon zest and parsley. Bring to a simmer and poach ham for about 7 minutes. Remove the meat, cool and cut into short, thin strips. Raise heat under liquid and reduce it, aromatics in place, to ⅔ cup. Drain and reserve.

Meanwhile, cut the almonds into pine-nut-like nibs. Toast for 5–10 minutes until pale brown in a preheated oven at 350°F.

Bring a large saucepan of salted water to a boil, add a dash of olive oil and simultaneously heat a smaller saucepan of water. Take a heavy, heat-proof bowl, add the egg yolks and ham-poaching liquid and beat together well. Place bowl over the small pan of water (keeping it just at a simmer) and beat yolks to a thick frothy mousse; a matter of 3–5 minutes. Remove from the water and beat sauce

for 1–2 minutes more. Taste for seasoning.

Set the bowl aside in a warm place, and plunge pasta into boiling salted water. Boil uncovered until *al dente* – anywhere from 1–12 minutes, depending on the noodles – drain, season, toss for several minutes in another bowl to cool. Give sabayon another beat and pour on most of it, tossing noodles with ham, nuts and herbs. Season again, and present pasta with extra sauce in a warmed boat. Serves 3–4.

VEAL CUTLETS BAKED IN FOIL

I usually find veal dry and uninteresting, but a cutlet baked with good condiments in a sealed bag of aluminum foil retains moisture and makes its own piquant sauce. Serve this when you're feeling rich and very hungry.

2 veal cutlets, on bone, from wing end of loin, each weighing about 1 lb and measuring 1–1¼ inches thick
vegetable oil
butter
1 small onion, peeled
2 large cloves garlic, peeled
4 rashers bacon
4 anchovy fillets
black pepper
2 tablespoons dry white vermouth

Sauté cutlets in a little oil and butter for 5 minutes on each side, just to color. Remove from the pan and cool. Mince the onion and garlic and sauté in the cutlets' oil and butter until golden and browning. Divide each rasher in half lengthwise.

Take two large sheets of foil, fold each in half and lay an X of bacon across each center. Place a cutlet on top, cover both cutlets with another X of bacon and wrap all bacon ends around veal. Halve the anchovy fillets lengthwise and lay the fillets across each cutlet. Grind on pep-

per, spread onion and garlic on top of the meat and sprinkle on vermouth.

Bring the edges of the foil up around each set of contents and fold into two loose but airtight bags. Bake in a preheated oven at 375°F for 25 minutes.

Present each bag, intact, on a hot plate; open foil at the table and the burst of aromas will rise to greet you. Have an extra plate to hand for discarding wrapping and accompany the cutlets with mashed potatoes. Serves 2.

POACHED CHICKEN WITH GINGER AND ORANGE

The sliced ginger under the skin and the zest of orange in its poaching liquid give this bird an unexpected and very delicate flavor.

3½ lb roasting chicken, dressed weight
2 oz piece fresh ginger root, peeled and finely sliced
1 carrot, peeled and sliced
1 onion, peeled and sliced
3 long strips orange zest, pith removed
2 parsley stems
4 black peppercorns
1 cup dry white wine
salt
6 tablespoons heavy cream
2 teaspoons arrowroot starch
2 cups sliced carrots
2 cups sliced broccoli
black pepper
butter

Remove any fat from the chicken cavity; wash and wipe inside and out. Peel a third of the ginger, slice this into very thin rounds; carefully loosen skin from chicken breasts and legs by working fingers beneath skin and push the slices into place all over the area. Truss the chicken with soft white string.

Place it in a heavy, deep flameproof casserole that holds it snugly. Add half the remaining ginger, cut up the carrot and onion, 2 strips of orange rind,

Fettuccine with ham

Chicken with ginger

parsley, peppercorns and wine. Pour in water to come halfway up the chicken and hold casserole, covered, in bottom of refrigerator overnight; this gives the flavors time to blend.

Next day, bring the casserole to room temperature and place on top of the stove, bringing the liquid to the simmer. Skim thoroughly, add salt and cover chicken breasts with a double thickness of washed and wrung out muslin, the ends of which should fall into the potential broth to draw this over the bird and baste it during cooking.

Lower heat until the liquid simmers slowly, cover casserole with a close-fitting lid and poach for 1 hour. Test the bird by pressing its flesh and seeing if you can move the legs in their sockets. If in doubt, poach for 5 minutes more.

Carefully strain off $2\frac{1}{2}$ cups of stock and keep chicken hot at the bottom of a very low oven. Keep the chicken in its casserole with a little stock, and with the muslin in place, while you make the sauce and prepare the vegetables.

Let the fat rise in the $2\frac{1}{2}$ cups stock as you beat the cream with the arrowroot starch in a small bowl. A sauce thickened with arrowroot is much subtler than the roux-based variety, which needs long, slow cooking to eliminate its taste of flour.

Thoroughly degrease the stock, beat some of this into the cream and arrowroot to warm them, and beat all together in a saucepan. Set this over a low heat, beating constantly until the sauce comes to a simmer. Add the remaining peeled and sliced ginger and orange zest to refresh these flavors, and let sauce simmer very gently, beating occasionally, for several minutes to reduce and thicken.

Meanwhile, simmer the carrots and broccoli in pans of salted water until tender. Drain and season, add a little butter, and hold.

When the sauce is ready – it should coat the back of a spoon – season and strain it into a heated boat. Drain, de-truss, and carve the chicken, removing ginger from under its skin. Serve with vegetables and sauce. Serves 4.

CELEBRATIONS

Celebration calls for special food – dishes which the cook loves to prepare, which friends will find hard to resist, or which anyone would recognize as a luxury.

Celebrations demand, too, a sense of occasion. At an indoor picnic, for instance, rain will scarcely dampen the whoosh of champagne or the elegant pleasures of a rolled soufflé, a wine-drenched Camembert, or a sparkling sweet jelly, while a springtime birthday that is centered around smoked salmon lasagne has a note of unusual exuberance. But self-indulgent pastimes can be truly simple: a slice of wholemeal toast spread with runny, peppery Brie, or a robust lamb stew that is easy to make and amiably adaptable once prepared.

Cooking with wine has always, for me, the atmosphere of celebration, particularly when the result looks as striking as a slim glass of strawberry cream surrounded by perfect fruits. But, for some of us, nothing else has the allure of a plate of miniature cakes and pastries, or chocolate in as many glorious forms as possible.

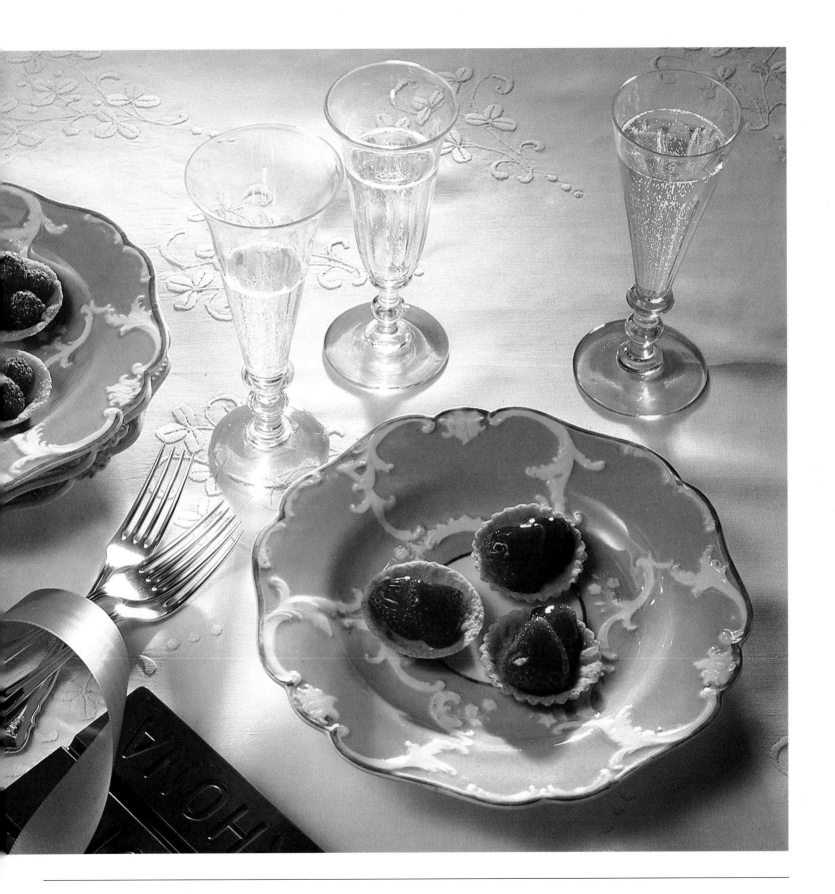

AN INDOOR PICNIC

I love picnics, and have given many – sometimes indoors, faced with last-minute showers or an out-and-out downpour. So I like to plan alternatives to the lawn and field; one way of having your spread and eating it without humidity is to borrow a conservatory, which gives the illusion of outdoors without its changeability.

CAMEMBERT AU MUSCADET

A smooth and surprising alternative to the cheese itself.

1½ Camembert cheeses, (8 oz size) soft and fairly ripe
Muscadet or other dry and fruity white wine
¾ cup sweet butter, softened
black pepper
1¼ cups blanched almonds
oyster crackers or saltines

Pierce the Camemberts all over with a fork, place in a wide bowl, and barely cover the cheese with wine. Leave to marinate for about 12 hours, turning periodically.

Drain off the wine, break up the cheese, and put, with butter, into a blender or the bowl of a food processor fitted with a steel blade. Add a tablespoon or two of the marinating wine (the rest can be added to stock or soup) and a few turns of the pepper mill. Blend until smooth. Taste and add pepper if necessary.

Turn the cheese out into a bowl – it will be a sticky mass – and refrigerate for about 30 minutes, or until firm enough to shape.

Meanwhile, chop the almonds fairly finely and place on a baking sheet. Toast in a preheated oven at 350°F for 5 or 6 minutes or until pale golden brown. Remove from the baking sheet and cool.

When the cheese has firmed, shape it with your hands to re-form a Camembert, cover it all over with the cooled nuts, and lower, on a piece of foil, into a plastic box. Put a lid on the box and refrigerate for several hours or overnight. Remove from the refrigerator and box in good time before eating, to allow cheese to develop its bouquet; on a hot day, try to keep cheese fairly cool once it has been out of the refrigerator for more than 20 minutes, so that the butter does not melt. Serve with oyster crackers or saltines. Serves 6.

LETTUCE AND VINAIGRETTE

To me, the best salad is simply a crisp, green lettuce and a very pungent vinaigrette; the kind that makes you want to wipe up every drop with good bread.

1–2 heads butterhead, loose-leaf or Romaine, depending on size of lettuce and appetites
red wine vinegar
Dijon mustard
2–3 cloves garlic
salt, preferably freshly-ground sea salt
black pepper
superfine sugar
5–6 tablespoons olive oil

Wash and thoroughly dry the lettuce; tear large leaves into smaller pieces and place in a large salad bowl, or hold in a damp cloth until ready to use.

Put about 1 tablespoon of vinegar into a small bowl. Add a generous 1 tablespoon of Dijon mustard. Bruise 2 garlic cloves with the handle of a heavy knife, peel, sprinkle with ½ teaspoon of salt, and with the blade of a small knife, work garlic and salt on the chopping board into a smooth paste. Add to the bowl.

Grind on a liberal amount of salt and pepper, add a teaspoon of superfine sugar, beat all together with a fork and slowly pour on the olive oil. The mustard will cause oil, vinegar, and seasonings to form a thick, creamy emulsion. After adding about 5 tablespoons oil, stop and taste. At this point I usually add more mustard and seasonings and sometimes more garlic! The ideal is very well-seasoned but not too acid; the sugar gives an interesting dimension to the flavor.

When you like the result, beat vigorously. The vinaigrette is ready to use, or can be stored, tightly covered, for weeks in the refrigerator. Bring to room temperature and beat well before pouring.

To serve salad, add a small amount of vinaigrette to a bowl of leaves and toss with your hands, if possible. In this way you can ensure that the leaves are just covered with dressing, without excess. Store the remainder for another time. Serves 6.

Clockwise from top: Lettuce and vinaigrette, Rice flour shortbreads, Cava molds with soft fruits, Marinated vegetables, Mackerel, fennel and anisette, Camembert au Muscadet, Rolled tomato soufflé

ROLLED TOMATO SOUFFLE WITH TOMATO AND PESTO SAUCES

A rolled soufflé is impressive and not difficult to make. A picnic encourages appetites, and you will probably be happier with a pair of soufflés. If so, make 1½ quantities of tomato sauce, double quantities of *pesto* and of soufflé filling, but make and bake each soufflé separately.

TOMATO SAUCE
1 medium onion, minced
2 large cloves garlic, minced
1 carrot, peeled and minced
1 stalk celery, minced
2 tablespoons butter
olive oil
1 can (28 oz) Italian plum tomatoes, with their juices
3 tablespoons dry white wine
2 teaspoons granulated sugar
salt
1 bay leaf
pinch of thyme
fresh parsley stems
black pepper

TOMATO SOUFFLE
5 tablespoons all-purpose flour
1½ cups milk
¾ cup of the tomato sauce
3 egg yolks
salt
black pepper
¾ cup shredded Gruyère cheese
5 egg whites

FILLING
2 shallots or white part of 2 scallions, minced
2 small cloves garlic, minced
1 tablespoon butter
¼ lb ham, chopped
½ cup coarsely chopped walnuts
⅓ cup heavy cream
salt
black pepper
¼ cup shredded Gruyère cheese

PESTO SAUCE
2 large bunches fresh basil, or all the leaves from one large basil plant
¼ cup pine-nuts
2 large cloves garlic, peeled and sliced
⅓–½ cup olive oil
salt
½ cup grated Parmesan cheese
1–2 tablespoons freshly grated pecorino cheese (a hard, sharp, sheeps' milk cheese sold by the piece in Italian delicatessens), to taste
3 tablespoons butter, softened

To make the tomato sauce, sweat the onion, garlic, carrot and celery in butter and a splash of olive oil in a large skillet, covered, for about 10 minutes, until onion becomes soft and golden.

Add the tomatoes and their liquid, the wine and sugar, about a ¼ teaspoon of salt and the herbs. Bring to a boil and simmer uncovered for 20–30 minutes, stirring occasionally. Don't allow the liquid to reduce too much.

Remove the bay and parsley, cool sauce slightly and liquidize. Put through a coarse strainer, add freshly-ground pepper and more salt if necessary. Yields about 2½ cups.

To make the soufflé, line a jelly roll pan measuring 13 × 9 inches with unbuttered parchment in a sheet large enough to extend above sides of pan.

Sift the flour into a small, heavy saucepan. Gradually beat in half the milk, beating absolutely smooth before adding the rest of the milk and beating well. Place the pan over a low heat and beat mixture until thick; let it boil for 30 seconds, beating constantly. Remove the soufflé mixture from heat and beat until smooth.

Beat in the tomato sauce, followed by the egg yolks. Season liberally with salt and pepper; more than you think necessary at this stage, to compensate for the bland egg whites.

Have the shredded Gruyère to hand and make sure it is not stuck together in clumps.

Beat the egg whites to peaks. Beat a quarter of the whites into the soufflé base to lighten it, then fold the lightened base quickly and deftly into the rest of the whites, retaining the volume, and adding the cheese as you go.

Pour the tomato soufflé mixture into the jelly roll pan and lightly spread to level it. Bake in a preheated oven at 375°F for about 40–45 minutes. The soufflé will rise and turn brown.

Meanwhile, prepare the filling. Sweat the minced shallots or scallions and garlic in butter, in a small saucepan, covered, for about 5 minutes until golden. Add the chopped ham, walnuts and cream. Let the cream reduce to form a sauce with the rest, then remove from heat and season to taste. Set aside to cool until you have completed the pesto sauce.

Moisten and wring out a teatowel and spread it onto a working surface.

Test the soufflé with a skewer plunged into the center; if the skewer is piping hot and dry to touch when applied to the back of your hand, the soufflé is ready.

Remove the soufflé from the oven and invert smartly onto a teatowel. Carefully peel off parchment paper with the aid of a spatula; the soufflé will probably stick around the edges but don't worry, just remove any particles which come away with the paper and patch the soufflé as needed; no one will suspect.

Spread with filling, sprinkle on the shredded Gruyère cheese and, using the damp cloth to help you, gently roll up the soufflé – *not* incorporating the towel into the roll. Carefully transfer the soufflé to a large piece of foil in which to store or transport it.

Serve the remaining tomato sauce with this, plus the *pesto* which you have made as follows.

Tear all of the basil leaves into two or three pieces, put into a blender or food processor along with pine-nuts, garlic, ⅓ cup olive oil and a large pinch of salt.

Cava molds

Marinated vegetables

Purée, add more olive oil if the mixture looks too stiff. The purée should retain a certain amount of texture.

Remove to a bowl and beat in the Parmesan. Grate in a small quantity of pecorino from the very hard fragment you have bought – you'll probably need 1 or 2 tablespoons but check and taste, as you don't want too much of its over-powering flavor. Finally, beat in the butter, sample and add more salt if necessary. The result should have a wonderful green color and garlicky flavor.

The beauty of a rolled soufflé is its versatility and ease of transport. You can slice and serve it cold for an outdoor picnic – it slices more neatly that way than when hot; or if near an oven, you can re-heat it foil-wrapped, at 350°F for 15 minutes, then slice and serve hot. The tomato sauce can be heated too, but not the *pesto*. Whatever your method, the rolled tomato soufflé and sauces are equally good. Serves 6.

MARINATED VEGETABLES

The acid in this marinade makes the vegetables piquant and crisp; best eaten in small quantities and garnished with a soft cheese like Dolcelatte.

¾ lb fat, flavorful carrots, peeled
salt
¾ lb medium zucchini
2 large cloves garlic
dried oregano
black pepper
2 tablespoons red wine vinegar
olive oil
6 oz Dolcelatte cheese

Cut the carrots into 2 inch lengths and drop into a pan of boiling, salted water. Simmer about 3 minutes; they should only half cook. Remove carrots, refresh under cold water to arrest cooking, and dry.

Wash but do not peel the zucchini,

trim, cut into 2 inch lengths, and drop into boiling, salted water. Simmer for about 2 minutes, drain when half cooked, refresh and dry.

Cut both vegetables lengthwise into slices about ¼ inch thick, and then cut slices into square sticks. Dry on paper towels and put into a deep bowl.

Bruise the garlic cloves with the handle of a heavy knife, peel and quarter them and add to the vegetables. Sprinkle on a large pinch of oregano and season with salt and pepper. Add wine vinegar and enough olive oil to coat the vegetables completely when turned repeatedly in the mixture.

Cover and refrigerate the vegetables and marinade for at least 12 hours, turning periodically. The vegetables will become very crisp and the garlic and oregano permeate the vegetables. Remove the garlic before serving at room temperature, garnished with crumbled Dolcelatte. Serves 6.

MACKEREL, FENNEL AND ANISETTE

Another marinade, which in this dish features the complementary flavors of mackerel and aniseed in vegetable and alcoholic forms.

---

2 lb mackerel fillets
3 medium bulbs fennel, with leaves if
  possible
½ teaspoon coriander seeds
¼ teaspoon celery seeds
8 black peppercorns
1 teaspoon sea salt
6–7 tablespoons vegetable oil
juice of 1 lime
scant 1 teaspoon anisette liqueur (I use
  Marie Brizard, available in
  miniatures)

Skin the mackerel fillets and remove all bones; cut into bite-size pieces. Wash and trim the fennel, saving the leaves and green of upper stems as a garnish. Cut the bulbs into small pieces and put with mackerel into a wide glass or porcelain dish.

Pound the coriander and celery seeds, peppercorns and salt in a mortar with a pestle and strew the results over fish and fennel. Dribble on the oil, lime juice and anisette; turn mixture well in marinade, cover and refrigerate overnight, turning periodically. The acid in the marinade will partly 'cook' the fish and the anisette will reinforce the taste of the fennel.

Line the broiler tray with foil and strew it with fish, fennel and enough marinade to moisten well. Don't try to crowd on too much at once, but broil the fish and fennel in several batches, about 2 minutes per side. Remove the mackerel, and broil the fennel longer, until slightly charred. When everything has been cooked, serve, with juices, unchilled, within a few hours of broiling. Garnish with the reserved fennel leaves and the thinly sliced green of the reserved fennel stems. Serves 6.

RICE FLOUR SHORTBREADS

Rice flour and a lot of butter gives these a rich crispness. They are a delightful accompaniment to the cava molds.

---

1 cup sweet butter, softened
grated zest of large lemon
½ cup superfine sugar
generous 1½ cups all-purpose flour
⅔ cup rice flour
pinch of salt

Cream butter and lemon zest, gradually cream in the sugar; sift together the flours and salt and beat into the butter.

Break off bits of dough and roll into balls the size of marbles. Flatten into circles about 1¾ inches in diameter on heavy baking sheets, score with a fork and bake in a preheated oven at 375°F for 10–15 minutes, until just beginning to brown. Leave the cookies on baking sheets for 2–3 minutes before removing with a spatula. Cool on racks and store in airtight tins. Makes about 48.

CAVA MOLDS WITH SOFT FRUITS

Champagne gelatin is a luxury, but champagne is a needless extravagance when cava, the Spanish *méthode champenoise*, is both a cheaper and a more successful alternative because of its grapy flavor. It must, however, be a dry and fruity one – run-of-the-mill sparkling wine will not do. Delightfully, bubbles prickle on the tongue as you eat the gelatin.

---

5 sheets gelatin
2 cups water
generous ½ cup granulated sugar
zest and juice of 1 lemon
1¼ cups cava, chilled – Conde de
  Caralt seco gives a good result
soft fruits for garnish: bananas, kiwis,
  strawberries, raspberries

Soften the gelatin in a jug of water and drain. Heat the 2 cups water in a saucepan, add gelatin and dissolve. Stir in sugar, pared and pithless lemon zest cut into strips and lemon juice. Heat mixture to just below boiling point, draw pan off the heat, cover and let steep for 30 minutes. Strain the liquid into a bowl through a fine strainer lined with a double thickness of muslin; discard the zest.

Cool gelatin almost to the setting point and stir in cava, retaining as much of the bubble as possible by not overbeating.

Spoon or pour into ramekins or other small molds; clear ones will show the gelatin's translucence to advantage. Refrigerate until set; don't make more than a day in advance because molds will then begin to lose their sparkle.

Serve them with the soft red fruits, and with sliced bananas and kiwi fruit, which can be cut up in advance, turned in lemon juice and transported to the site of your picnic in small containers. Makes 8.

CHOCOLATE

I can think of few self-indulgences as versatile, or satisfying, as chocolate. It comforts and impresses; from the candy store bar, eaten on a Friday evening train to the country, to the most sophisticated Parisian bitter chocolate cake eaten in a smart patisserie.

The recipes given here are based on a small number of ingredients, which must be the best: chocolate made with cocoa butter, not vegetable oil; heavy cream, sweet butter; vanilla and almond extracts, not 'flavorings'; Kirsch, Grand Marnier and good dark rum. It's luxury, and worth it.

CHOCOLATE-CHEESE BROWNIES

CHOCOLATE LAYER

6 squares (6 oz) semisweet dark chocolate, broken up
3 tablespoons sweet butter
2 eggs
generous $\frac{3}{4}$ cup superfine sugar
$\frac{2}{3}$ cup all-purpose plain flour
$\frac{1}{4}$ teaspoon salt
$\frac{1}{2}$ teaspoon baking powder
$\frac{1}{2}$ teaspoon vanilla extract
few drops almond extract
$\frac{1}{2}$ cup coarsely chopped walnuts

CHEESE LAYER

$\frac{1}{4}$ cup sweet butter, softened
$\frac{3}{4}$ cup Ricotta or softened cream cheese
generous $\frac{1}{4}$ cup superfine sugar
2 eggs, beaten
1 teaspoon vanilla extract
2 tablespoons all-purpose flour, sifted
$\frac{1}{4}$ teaspoon salt

Melt the chocolate and the butter in a small, heavy saucepan which you have set, covered, in a larger pan of just-boiled water. Beat the chocolate until smooth and set aside to cool.

For the cheese layer, cream the butter with the cheese, gradually beat in sugar, beaten eggs and vanilla, creaming thoroughly after each addition. Blend the sifted flour and salt. The mixture will be quite runny. Set aside.

For the chocolate layer, beat the eggs, gradually adding the superfine sugar, until very thick, light, and increased in bulk. This is best done with a hand-held electric mixer. Sift together the flour, salt and baking powder and blend into the egg, beating with a wire whip if necessary to eliminate lumps. Blend in the cooled chocolate and butter, the extracts, then the walnuts.

Spread half the chocolate batter into a well-buttered 8 inch square pan. Top with cheese mixture and spoon the remaining chocolate on top. Zig-zag a wide-bladed knife through batter to get a marbled effect.

Bake at 350°F for 25–30 minutes until *just* cooked – a knife inserted in the center should come out clean and the top will have begun to crack. Let the pan cool and cut into 20 small brownies.

CHOCOLATE-DIPPED STRAWBERRIES

20 perfect strawberries, with stems
about 12 squares (12 oz) semisweet dark chocolate, 6 squares (6 oz) finely chopped, 6 squares (6 oz) finely grated

Make sure that the strawberries are ripe, firm, clean, and completely dry before dipping in chocolate, otherwise the results will be imperfect.

Put the finely-chopped chocolate into a small heavy saucepan with a tight-fitting lid that will keep out moisture. Set this into a pan of just-boiled water and melt the chocolate as for the chocolate-cheese brownies; be sure to keep steam away from the chocolate, as it alters the consistency.

When melting is achieved, remove the pan from water and beat the chocolate until smooth. Test the temperature with a thermometer; it should be 113°F. If it is lower, return the pan to water and cover until this temperature is reached. Take off the heat and beat in the finely-grated chocolate, a spoonful at a time, until the temperature is lowered to 79°F. Return briefly to the hot pan, and stir with the thermometer in, until the temperature reaches 90–92°F. These temperatures are important and should be accurately judged. By tempering the chocolate in this controlled way you are re-forming the correct emulsion of cocoa butter and chocolate solids, necessary to give the dipped strawberries a hard surface with a professional sheen and no white streaks.

Holding each strawberry by its stem, dip quickly into chocolate to cover about three-quarters of its surface, and place on waxed paper on a baking sheet. The chocolate should harden in about 5 minutes, but if not, put the strawberries briefly into a refrigerator. Remove and store in cool, dry place (not the refrigerator). Don't allow the strawberries to touch each other. They do not keep and should be eaten on the day made. Makes about 20.

PAIR OF CHOCOLATE CHESTNUT ROLLS

CHOCOLATE SPONGE CAKE
6 eggs
1 cup superfine sugar
½ cup plus 2 tablespoons unsweetened cocoa
pinch of salt

CHESTNUT BUTTERCREAM
½ cup granulated sugar
3 tablespoons water
4 egg yolks
about ¾ cup sweet butter, softened
about ¾ cup unsweetened chestnut purée

TO FINISH
confectioner's sugar

Line two jelly roll pans, each measuring 13 × 9 inches, with parchment paper large enough to extend above sides.

Using the ingredients for the cake, separate the eggs and beat the yolks, gradually adding ¾ cup of the sugar, until very light, thick, and increased in bulk. Sift in the cocoa and salt and beat mixture with a wooden spoon until well-blended.

Half-beat the whites, adding the remaining sugar until stiff peaks form. Beat about a third of whites into cocoa mixture to lighten it; pour this onto the rest of the whites and fold together deftly and quickly.

Divide the batter between the cake

Clockwise from top: Chocolate chip cookies, Chocolate chestnut rolls, Chocolate-cheese brownies, Chocolate-dipped strawberries, Chocolate and walnut cake, Frozen chocolate mousse, Le Paradis

pans, spreading evenly, tap each pan smartly against working surface to settle the contents. Bake on two shelves of a preheated oven at 375°F for about 25 minutes or until the cake on the top shelf tests done (the cake on the lower shelf will take longer). Turn each out onto a separate teatowel which has been covered with a sheet of parchment paper. Peel the parchment paper carefully from the back of each cake, and lay a fresh sheet over it. Roll up each towel around its sponge and set to cool.

While the cakes are baking, prepare the buttercream. Make a syrup by boiling sugar and water up to 245°F, while beating yolks until thickened and light. Beat the syrup into the yolks and beat the mixture for several minutes until thick and cold. It will grow significantly in volume. Beat in the soft butter bit by bit, until the buttercream suddenly comes together and is firm and spreadable. You may need to add a little more butter than the ¾ cup in order to achieve this. Strain the chestnut purée directly into the buttercream, and beat to incorporate.

Unroll each sponge, remove the inner parchment paper and divide the buttercream between the two, spreading thickly to edges. Roll up each cake and don't worry if they crack a little. Trim the ends with a serrated knife, sift a light coating of confectioners' sugar over both. Serve thinly sliced. Serves 8.

CHOCOLATE CHIP COOKIES

1 cup sweet butter, softened
generous ½ cup superfine sugar
1 cup packed, sifted dark brown sugar
2 eggs, beaten
1 tablespoon vanilla extract
2 cups all-purpose flour
1 teaspoon baking soda
1 teaspoon salt
1½ cups coarsely chopped walnuts
1⅔ cups chocolate chips

Cream butter well, gradually add the two sugars, the eggs and vanilla, creaming thoroughly after each addition. Sift together the dry ingredients and fold into the rest, followed by the walnuts and chocolate chips.

Drop small spoonfuls onto heavy baking sheets; flatten slightly and leave space between the cookies.

Bake in a preheated oven at 375°F for about 10 minutes until just browning and still chewy. Remove from the oven, but leave on baking sheets for about 1 minute, then cool on wire racks. Makes about 48.

FROZEN CHOCOLATE MOUSSE

9 squares (9 oz) semisweet dark chocolate, broken up
⅔ cup sweet butter
1 tablespoon dark rum
4 egg yolks
6 egg whites
scant ¼ cup icing sugar

TO SERVE
chocolate coffee beans
caramel custard (see page 122)

Oil the sides of a loaf pan measuring 8½ × 3 × 3 inches and line the bottom of the pan with a strip of unoiled waxed paper.

Melt the chocolate with the butter, in a small, heavy saucepan which you have set, covered, into a larger pan of just-boiled water. Reheat the water as necessary to melt chocolate completely. When ready, beat smooth, remove the saucepan from the water, and beat the mixture for 1–2 minutes to cool slightly.

Add a dash of rum – no more than about 1 tablespoon – and the egg yolks. Beat again to thicken. When cool, beat the egg whites to soft peaks and beat in the icing sugar until firm peaks form. Beat about a quarter of the whites into the chocolate base to lighten it, then pour the chocolate onto the whites, folding them together quickly and deftly. Pour the mousse into the prepared pan and freeze overnight.

To serve, plunge the pan quickly into a bowl of warm water, run a knife around the four sides, and turn the mousse out onto a platter. Peel off the waxed paper. Strew chocolate coffee beans around the mousse, and slice it thinly with a sharp, heated knife, adding a few coffee beans and the caramel custard to each serving. Serves 6–8.

CARAMEL CUSTARD

scant 1 cup granulated sugar
8 egg yolks
vanilla bean, split
2½ cups milk

Make a caramel with the sugar and a little water, bringing it up to a good color (370°F). Meanwhile, beat the yolks until thick and pale, while infusing the vanilla bean in the milk brought up to the scalding point in a heavy saucepan.

When the caramel is ready, remove from heat, take the bean from the milk, and, covering hands with a cloth, pour some of the hot milk into the caramel. It will bubble and froth alarmingly. Slowly pour on the rest of the milk and return mixture to the heat. Bring back to a boil and beat thoroughly to dissolve any pieces of caramel which may have stuck to the pan.

Pour this slowly onto yolks, beating fast, then put the mixture back into the milk pan. Over a high heat beat vigorously, bringing the custard up to its first boil and sudden thickening. Immediately remove custard from the heat and strain into a bowl to prevent curdling. Beat the custard afterward to cool rapidly.

Chill the custard thoroughly and serve in a jug. Serves 6–8 with mousse.

LE PARADIS

CHOCOLATE SPONGE
3 eggs
½ cup superfine sugar
4 tablespoons unsweetened cocoa
pinch of salt

CHOCOLATE MOUSSE
10½ squares (10½ oz) semisweet dark chocolate, broken up
¾ cup plus 1 tablespoon sweet butter
5 egg yolks
dash of dark rum
1¼ sheets gelatin
6 egg whites
1½ tablespoons confectioners' sugar

GENOISE
scant ¼ cup all-purpose flour
¼ cup potato flour
pinch of salt
2 tablespoons sweet butter
3 eggs
½ cup superfine sugar

CREME CHANTILLY
1 sheet gelatin
1⅔ cup heavy cream
about 2 tablespoons superfine sugar
Grand Marnier
Kirsch

GLAZE
7 squares (7 oz) semisweet dark chocolate, broken up
¼ cup sweet butter
capful of vegetable oil

LEAVES
12–16 rose leaves
2 small bars semisweet dark chocolate

Make the chocolate sponge exactly as for Chocolate Chestnut Roll (see page 121) but using only one lined 13 × 9 inch jelly roll pan. When baked, turn cake out on to teatowels and parchment paper, cover with another towel and don't roll up.

While sponge is baking, make a

chocolate mousse exactly as for the Frozen Chocolate Mousse with Caramel Custard (see page 121), but using the quantities stated here. After adding the yolks and rum to mixture, beat in soaked sheets of gelatin, which have been dissolved in a little hot water. Then proceed with the recipe. When the mousse is finished, refrigerate it in a mixing bowl until ready to use.

For the *génoise*, line the same size jelly roll pan with parchment paper as for the sponge. Sift the flours and salt together twice and reserve. Melt the butter in a small metal cup and let cool. Put the eggs into a medium-size heatproof mixing bowl and set bowl on top of a small saucepan of boiling water.

Begin to beat the eggs with a large wire whip or with a hand-held electric mixer set to high speed. After 1 minute gradually add the sugar and continue to beat until the mixture has grown thick and pale and begins to form a ribbon when the mixer is raised. This takes about 5–10 minutes. Keep checking that the mixture is not getting too hot.

Remove the bowl from the pan and keep beating until the eggs and sugar are completely cold, by which time the volume will have tripled. This takes about 15 minutes with an electric mixer, or twice that time by hand.

Gradually sift the dry ingredients directly into bowl, folding them deftly with your hand – this is the gentlest and most thorough method of folding a *génoise*, with the least loss of volume. Fold in the melted butter, pour into the lined pan, spread evenly, rap smartly on working surface. Bake in a preheated oven at 375°F for about 25–30 minutes or until cake tests done. Turn out as for the sponge.

While the *génoise* is cooling, make *crème chantilly*. Dissolve soaked gelatin in a little hot water, cool slightly and add a few tablespoons cream. Whip the rest of cream to a soft shape, add the sugar and just a little Grand Marnier – this should be only slightly sweet and just suggest the flavor of Grand Marnier – whip in the liquid gelatin-cream mixture and beat until firm but spreadable. Refrigerate until ready to use.

Choose a 9 inch square cake pan with high sides, and line the bottom with unbuttered waxed paper, cut exactly to size. Cut the chocolate sponge and *génoise*, which should have cooled by now, to fit closely inside the pan. Split the sponge into two very thin layers with a long serrated knife. Cut *génoise* into three such layers (use the crusty top one for some other purpose). Do this as carefully as possible, but if the layers break up a bit, do not worry; they can be easily patched in assembling the cake.

Put the better of the two *génoise* layers onto the waxed paper inside the pan, and lightly moisten with a little water that has been sparingly flavored with Kirsch. Apply this mixture with a pastry brush, using just enough to moisten the cake. Reserve a little chocolate mousse – about 2 tablespoons' worth, with which to stick leaves down later – and spread half of the remaining mousse evenly over the whole of the *génoise*. Place the poorer of two chocolate layers on top of the mousse and moisten with Kirsch and water. Spread all of the *chantilly* over sponge, cover with second layer of *génoise*, moisten, and spread on remaining mousse. Cover with the second chocolate layer, and press assembly so that cake when turned out will be flat and even. Refrigerate for several hours to set.

Turn the cake out and make the glaze. Melt the chocolate and butter, add oil and stir. Allow the temperature of mixture to fall to 91°F, then pour icing over top of cake and spread smoothly. Refrigerate.

Wash and dry the rose leaves. Melt semisweet chocolate on a plate over hot water. Take each leaf by its stem and drag it shiny side down, through the chocolate until thickly coated. Dry on waxed paper in a refrigerator until hard, then peel off rose leaves from stem end.

Remove the cake from the refrigerator when glaze has set, and with a long sharp knife, cut off the four sides to make an attractive square, heating the blade in the steam of a kettle before each cut and being careful not to drag the knife through the cake while doing this, lest you blur the lines of layering. Transfer to a flat serving plate, fill a small plain-tipped pastry bag with the reserved mousse and pipe a little mousse onto four corners of cake so that three or four leaves can be stuck in clusters at each. Refrigerate cake until about half an hour before serving. Serves 8.

CHOCOLATE AND WALNUT CAKE

CAKE
6 squares (6 oz) semisweet dark chocolate, broken up
¾ cup sweet butter
3 eggs
1 cup superfine sugar
¼ cup finely ground walnuts, freshly prepared
5 tablespoons all-purpose flour
1 tablespoon potato flour
pinch of salt
1 extra egg white

GANACHE
8 squares (8 oz) semisweet dark chocolate
1 cup heavy cream

TO FINISH
handful of walnut halves

Use a round cake pan, 8 inches in diameter and 1¾ inches deep, with a removable bottom. Butter the sides of the pan. Cut a circle of parchment paper to fit bottom exactly. Butter and flour it on one side, and flour sides of the pan. Separate the eggs.

Melt the chocolate and butter as for the Chocolate-cheese Brownies, while beating yolks and all but 1 tablespoon sugar, with an electric mixer, until very pale, thick, and increased in volume. Beat the chocolate and butter smooth, cool slightly and blend into the yolks and sugar. When this mixture is thoroughly cool, sift together the walnuts, the two flours and salt, and beat these into the base.

Beat the egg whites to soft peaks, beat in the extra tablespoon of superfine sugar and beat whites stiff. Fold with the base, pour into pan and bake in a preheated oven at 375°F for about 40–45 minutes until the top has risen and begun to crack, and a fine metal skewer inserted into the center tests oily, and not dry. The middle should remain slightly under-cooked. Cool in the pan on a wire rack. The top will crack and separate from the body of the cake, which is normal.

When cold, push the cake up from the side of the pan, reverse it onto a plate, remove the bottom of pan and peel off the parchment paper; invert the cake onto a rack. Replace any parts of the top which may come off; make the *ganache*.

Break up the chocolate and put with the cream into a small, heavy saucepan directly over a low heat. As chocolate starts to melt, beat the mixture with a wire whip. By the time the cream comes to a boil, the chocolate will have melted. Remove from the heat and beat smooth. Pour into a medium-size bowl and cool, stirring occasionally.

When cool, beat at high speed with a hand-held electric mixer for about 5 minutes, until mixture just holds soft peaks. It will lighten and increase in bulk. Don't overbeat, or *ganache* will stiffen. As it hardens fast apply *ganache* quickly to top, and the side of the cake. Smooth the top, make pattern with a wide-bladed knife, and decorate with half-walnuts. Cut into small slices; this cake is rich and very filling. Serves 8.

A BIRTHDAY PARTY

My birthday is in May, and this is the sort of party I enjoy: green and snappy, with foretastes of summer in the flavors, textures and coloring.

SMOKED SALMON LASAGNE

This is light and exotic and easily made with the help of a food processor. I find Barilla lasagne is the best brand, available from good Italian grocers.

> about 6 oz green lasagne
> about 6 oz white lasagne
> salt
> vegetable oil
> $\frac{1}{2}$ cup walnuts
> 1 bunch of fresh cilantro
> 2 cups whole-milk Ricotta cheese
> 1 egg yolk
> black pepper
> 3 oz smoked salmon, very thinly sliced and finely shredded
> 3 cups shredded Mozzarella cheese
> $\frac{1}{2}$ cup freshly grated Parmesan cheese
> $\frac{1}{4}$ cup melted butter

Copiously butter a 6–9 cup heavy baking dish measuring about $9 \times 12 \times 2$ inches.

Boil the lasagne, a few pieces at a time, in two large pans of salted water with a good spoonful of oil in each, for about 10 minutes per batch. Remove the lasagne from the water with a wide spatula and drain, side by side, on paper towels.

Finely chop the walnuts and cilantro leaves in a food processor. Beat the Ricotta cheese with the egg yolk, walnuts and cilantro leaves. Season to taste.

Line the baking dish with a layer of white pasta, the pieces overlapping by about $\frac{1}{2}$ inch and lining halfway up sides. With wet fingers, spread half the Ricotta mixture. Cover with overlapping pieces of green lasagne. Strew the salmon over the pasta.

Sprinkle half the Mozzarella over the salmon. Cover with half of Parmesan, dribble on half the melted butter and season.

Add a layer of white lasagne, spread on remaining Ricotta, cover with green lasagne and rest of cheeses and butter. Season well.

This dish can be assembled and refrigerated, foil-covered, overnight. Bring to room temperature before baking. Bake, still covered, in a preheated oven at 350°F for 15 minutes. Remove the foil and return to the oven for about 35 minutes until lasagne is very hot. Brown under a preheated broiler if necessary. Leave to rest for a few minutes before slicing. Serve salmon lasagne with a green salad made with a mixture of leaves. Serves 6.

GREEN SALAD

I love the Smoked Salmon Lasagne served simply with this. Arrange young Romaine lettuce leaves, oakleaf lettuce and corn salad or lamb's lettuce on a large glass platter. Purslane would be wonderful in the summer with one or two other kinds of leaves. Use whatever leaves are in season that take your fancy. Strew on scissored chives. Make up a vinaigrette dressing using 1 part lemon juice to 3 parts olive oil and several spoonfuls of Dijon mustard, plus seasoning and more chives. Pour over salad and toss to coat leaves.

BUTTERMILK VICHYSSOISE WITH WATERCRESS

I think that vichyssoise, a chilled soup, is much better – and lighter – finished with buttermilk instead of cream. A few leaves of watercress blended in shortly before serving intensify both the color and flavor marvelously.

> generous $\frac{3}{4}$ lb potatoes, peeled weight, thinly sliced
> $\frac{1}{2}$ lb onions, peeled weight, thinly sliced
> $4\frac{1}{2}$ pints homemade chicken broth, as prepared on page 100, fairly weak; or half chicken broth of normal strength and half water
> salt
> $1\frac{1}{4}$ lb leeks, trimmed weight, white part plus part of green
> black pepper
> $\frac{3}{4}$–1 cup buttermilk
> lemon juice
> watercress

Put the sliced potatoes and onions into a large, heavy pot (or two smaller ones), with the broth or broth and water mix. Add salt, half cover, and bring to a boil. Reduce heat and simmer very briefly, for 5 minutes before adding the leeks.

When trimming the leeks, save a little of the inner green for garnish, wash the leeks well and chop. Add to the broth, bring back to simmer, and cook for about 5–7 minutes until all the vegetables are done. Cool the soup slightly, then liquidize until smooth, season to taste.

Pass the mixture through a coarse strainer, forcing through all but the most fibrous parts of the purée. Add the buttermilk and a tablespoon lemon juice to sharpen the taste. Adjust the season-

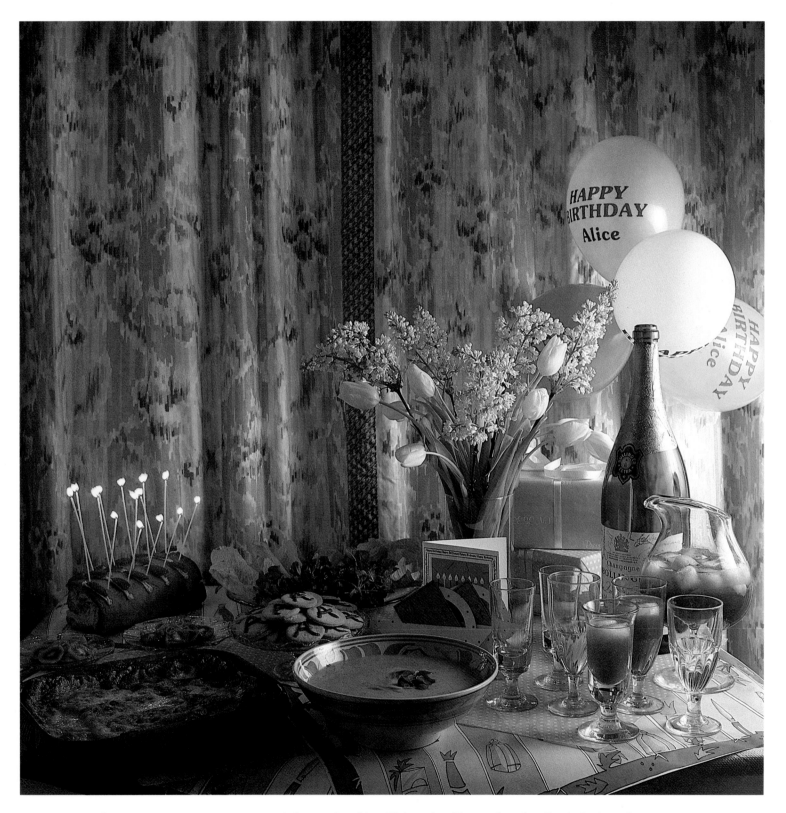

Clockwise from top: Kiwis in syrup, Green salad, Initial cookies, Vichyssoise, Vermouth cooler, Smoked salmon lasagne, Hedgehog cake

ing, remembering that soup thickens as it cools and that chilling dulls flavor.

Chill thoroughly. Shortly before serving, blanch a small handful of watercress leaves for 10 seconds in rapidly boiling water. Drain, refresh them and squeeze dry. Purée the watercress in a food processor, add a little soup and whiz again. Stir this well into the vichyssoise; its color and flavor should intensify subtly. Adjust the seasoning. Ladle the soup into freezer-chilled bowls. Garnish with watercress leaves and a little blanched and refreshed julienned green of the the leek. Serves 6–8.

THE HEDGEHOG

The cake is a jelly roll of sponge and strawberry buttercream, studded with strawberries and, naturally, candles. Like a hedgehog, it should look friendly and rather lovable.

SPONGE CAKE
$\frac{1}{3}$ cup potato flour
$\frac{1}{3}$ cup all-purpose flour
pinch of salt
2 tablespoons sweet butter
4 eggs
$\frac{2}{3}$ cup superfine sugar

SYRUP
1 tablespoon granulated sugar
2 tablespoons boiling water
Kirsch

BUTTERCREAM
1 cup milk, heated
3 egg yolks
scant $\frac{1}{2}$ cup superfine sugar
1 cup sweet butter, softened
$\frac{1}{3}$ pint fresh strawberries,
    or frozen ones thawed
    and drained
red food coloring

TO FINISH
$\frac{1}{4}$ pint fresh strawberries

Line a jelly roll pan of 13 × 9 inches with an unbuttered sheet of parchment paper, cut to extend above the sides of the pan.

To make the sponge, sift the flours and salt together three times and reserve them on a piece of waxed paper. Melt and cool butter.

Break the eggs into a large heatproof bowl and beat them briefly, using a hand-held electric mixer. Set bowl over a small saucepan containing simmering water and beat eggs at highest speed gradually adding sugar.

Beat the mixture until triple in bulk, remove the bowl from heat and continue beating until eggs and sugar are cold. Using a flexible rubber spatula, quickly start to fold in the sifted ingredients, tipping them gradually down their piece of waxed paper into the bowl. Fold in the butter until just combined so as not to lose the volume. Pour the mixture across the surface of the paper-lined pan, smoothing it quickly. All movements should be deft and economical.

Tap the pan against a working surface to settle and level its contents. Bake in a preheated oven at 375°F for 20–25 minutes, reducing the oven temperature to 350°F after 20 minutes if the top is browning too much.

Test the cake with a thin trussing needle, and if done, turn out the cake onto a teatowel that has been covered with a sheet of parchment paper. Peel the paper carefully away from the bottom of the cake. Lay a fresh sheet of parchment paper over the cake and, starting at one of the short ends, roll up the towel around the sponge. Cool.

To make the syrup, dissolve the sugar in the boiling water. When cold, add enough Kirsch to flavor.

To make the buttercream, prepare a very light custard with milk, yolks and sugar (beating egg yolks and superfine sugar together for several minutes before pouring on hot milk will achieve this). See page 34 for the basic method ignoring hazelnuts, vanilla and Kirsch. Strain and cool.

Cream the butter until very soft. Gradually beat and whip in the custard until the mixture is the consistency of a spreadable cream. Purée the strawberries until smooth and add just enough to the buttercream to impart their flavor – probably less than the full amount. If necessary, beat in the tiniest drop of red food coloring.

Unroll the cooled sponge, remove the parchment paper and brush the syrup over the entire inner surface of cake. Spread the buttercream thickly right to the edges. Reroll the cake and don't worry if it cracks slightly. Fit a $\frac{1}{8}$–$\frac{1}{4}$ inch plain tip onto a pastry bag, pile in some buttercream and pipe the roll with diagonal stripes. Cut fresh strawberries into 'darts' and stud these over the stripes. Prepare and assemble cake within a few hours of eating. Serves 6.

KIWIS IN SYRUP

Someone asked me recently if I'd taken the pledge against kiwi fruit; I must have, unconsciously, as there are so few in this book. The question amused me so much that I actually began to think about this very agreeable 'gooseberry' which has been vulgarized by over-exploitation. The combination of flavors here goes well with Initial Cookies.

Kiwis in syrup

*1 cup fruity, but not sweet, white or
    rosé wine*
*3 tablespoons clear honey, not heather
    or lavender-scented*
strip of lemon zest, without pith
6 (3 oz each) kiwi fruit

Simmer the wine, honey and finely-julienned lemon zest until the liquid has reduced to about $\frac{3}{4}$ cup and tastes balanced and pleasantly sweet.

Trim kiwi fruits and peel away the skin in strips from end to end, using a small, sharp knife. Slice the fruit across, put into the syrup and leave to cool.

To serve, divide the drained slices among six dessert plates, garnish with a few strands of lemon julienne and spoon over a little syrup. The syrup can be prepared in advance, refrigerated and reheated when required.

Serves 6. For 8 portions, add two more kiwi fruits and increase the syrup quantities by a third.

INITIAL COOKIES

When the cake has no inscription, these are the cookies to follow it. Short and delicious.

1 cup sweet butter, softened
scant 1 cup superfine sugar
2 eggs, lightly whisked
*1 teaspoon vanilla extract,
    not 'flavoring'*
2$\frac{1}{4}$ cups all-purpose flour
$\frac{1}{4}$ teaspoon baking powder
large pinch of salt
*1$\frac{1}{2}$ squares (1$\frac{1}{2}$ oz) semisweet dark
    chocolate, melted and cooled*

Cream the butter, gradually beat in the sugar, then the eggs and vanilla. Sift the flour, baking powder and salt, then beat into the butter and sugar mixture to form a dough. Weigh the dough, cut off three-quarters and work the chocolate into the remaining quarter of dough.

Initial cookies

Divide the vanilla dough in half, wrap the halves separately and refrigerate them until firm but not hard. Roll out one piece to $\frac{1}{4}$ inch thick on a floured board. Cut out circles with a 2 inch cutter and transfer those to heavy baking sheets; space the cookies well since they will spread slightly in the oven.

Soften the chocolate dough by working it with a wooden spoon in a bowl set over a saucepan of very hot water. Mash and beat until dough becomes very malleable, like the consistency of taffy, but not so hot that the butter oozes. Spoon the chocolate dough into a pastry bag fitted with a $\frac{1}{8}$ inch plain tip, and pipe an initial onto each cookie, tidying the shapes of letters as you go along with the tip of a sharp knife.

Refrigerate the cookies for about 7 minutes to firm and preserve their shape. Bake them in a preheated oven at 350°F for 10 minutes or until the edges brown. Remove from sheets and cool completely on wire racks.

Keep the chocolate-filled bag in a warm place between each use. Roll out the remaining vanilla dough, reroll the off-cuts, and proceed as above until all the cookies are baked. These cookies keep for weeks in airtight tins. Serve with kiwis in syrup. Makes about 72.

VERMOUTH COOLER

The mixture of liquors for this aperitif sounds rather alarming, but results are smooth and refreshing, with a welcome *pétillance*. Champagne can be served to those who like their drinks more orthodox.

$\frac{3}{4}$ cup Italian red vermouth
$\frac{3}{4}$ cup French dry white vermouth
*6 tablespoons crème de framboise
    (raspberry liqueur)*
*1 cup plus 2 tablespoons fresh orange
    juice*
grenadine syrup
spiral of lemon zest, without pith
2$\frac{1}{2}$ cups Perrier water, chilled
lots of ice

Mix together the red and white vermouth, liqueur and orange juice. Add a little grenadine syrup to improve the color, immerse the lemon zest and put to cool. Just before serving, pour the drink into a handsome jug, top up with Perrier to taste; you may prefer slightly more or less than 2$\frac{1}{2}$ cups. Stir, add more grenadine if the color needs brightening, then drop in the ice.

Makes enough for 6 glasses-plus. To serve 8 people, or 6 more generously, make up to 1$\frac{1}{2}$ or even double quantities of the cooler.

Vermouth cooler

COOKING WITH WINE

Wine and its derivatives enhance the quality of food in as many ways as you would expect from a family in which champagne is a cousin to vinegar, and vermouth – a wine enhanced with barks, herbs and spices – is related to that famous wine-distillate, Cognac.

In these recipes I have used wine and some of the members of its network of kin as condiments or as aromatic poaching liquids that turn themselves into flavorful sauces.

ASPARAGUS VINAIGRETTE

A classic, using oil and vinegar – the wine derivative *vin aigre*, or 'sour wine' – with sorrel and chopped egg, as unusual accents to the splendor of asparagus.

---

2 tablespoons red wine vinegar
salt
black pepper
$\frac{1}{2}$ cup olive oil
1 cup very small, young sorrel leaves
2 hard-boiled eggs
2 lb fresh green asparagus

Make the vinaigrette about 2 hours before serving by mixing together vinegar, salt and pepper, beating in the oil. Stem the sorrel, wash and dry the leaves, shred them very finely and add to the oil and vinegar. Stir well and let sit, stirring occasionally.

Peel, halve and coarsely chop the eggs, doing yolks and whites separately. Cover and reserve.

Cut away the first $\frac{1}{2}$–1 inch of the asparagus' tough stem ends and use a swivel peeler to pare each stalk. Make them up into string-tied bundles of 6–8 stalks each and immerse bundles in a large casserole of boiling, salted water. Simmer for 5–10 minutes, uncovered, until asparagus is just tender and still bright green. Put the bundles onto paper towels, cut the strings, drain and pat the asparagus dry.

Strew on the egg and serve at room temperature, the lower half of the stalks lightly sauced with vinaigrette. Serves 4.

MACKEREL IN WHITE WINE

Another classic, this time from northern France, the fish poached in a very aromatic court-bouillon which jellies as the dish cools.

COURT-BOUILLON
$2\frac{1}{2}$ cups trocken or other dry white
wine
1 large wine glass of water
dash white wine vinegar
3 cloves
1 bay leaf
about 6 fresh cilantro leaves
3 slices lemon
2 thin slices green pepper
1 large carrot, peeled
1 large onion, peeled and very thinly
sliced
pinch of salt
3 black peppercorns

3 fresh mackerel, 1 lb each, drawn

TO FINISH
1 lemon
leaves of fresh cilantro

Put court-bouillon ingredients into a saucepan – the carrot can be fluted after peeling by running a lemon decorator called in French a *couteau à canneler* down its sides. Bring them to the boil and simmer 10 minutes.

Meanwhile, remove mackerels' heads and tails and cut the bodies across into $1\frac{1}{4}$ inch sections. Wash away any traces of blood. Arrange pieces in one compact layer over the bottom of a wide heavy casserole or saucepan and pour on the court-bouillon and all of its trimmings.

Bring to a boil, lower heat to a bare simmer and poach the mackerel, uncovered, for about 10 minutes, or until just cooked through. Turn the pieces over once, very carefully, during poaching.

Transfer mackerel to one or two rimmed china dishes and pour over them the court-bouillon and its elements; they should cover the fish. Let cool and refrigerate, covered, overnight.

Remove from the refrigerator 30 minutes before serving, by which time the liquid will have jellied. Transfer fish to one or two serving plates. Discard lemon slices, bay leaf and cilantro, plus cloves and peppercorns if you can locate them, and decorate the mackerel with onion, green pepper and carrot. Spoon on jelly and adorn plates with fresh slices from a lemon fluted before cutting, and fresh leaves of cilantro. Serves 5–6 as a substantial first course.

Clockwise from top: Mackerel in white wine, Asparagus vinaigrette, Stuffed neck of lamb, Terrine of pork and prunes

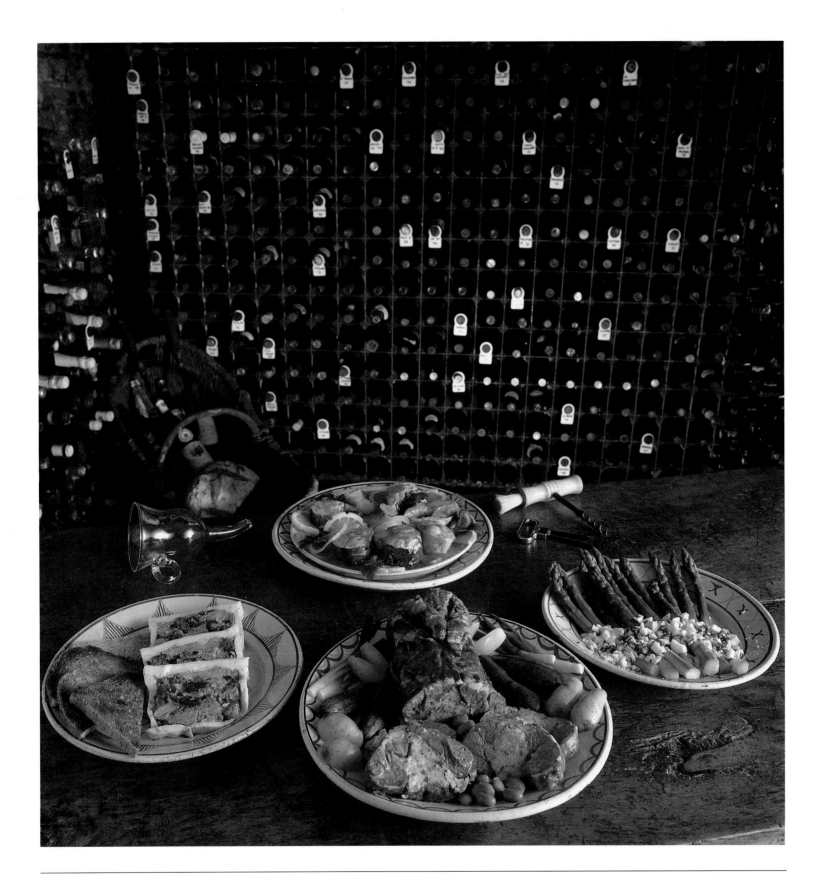

TERRINE OF PORK AND PRUNES

Pork tenderloin with prunes is beloved of the Touraine French and the Danes. I've used these ingredients to make a pair of terrines, the gamey sweetness heightened by garlic and a few tablespoons of red Dubonnet.

$1\frac{3}{4}$–2 cups large prunes
1 tea bag
2 pork tenderloins, to yield a total of about 17 oz after trimming
13 oz rindless pork sides, to weigh 9–10 oz after trimming
2 oz bacon, preferably unsmoked
1 large clove garlic, peeled
$\frac{1}{4}$ cup red Dubonnet
salt
black pepper
$\frac{3}{4}$ lb pork back fat, thinly sliced in sheets
butter
$\frac{1}{2}$ lb lard

Put prunes into a saucepan. Use tea bag to make about 2 cups of very strong tea, pour this to cover the prunes, bring to a boil and poach fruit for about 1 minute. Turn off the heat and let prunes soak for 1 hour.

Meanwhile, trim the two cuts of pork of all nerve tissue – a little on the tenderloins, quite a lot on the pork sides – and cut them into small pieces, with the bacon.

Run the meats through the coarse disc of a meat grinder, or food processor fitted with its steel blade, until coarsely chopped. Remove the combined meats to a bowl and pick out any nerve threads that may remain.

Drain the prunes well, pit and chop them, but not too finely. Mince the garlic and add to the meats with the prunes, Dubonnet and some salt and pepper. Mix thoroughly with your hands. Let the forcemeat marinate, covered and refrigerated, for a few hours.

Line the bottom and sides of two $3\frac{3}{4}$ cup oblong terrines with the sheets of back fat, saving some for the tops.

Test forcemeat for seasoning by frying a small ball of it in butter until cooked through; add more seasoning if necessary, remembering that chilling will dull the subtlety of flavors.

Pack the mixture into both terrines, rap them on the working surface to settle contents, and with a wet hand smooth over the tops.

Cover with remaining back fat, a double thickness of foil, and the terrine lids. Place in a bain-marie. Bake in a preheated oven at 300°F for 2 hours, removing the lid and foil for the last 15 minutes of cooking.

Lift from bain-marie, peel fat from the tops, and cover with foil-wrapped, weighted boards that can rest on the meat. When cool, refrigerate overnight, still weighted.

The next day, clean the rims of the containers, melt lard and pour it over the tops to seal meat completely.

Let the flavors mature for 3–4 days before slicing to serve with toast and butter. Remove the surrounding fat before eating. (The terrines will keep, refrigerated, for 2 weeks.) Each terrine serves 4–6.

STUFFED NECK OF LAMB WITH EARLY SUMMER VEGETABLES

Lamb from the middle neck is a firm, gelatinous meat that needs long, slow cooking to realize its succulent flavor. One of the least expensive cuts, it is subtle and delicious when boned and rolled around a stuffing of lemon, cheese and herbs, then poached in red wine. The acidity of the wine will help to tenderize the meat, which is delicious sauced with the poaching liquid and served with seasonal vegetables.

---

about $3\frac{3}{4}$ lb neck of young lamb, in one unboned piece
$3\frac{3}{4}$ cup lamb stock made from neck bones after removal, a peeled carrot and onion, pinch of thyme, bay leaf, parsley stems, salt
salt
black pepper
2 carrots, peeled
1 large onion, peeled and stuck with 3 cloves
2 cloves garlic, unpeeled
pinch of thyme
1 bay leaf
up to 1 bottle of fruity red wine
about $\frac{1}{2}$ teaspoon arrowroot

STUFFING
4 oz cream cheese
$\frac{1}{4}$ cup butter, softened
1 cup soft white bread crumbs
1 large clove garlic, minced
chopped fresh herbs – parsley, tarragon or chives – to taste
grated zest of 1 small lemon
finely ground meat trimmings from the neck bones
salt
black pepper
1 egg

VEGETABLES
about 5 oz each young vegetables: scallions, shelled broad beans, small turnips, tiny zucchini, new potatoes

---

Get your butcher to bone the lamb, taking care to pierce its flesh as little as possible (tell him it's to be stuffed). Also get him to chop up the vertebrae and give them to you with the rib bones. Or, if you are adept at boning, do this yourself and cut the vertebrae into two or three lengths.

Beat and knead together stuffing ingredients, season well and bind with enough egg to hold them firm.

Meanwhile, make a lamb stock in the usual way with bones and the

Strawberry not-so-foolish

necessary over a high heat; add a little red wine to refresh the flavor if need be. Simmer away the alcohol. Thicken slightly with arrowroot flour slaked in water; season and keep hot.

Simultaneously poach each vegetable until just tender in remaining lamb stock (which can subsequently be used for soup), and keep vegetables hot.

De-truss and unwrap lamb, 'seam' side down, and rapidly carve it into $\frac{1}{2}$ inch slices. Arrange these over a hot platter, surround with the vegetables, spoon on a little sauce, and pass remainder in a warmed boat. Serves 4–5.

STRAWBERRY NOT-SO-FOOLISH

A fool with a difference: the strawberries are first soaked in *crème de framboise*, or raspberry liqueur, with which they have a true affinity, or in default of this, an orange-based liqueur such as Grand Marnier.

$\frac{3}{4}$ *pint ripe and flavorful strawberries, plus extra ones for garnish*

3–4 tablespoons crème de framboise or Grand Marnier

2–4 tablespoons or more superfine sugar, depending on sweetness of berries

$\frac{1}{2}$ *cup heavy cream*

Wash, hull and quarter strawberries and soak for 1 hour in 3 tablespoons crème de framboise or Grand Marnier, plus 2 tablespoons sugar. Stir once or twice to ensure that the flavor of the alcohol permeates the berries.

Purée the mixture in a blender, add more liqueur and sugar to taste; neither should be obvious, but should complement and give 'texture' to the berries.

Whip the cream, fold all together, spoon into glasses and chill, tightly-covered with plastic wrap, for several hours. Serve very cold, on plates strewn with extra strawberries. Serves 3–4.

aromatics listed, plus a little salt. Simmer for 3–4 hours, skimming often.

Open out the neck, boned side up, incise its thick parts and flatten the meat with your hands. Season it and cover it with stuffing. Fold over the long sides to enclose this, turn lamb over onto the center of a double thickness of muslin measuring about 16 × 16 inches, wrap muslin tightly round it to form a long roll. Tie one end of roll with string, loop the string five times around length of the roll, tie second end, loop string back underneath and tie it round the first knot. Trim the parcel ends.

When the lamb stock is ready, strain and degrease it. Put rolled neck into a heavy oval casserole into which it fits snugly, add carrots, onion, garlic, herbs, enough wine to half-cover the meat, and $1\frac{1}{4}$—2 cups lamb stock. Sprinkle in a little salt, bring liquid to a simmer on the stove, and poach lamb in the lower middle of an oven preheated to 325°F for $2\frac{1}{2}$–3 hours, with the lid of casserole slightly ajar until tender. Turn the parcel over every 30 minutes. Test by piercing meat carefully with a trussing needle.

Prepare vegetables by trimming scallions, skinning beans, cutting turnips into small olives, and cleaning zucchini and potatoes. Reserve vegetables in bowls of cold water. When the meat is ready, remove it from the casserole and let it rest, still wrapped, in a warm place for 15 minutes.

Strain and thoroughly degrease the poaching liquid, taste and reduce if

SELF-INDULGENCE

Self-indulgence is all about pleasure and ease; a symbolic sun-bath with no particular high season. For me, such pleasure is based on the details of perfection: a flûte of well chilled pink champagne, or the cool segments of a tiny Cavaillon melon whose ripeness I savored, one hot summer's day, with the house aperitif of a southern French restaurant.

Indulgence is based, too, on cooking and serving something well, for oneself and the delight of others. Below are some of my own candidates for the exercise of self-indulgence the year round.

GNOCCHI AND SALSA DI NOCI

On a working trip to Tuscany, my husband and I each ate a plate of pasta at the restaurant of the Fattoria di Montagliari, south of Florence. Hugo's plate was ravioli in a delicious *salsa di noci*, a walnut sauce for which Signor Giovanni Cappelli kindly gave me the recipe. I've put this with potato *gnocchi*, an Italian form of dumpling which I take great pleasure in making. If this kind of self-indulgent labor is not for you, have the sauce with some sort of ready made pasta; it's very agreeable with many. My technique with *gnocchi* is based on Marcella Hazan's.

WALNUT SAUCE
6½ oz shelled walnuts
3½ oz pine-nuts
cold-pressed extra virgin olive oil
⅓ cup grated pecorino cheese
20 basil leaves, chopped
6 tablespoons light cream
black pepper
salt (optional)

GNOCCHI
1½ lb floury potatoes
salt
all-purpose flour

TO FINISH
3 tablespoons grated pecorino cheese
basil leaves

Put both nuts into the food processor fitted with its steel blade. Process them, with olive oil to moisten, until the nuts are quite finely ground but are not an oily paste. Remove the nuts to a bowl, beat in the cheese, the 20 chopped basil leaves and the cream. Add more oil if needed; the sauce should remain quite thick. Season to taste, remembering that the cheese is salty. Cover the bowl with plastic wrap and reserve. (The sauce can be made in a pestle and mortar.)

To make the *gnocchi*, boil the unskinned potatoes in salted water until tender. Drain and peel as soon as you can touch them. While still hot, purée through a food mill or ricer into a deep bowl. Sift on about 1 cup flour, work this into the potato and knead until smooth. You may need to add several more tablespoons flour if the potatoes are particularly absorbent, but stop when the mixture feels soft, smooth and still a little sticky. On a large floured board, form the dough into rolls the thickness of your thumb; leave to rest for 30 minutes.

Bring a large pan of salted water to a boil and begin to shape *gnocchi*. The method sounds involved but is actually not difficult; you'll quickly learn the technique.

Use a floured knife to cut rolls into ¾ inch lengths. Throughout the process which follows, repeatedly flour, as needed, the *gnocchi*, the board, your hands and the fork with which you'll be working.

Choose a fork with long, slim, rounded tines. Hold the fork sideways in your non-dominant hand (left hand if you're right-handed), with the concave face toward you. With the index finger of your other hand, press a dumpling to the inside curve of the fork, just inside the points of tines; your index finger should be aligned to the fork's plane. When dumpling is in place, smartly flip it with the tip of your index finger along the tines of the fork, toward the handle. As it rolls to the fork's base, let the dumpling drop to the board. You'll get a sort of shell-like result.

Keep making these *gnocchi* – with increasing dexterity – until all the dough has been used. Heat four plates.

Uncover the walnut sauce, ladle and beat in enough of the boiling water from the pan to give the sauce a fairly loose consistency. Rapidly spoon a wreath of this onto each plate; keep the plates in a warm place.

Drop the *gnocchi*, about 24 at a time, into the pan of boiling water. They will rapidly rise to the surface. Simmer for 10 seconds more, lift them out with a slotted spoon, drain well and transfer directly to the plates. Boil all *gnocchi* in this way and, when plates are well-filled, season copiously, sprinkle over the pecorino cheese and basil leaves. Serves 4 as an appetizer.

Clockwise from top: Gnocchi and salsa di noci, Carrot and cucumber soup, Gâteau Victoire au chocolat, Armenian lamb with rice pilaf

CRANBERICO

This cocktail uses cranberry juice, which should be sought in food shops with a sophisticated range of goods.

2½ cups cranberry juice cocktail
¾ cup white Bacardi rum
¾ cup Perrier water
lemon juice
plenty of ice

Mix the cranberry juice cocktail, rum and Perrier water in a glass serving jug. Add lemon juice to taste, and ice. Pour out six glassfuls, including ice, and serve. Serves 6.

TRUFFLE TOAST

Each January, Jacques and Pierre-Jean Pébeyre and their wives host the Fête de la Truffe at Cahors in south-western France. The Pébeyres are to truffles what the Windsors are to royalty, and their hospitality is warm and generous.

At the family's truffle-processing plant during a recent fête, we inspected black and aromatic truffles of all sizes, and were served with fingers of hot, truffled toast. Ambrosial!

a whole black canned or bottled truffle
    with its juice
thinly sliced good quality bread
butter
salt and black pepper

Thinly slice the truffle, reserving its juice. Toast and butter the bread, remove crusts and cut into fingers. Lay several slices of truffle on each. Spoon the juices over the truffle. Season and eat.

BRIE TOAST

One night at the 21 Club in New York I ate nothing more than ripe peppery Brie on slices of toasted brown bread.

unpasteurized Brie, ripe and if possible
    runny
wholewheat bread
butter
black pepper

Remove the rind from the cheese. Slice, toast and butter the bread. Spread with Brie, grind on pepper and eat.

FETTUNTA

During that recent spring working trip to Tuscany, I tasted some admirable food. The *fettunta*, around Florence, is a garlic-rubbed and toasted slice of bread on which, in December, the newly-pressed olive oil is poured for sampling. In the summer, a *fettunta* – or *bruschetta*, as it's called in the neighboring provinces of Umbria and Lazio – is often prepared with oil from the last year's harvest. Basil and tomatoes are added, and if all the elements are of the best, the result is magnificent.

white 'country' bread from an Italian-
    run delicatessen
cold-pressed extra virgin olive oil
salt
black pepper
1 clove garlic, peeled and halved
basil leaves
ripe, flavorful tomatoes, sliced

Thickly slice bread. Pour the oil into a deep dish and season well. Press both sides of each slice into the pool of oil. The oil should lightly soak each piece.

Lay the bread on foil on a heavy baking sheet. Toast in a preheated oven at 375°F for 15–20 minutes, turning over once. Remove from the oven, rub each slice with the cut side of the halved clove of garlic. When toast has cooled slightly, cover with basil leaves and tomato slices.

Season to taste, pour on more oil and eat the *fettunta* without delay with fingers or knife and fork.

ARMENIAN LAMB WITH RICE PILAF

I've used this recipe for ages, and am so familiar with it that I can't even remember its origins.

It has the excellent virtues of ease of preparation and improvement with age, reheating with superior results on the second or even third day after making. To the self-indulgent, such good nature can be an important quality in cooking; I highly recommend this comforting dish.

LAMB
1 boned shoulder of lamb
3 tablespoons vegetable oil
3 tablespoons butter
2 medium onions, peeled and sliced
1 large clove garlic, peeled and sliced
2 teaspoons all-purpose flour
1 teaspoon ground cumin
½ teaspoon ground cloves
2 cups stock, made with bones from
    the shoulder and a chicken quarter
2 tablespoons tomato paste
salt
black pepper

PILAF
generous 1 tablespoon butter
a liberal pinch of saffron threads
1 small onion, peeled and minced
1¼ cups long-grain rice
2 cups chicken stock, made as above
salt
½ cup shelled pistachio nuts
⅓ cup dried currants
black pepper

Trim the lamb of skin, excess fat and connective tissue. Cut into small cubes; if you have a devoted butcher, he may do all this for you.

Heat 1 tablespoon of the oil in a wide, flameproof casserole, add 1 tablespoon of the butter and, when foaming, lightly brown half the meat. Remove from the casserole. Add the same amount of oil and butter, brown the remaining lamb, then remove.

Melt the rest of butter with oil in the cleaned casserole, sweat onion and garlic until soft and golden. Stir in the flour and spices, stir over a low heat for 3–4 minutes. Remove from the heat, beat in stock plus the tomato paste to form a smooth sauce; return to heat and bring the sauce to simmering point. Add the meat, some salt; stir well. Cook, partially covered, in a preheated oven at 325°F for 2 hours, stirring occasionally, until the meat is tender. Adjust the seasoning, cool, and refrigerate for 2–3 days.

When preparing to serve, remove the fat from the top of lamb and its sauce. Work a few tablespoons of water into the casserole and slowly reheat on top of the stove while making pilaf.

To make the pilaf, melt the butter in a heavy saucepan, stir in the saffron and onion and sweat until the onion has

Cranberico, Toasts, Fettunta

softened. Wash and drain the rice, combine with the onion and stir over low heat for 2–3 minutes to begin cooking. Add the stock and salt, stir well, turn the heat very low, cover and leave undisturbed for 20 minutes. The rice should absorb all the stock and emerge cooked.

Blanch the pistachios for 1 minute in boiling water, then skin and shred. Fork the currants and nuts into the pilaf and season to taste.

Present the lamb flanked with the pilaf. Serves 4.

CARROT AND CUCUMBER SOUP WITH BUTTERMILK

I love cold vegetable soups finished with buttermilk, so this must be a logical self-indulgence.

---

3 cups sliced carrots
1 cup sliced onion
5 cups light chicken broth, made as on
    page 100
salt
9 oz cucumber, peeled and seeded
    weight
black pepper
pinch of superfine sugar (optional)
fresh dill
1½–1¾ cups buttermilk
1–2 teaspoons lemon juice
smetana or sour cream

Put the carrots, onion and broth into a saucepan. Add salt, bring to a boil and simmer until the vegetables are just cooked. Cool slightly.

Meanwhile, grate the cucumber flesh; squeeze away as much of its liquid as possible.

When soup base has cooled, purée with the cucumber until smooth in a blender or food processor. Season, add a small pinch of sugar if you think the soup needs it, plus some fronds of dill. If your blender is large enough, work in 1½ cups buttermilk; otherwise remove the soup to a bowl and beat in the buttermilk, judging whether to include the remainder. Add lemon juice to taste and adjust the seasoning.

Chill soup for several hours. Beat before ladling into soup plates. Swirl a spoonful of smetana or sour cream in the center of each portion and add a frond of dill. Serves 5–6.

GATEAU VICTOIRE AU CHOCOLAT

This is one of the ultimate chocolate cakes, a recipe from *Julia Child & Company*, made entirely without flour. I've adapted it; the result is bitter and agreeably light, with a surprising, almost custard-like texture.

---

1 tablespoon instant coffee granules
¼ cup hot water
14 squares (14 oz) semisweet dark
    chocolate, broken up
½ cup unsweetened cocoa, sifted
2 tablespoons dark rum
6 eggs
½ cup superfine sugar
1 cup heavy cream
1 tablespoon vanilla extract (not
    'flavoring')
confectioners' sugar

TO SERVE
whipped cream
dark rum

Butter the sides of a 9 × 9 inch cake pan, about 2 inches deep. Line the base with buttered parchment paper.

Dissolve the coffee in hot water in a heavy saucepan. Add the chocolate, cocoa and rum. Cover the pan and set into a larger one of just-boiled water. Reheat the water to melt the chocolate.

Beat the eggs and sugar in a large bowl, using an electric mixer, for about 10 minutes, until the mixture has reached the consistency of lightly whipped cream. Whip the heavy cream until very soft peaks form, then beat in the vanilla.

When the chocolate has melted, beat it with a wooden spoon; the result should be smooth, if a little resistant to the spoon. Blend the chocolate into eggs and sugar, folding rapidly and, when partially incorporated, fold in whipped cream until just combined.

Pour into the cake pan and place inside a bain-marie of simmering water to reach halfway up the sides of the pan. Bake in lower center of a preheated oven at 350°F for about 1–1¼ hours or until the cake has risen and cracked slightly, and a skewer inserted into the center tests clean.

Switch off the oven and leave the door ajar, allowing the cake and bain-marie to remain inside for 30 minutes. The cake will sink slowly and evenly back to its original volume. Remove from oven and leave to stand still in the bain-marie for 30 minutes before unmolding.

The cake can be turned out and served at this stage, still rather warm; you can also bake it a day in advance and reheat, still in the tin but minus the bain-marie, in a preheated oven at 240°F for 15 minutes.

Whichever plan you choose, turn the cake from the tin onto a board. Peel off the paper and turn back onto a flat serving plate. Work deftly but carefully, as the cake is very fragile. Dust with sifted confectioners' sugar and slice into rectangles. Serve with lightly whipped cream flavored with a dash of rum. Serves 10.

PASTRIES IN MINIATURE

When you present guests with an array of small cakes and tiny tarts, you are opening a jewel-box of temptations for the eye and palate. With some lemon curd, shortbread and pastry cream, fresh or dried fruits and a little sleight of hand, you will bring particular elegance and charm to teas and wedding breakfasts.

SUCCES

This is a kind of light and chewy almond meringue sandwiched with coffee buttercream.

SUCCES BASES
scant 1 cup confectioners' sugar
1 cup plus 3 tablespoons superfine
   sugar
1 cup finely ground almonds
6 egg whites
$\frac{1}{4}$ cup milk

COFFEE BUTTERCREAM
$\frac{1}{2}$ cup granulated sugar
3 tablespoons water
4 egg yolks
$\frac{3}{4}$–1 cup sweet butter, softened
1 tablespoon good instant coffee
   granules, dissolved in $\frac{1}{2}$ tablespoon
   boiling water

TOPPING
1 tablespoon unsweetened cocoa
$\frac{1}{4}$ cup confectioner's sugar
instant coffee granules

Cover heavy baking sheets with non-stick baking parchment. Using a pencil, trace about 40 circles, well spaced, on the parchment. Sift together confectioners' sugar $\frac{3}{4}$ cup plus 3 tablespoons superfine sugar and almonds.

In a second bowl, beat the egg whites until soft peaks form. Gradually beat in the remaining sugar and keep beating until the whites are very firm.

Add the milk to the sifted ingredients and knead together with your hands. Lighten this by beating in about a quarter of the whites. Pour almond mixture onto the remaining whites and fold together deftly. Fill a large pastry bag fitted with a serrated $\frac{1}{4}$ inch tip with the succès mixture and pipe onto the circles on the baking sheets. Bake in a preheated oven at 290°F for about 35–40 minutes until turning a pale biscuit color (the meringues in lower part of the oven will take longer). With a spatula, carefully remove the baked bases from the parchment and cool on wire racks; they should be chewy, not hard. These bases will keep for about 2 weeks if they are stored, unfilled, in an airtight tin.

For the buttercream, make a syrup with the sugar and water and bring it up to 245°F. Beat the yolks until thickened and light. Beat the syrup into the yolks and beat the mixture for several minutes until thick and cold. It will grow in volume. Beat in the soft butter gradually until the buttercream suddenly comes together and is firm and spreadable (you *may* need to add more butter than 1 cup to achieve this). Beat in the dissolved coffee.

Fit a pastry bag with a $\frac{1}{4}$ inch serrated tip and pipe a generous amount of buttercream onto 20 succès bases, slightly overlapping the edges. Cover with remaining rounds of succès.

For the topping, sift together the cocoa and icing sugar. Press 2–3 teaspoons coffee granules through a fine strainer and add to cocoa mixture to taste.

Cut waxed paper into thin strips and arrange on top of each succès in a criss-cross pattern. Sift over the cocoa and confectioners' sugar mixture. Carefully remove strips and you will have an instant decoration. Some of the cocoa will have settled alluringly onto the buttercream which shows around edges of each succès. Eat on the day of making. Makes about 20 succès.

LEMON CURD TARTS

SHORTCRUST PASTRY
*quantities and method as in Jewel
Tarts recipe on page 140*

LEMON CURD
3 eggs
strained juice and grated zest of
   2 lemons
$\frac{3}{4}$ cup superfine sugar
$\frac{1}{4}$ cup sweet butter, softened

Bake, cool and turn out the small tart cases of various shapes as for Jewel Tarts (see page 140).

In a small bowl, beat the eggs, beat in the lemon juice and zest, sugar and butter. Pour into a small heavy saucepan, set into a larger pan of simmering water. Beat the mixture until it thickens to the consistency of a thick cream sauce. Pour into a bowl and beat well to ensure that there are no lumps.

Place the tart cases onto baking sheets and fill with the hot curd. Heat the filled tarts very briefly in a preheated oven at 350°F for 1–2 minutes. Remove and cool on wire racks.

Eat within a few hours of making. Makes 20–30 of assorted sizes.

An assortment of miniature pastries

CASINOS

A cheesy mousse between layers of *génoise* (sponge cake) and jelly roll.

GENOISE
6 eggs
¾ cup superfine sugar
1 cup superfine sugar
scant ½ cup all-purpose flour
large pinch of salt
2 tablespoons sweet butter, melted and cooled

CREME AU FROMAGE
5 tablespoons granulated sugar
4 egg yolks
3½ sheets gelatin
1 cup fromage blanc
1 cup heavy cream

TO FINISH
½–¾ cup currant jelly

Line two jelly roll pans, each measuring 13 × 9 inches, with parchment paper in sheets large enough to extend above the sides of the pan.

For the *génoise*, place the eggs in a large china or metal mixing bowl set over a small saucepan of boiling water. Using a hand-held electric beater, whip the eggs at highest speed, gradually adding the sugar. Continue beating until the eggs become very light, thick, increased in volume and rather warm. Remove the bowl from the heat and beat until the mixture is cold. The mixture will form a slowly dissolving ribbon when beaters are lifted.

Sift the dry ingredients together three times. Fold them into eggs and fold in the melted butter. Divide half the mixture between the two cake pans, spreading evenly. Tap each pan smartly against the working surface to settle and level the mixture. Bake on two shelves of a preheated oven at 375°F for 20–25 minutes or until the cake on the top shelf is done. (The cake on the lower shelf will take longer.) Turn out onto separate tea towels covered with sheets of parchment paper. Peel the parchment paper carefully off the back of each cake, and lay more sheets of parchment paper over them. Starting at a short end, roll the towel around one of the two sponges and leave it to cool.

Repeat the process with the remaining *génoise* mixture, but do not make a roll with the fourth cake (set aside and use for another purpose).

Undo the rolled, cooled *génoise*, remove parchment paper and spread cake with a thin layer of hot, strained currant jelly. Roll up snugly, wrap in waxed paper cut to size and store for several hours in the refrigerator. Butter interiors of 16 round metal molds, each of 6 tablespoons capacity, and line the bottom of each with a circle of buttered parchment paper.

For the *crème au fromage*, make a syrup with the sugar and a dash of water brought up to 245°F. Beat the egg yolks until thickened and light. Soften the gelatin in a jug of water. Beat the syrup onto the yolks and beat the mixture for several minutes until thick and cold. Drain the gelatin, dissolve it in a little water over low heat and beat it into the yolks. Beat the *fromage blanc* until smooth and add this to yolks. Whip the cream until soft peaks form and beat into the egg and cheese base. It will by this time be thick and hold its shape.

Fill each mold almost to the top with *crème au fromage*. Cut 16 circles of *génoise*, fit one just inside the top of each mold and refrigerate for several hours.

When it is nearly time to serve, remove the jelly roll from the waxed paper and, with a serrated knife, cut into slices about ⅜ inch thick. Paint the top and sides of each slice with heated and strained currant jelly.

Dip each mold briefly into hot water, turn out the contents onto a plate and peel the paper off what is now the top. Cover each top with a glazed slice of roll, which should just fit, and serve. Makes about 16.

MINIATURE FRUIT CAKES

The world's fastest and easiest.

1 egg
generous ¼ cup superfine sugar
1 teaspoon vanilla extract (not 'flavoring')
¼ cup sweet butter, melted and cooled
1 cup all-purpose flour
¼ teaspoon salt
½ teaspoon apple pie spice
½ cup buttermilk
½ teaspoon baking soda
1½ cups mincemeat
¼ cup raisins
¼ cup candied cherries, quartered
⅓ cup candied citron, chopped
⅓ cup coarsely chopped walnuts

Beat together the egg, sugar, vanilla and butter. Sift the flour, salt and spice together. Mix the buttermilk with the baking soda and alternately with the sifted dry ingredients, beat this into the egg mixture. Fold in the mincemeat, fruits and nuts.

Butter 22 small brioche pans, measuring 1½ inches across the base. Fill three-quarters of each pan with the cake mixture and place on baking sheets. Bake in a preheated oven at 350°F for 20–25 minutes. Leave to cool a few minutes before sliding a knife around the edges of the pans and carefully removing the cakes. These keep for months in airtight containers. Makes about 22.

JEWEL TARTS

Each tart is filled with a dollop of *crème pâtissière*, or pastry cream, to keep the moisture from the fruit from softening the pastry. Makes about 20–30 small tarts of varying sizes, which should be assembled within a few hours of eating.

SHORTCRUST PASTRY

2 cups all-purpose flour
¼ cup superfine sugar
large pinch of salt
¾ cup sweet butter, softened
yolks of 2 hard-boiled eggs, sifted
1 egg

PASTRY CREAM

3 egg yolks
generous ¼ cup superfine sugar
1 cup plus 2 tablespoons milk
vanilla bean, split
1 tablespoon all-purpose flour
1 tablespoon potato flour

TO FINISH

¼ cup heavy cream
1 tablespoon confectioners' sugar
Kirsch
seasonal fresh fruits such as kiwi fruit, blueberries, blackberries, red currants, raspberries, strawberries
⅓–½ cup apricot jam
⅓–½ cup currant jelly

To make the pastry, sift the flour, sugar and salt onto a pastry board. Make a well in the center, put the butter into the well and make a trough in the butter. Add the strained yolks and whole egg.

With one hand, work the butter, yolks and egg swiftly together into a sticky mass. With a spatula, toss and chop the flour gradually into butter and egg until it begins to look like pastry.

With both hands, bring the dough together. Add a few drops of water if necessary to make it adhere, then knead briefly and form into a ball of dough. Wrap the pastry in foil and a plastic bag and refrigerate for several hours over-night if possible.

To make the pastry cream, beat the yolks and sugar to the ribbon stage. Put the milk into a pan with the split vanilla bean and scald. Sift the flour and potato flour (the latter makes for lighter pastry cream) onto the yolks and sugar. Beat well, then pour on the strained milk (minus the vanilla bean) and transfer the pastry cream mixture to a small heavy saucepan.

Over a very low heat, beat the pastry cream until it thickens and boils, beating vigorously to avoid the slightest lump. Boil for 60 seconds, beating, then turn out onto a plate. Cover the top with plastic wrap to prevent the formation of a skin. Cool completely.

Bring the pastry to room tempera-ture, roll out and line small tart pans of varying sizes and shapes. Chill for 30 minutes.

Place pieces of foil weighted with dried beans inside each pan. Bake blind in a preheated oven at 350°F for 15–20 minutes, removing the foil and beans when the pastry has set. Continue baking the tart shells until golden, browning and completely cooked. Cool and remove the tarts from the pans.

Take 1 cup pastry cream and beat to aerate. Half whip the heavy cream, beat in the confectioners' sugar with a scant

Jewel tarts

dash of Kirsch. Beat into pastry cream. Beat until completely smooth and light – if there is even a suspicion of a lump, pass through a fine strainer.

Fill each tart shell with pastry cream and top with fruit. I often use uncooked blueberries and ⅛ inch thick slices of kiwi fruit.

Brush the tops of the kiwi and blueberry tarts with simmered and strained apricot jam. The tops of the black or red fruit tarts should be brushed with simmered and strained currant jelly. Makes 20–30 tarts.

HEARTS

Crumbly and buttery shortbreads.

½ cup sweet butter, softened
generous ¼ cup superfine sugar
grated zest of 1 small lemon
½ teaspoon vanilla extract (not 'flavoring')
1½ cups all-purpose flour
pinch of salt
milk

Cream together the butter, sugar, lemon zest and vanilla. Sift together the flour and salt and mix gradually into butter mixture, beating well after each addition to combine thoroughly.

When all the flour is incorporated, knead the dough diligently until it ceases to cling to the hand. Add a few drops milk if necessary to moisten. Divide into two balls, wrap separately in waxed paper and refrigerate for 1 hour.

Roll each pastry ball out to ¾ inch thick on a floured pastry board. With a small heart cutter, cut out cookies, flouring the cutter each time, until all the dough is used.

Place on heavy baking sheets. Bake in a preheated oven at 350°F for about 20 minutes or until just turning golden brown. Cool on wire racks. These cook-ies keep for months in an airtight tin. Makes about 48.

Succès

Hearts and cornets

GANACHE CONES

These are made with mixture for *cigarettes russes*, each cookie turned around a tapering cone mold instead of the handle of a wooden spoon. An excellent use for leftover egg whites!

6 tablespoons sweet butter, softened
⅔ cup icing sugar
½ cup all-purpose flour
pinch of salt
3 egg whites
½ teaspoon vanilla extract (not 'flavoring')

GANACHE

5 squares (5 oz) semisweet dark chocolate
⅔ cup heavy cream

Cover heavy baking sheets with baking parchment. Cream the butter and sugar. Sift the flour and salt together. Gradually beat the egg whites into the butter mixture, then fold in the flour. Beat in the vanilla.

Drop by teaspoons onto the baking parchment at well-spaced intervals. Spread into very thin circles of even thickness and about 3 inches in diameter. Bake in a preheated oven at 400°F for 5 minutes or until the edges turn golden brown. Remove one baking sheet from oven and, working quickly, flip a cookie off the paper, turn over and roll around the pointed tip of a metal cone mold, 5 inches in length. It helps to have asbestos fingers, because the cookie must be soft and hot to roll properly. Remove from mold and cool on a wire rack. Quickly proceed with the remaining cookies, one by one. If they harden before being rolled, return briefly to the oven to soften.

To make the *ganache*, break up chocolate and put with cream into a small, heavy saucepan. Place directly over a low heat. As the chocolate starts to melt, beat the mixture with a wire whip.

By the time the cream comes to boil, the chocolate will have melted. Remove from heat and beat until smooth. Pour into a small bowl and cool. When cold, beat at high speed with a hand-held electric beater until the mixture holds soft peaks, has lightened and increased in bulk.

Spoon into a pastry bag fitted with a ¼ inch serrated tip and pipe a rosette into the open end of each cornet. Refrigerate to firm the *ganache*. Remove from refrigerator about 15 minutes before serving. Eat on the day assembled. Makes about 36 cones.

INDEX

ACKNOWLEDGEMENTS

I would like to thank the editors of *House & Garden*, particularly Leonie Highton and
Vicky Jones, for making this work both possible and enjoyable, and the many
generous suppliers and organizations which are listed below.

LONDON

Stephen Long Antiques

Edward Goodyear Flowers

Portmeirion Antiques

Bayly's Gallery

Linen Hire

Mollie Evans Antiques

Elizabeth David Kitchen Utensils

Souleiado

The Lacquer Chest

J.M. Turnell

John Baily & Son, Poulters

Frank Godfrey, Butchers

The Conran Shop

Sue Norman Antiques

Kenneth Turner Flowers

Valimex

Table Props

Britannia Antiques

The Golden Horn Restaurant

Robert Young Antiques

Tobias & the Angel

The Craftsmen Potters Shop

Knoodles

Schwartzsackinandcoltd

Lillywhites

Paperchase

Henry Willis Antique Silver

Jones Jewellers

Liberty

Divertimenti Cooking Utensils

Lonsdale Advertising

The Tunisian Tourist Board

Anthony Blake Studio

John B Benson, Architect

Tables Laid

PROVINCES AND ABROAD

Stuart Cousens
The Village Pottery
West Chiltington
West Sussex

Audrey Wilkerson
Admington
Warwickshire

Gwyn Davies
The Dairy Crest Creamery
Felinfach, Lampeter, Dyfed

Raven Products
Daws End
Marlow Common
Buckinghamshire

Johnny Grey
Grey and Co, Kitchen Furniture
    Designers
Wool House, Stedham
Midhurst, Sussex

Chocolaterie Valrhona
14 avenue du Président Rossevelt
26600 Tain l'Hermitage
France

PHOTOGRAPHERS' CREDITS

Clive Frost: pages 87, 88, 90, 91, 92

Christine Hanscomb: pages 2 (bottom
left) 11, 12, 13, 25, 27, 28, 56, 58, 59, 95,
97

Graham Kirk: pages 2 (top left) 2
(bottom right) 7 (top) 69, 71, 79, 80, 81,
83, 84, 85, 112/113, 133, 135

James Mortimer: pages 15, 16, 17, 18,
20, 21, 22, 23, 31, 32, 33, 35, 37, 38, 39,
41, 43, 44, 46, 51, 53, 54, 65, 67, 73, 75,
99, 101, 104, 106, 107, 109, 111, 115,
117, 120, 125, 126, 127, 131, 138, 140,
141

George Seper: pages 2 (top right) 61, 63

Clive Streeter: pages front cover, 6, 7,
(bottom) 8/9, 48/49, 76/77